CONTENTS

ACKNOWLEDGEMENTS

My agent Susan Mears, Michael Mann and Deborah Hercun and the staff at Watkins Publishing, Norma and Bruce Burgess for their ongoing support, the staff of Watkins Bookshop in London, the British Library and the Vatican Library and archives.

INTRODUCTION

For over two decades my research has woven in and out of prophecy and in my previous book, entitled *Inside the Priory of Sion* (Watkins Publishing, 2011), I delved deeply into the prophecies of the apocalypse from biblical texts and other sources. My investigations also included prophecies derived from witnesses of Virgin Mary apparitions and from the saints who had recorded visions of the End Times, some of which you will encounter in the pages before you.

As part of that research I read the *Prophecy of the Popes* as attributed to the 12th-century monk St Malachy, and found there were many interesting facets of his story that were far beyond the scope of my first book.

PROPHECY

We think of prophecy as a revealing of information that can include warnings or spiritual insights from a time gone by, where it was once held as a conduit to divine revelation. In the Old Testament the will of God was revealed to the prophets through communication with the Holy Spirit. The prophets were revered and the wisdom they imparted considered of the highest authority.

In recent times prophecy has fallen out of favour within the Catholic Church. Respect is still given to the biblical prophets such as Isaiah and St John of Patmos, to whom is attributed the Book of Revelation, but since biblical times the Catholic Church has refused to condone any further prophetic revelation as being credible, regardless of if it were from a saint, pope or seer. Christianity was built upon the Messiah, whose coming was prophesised in the Old Testament in the books of Daniel and Isaiah, but this foundation has not been built upon since antiquity.

For the last two millennia prophets have continued to add to the great body of prophetic work, intent on revealing our possible futures. Hildegard von Bingen, Nostradamus, many saints and even some of the popes were compelled to share their visions. Among these stands St Malachy of Armagh, a devout Catholic who helped to reform Ireland during the dark days of the 12th century.

St Malachy of Armagh was the first saint to be born in Ireland and is considered a leading reformer who overcame many challenges to bring the Irish Church in line with Rome. His life and work were recorded by his contemporary and friend, St Bernard of Clairvaux, who considered Malachy to be on a par with the apostles in terms of teaching and setting an example to those who followed him. St Bernard also recounts how Malachy was known to perform miracles of healing and to prophesise, and it is this aspect of his life that we take an interest in.

According to later historians Malachy had received a vision during a visit to Rome, wherein he had witnessed every pope from that day in 1139 to the Last Judgement. These were recorded as 112 brief Latin phrases that in some way represented a corresponding pope. It is said that Malachy gifted these prophecies to Pope Innocent II as a source of comfort through the troubled period the papacy was experiencing and then they were deposited in the Vatican and forgotten about for 400 years.

THE RELEASE

The prophecies were rediscovered in the Vatican archives in 1590, and in 1595 a series of prophecies were revealed by Arnold de Wyon in his publication *Lignum Vitae*. De Wyon claimed that these were the authentic prophecies as had been penned in the 12th century by St Malachy.

Since their appearance the prophecies have fascinated those inside and outside of the Church. Some cardinals have played upon some relevant aspect of their life in the hope that others might be influenced in choosing them as the next pope. Others have dismissed them as a forgery.

The release of the prophecies was not without intrigue. Their sudden 'rediscovery' in the 16th century allowed them to be used as propaganda in the campaign to promote Pope Gregory XIV to the throne. Since that time debate has raged over whether the prophecies were a fabrication purely invented for this purpose, and if Malachy was the true author.

ACCURACY

When the prophecies were published in 1595 the corresponding pope for each prophecy up to that date was known and de Wyon had explained the link between each pope – and sometimes antipopes – and the corresponding prophecy. The last named pope is Clement VIII, who was pontiff from 1592–1605. In the centuries since their publication many have poured over these sayings seeking evidence to identify current candidates as forthcoming popes. The brevity of the text in the Latin phrases allows for some room for interpretation, but many are very specific and in no way as vague as one might expect. For a document that is at least 400 years old there is a certain degree of accuracy without the need to find convoluted explanations for how a prophecy might fit a pope.

Even as recently as the 20th century there are popes who seem perfectly allied to their prophetic motto. For sceptics this raises the questions of how much influence the prophecies have over papal elections and if the cardinals are colluding in some way to see the prophecy come to fruition.

THE FINAL POPE

It is possible that some of the papal elections were contrived to fit the prophecies, but unlikely in recent years as the final prophecy foretells of the End Times. The *Prophecy of the Popes* joins that long tradition of apocalyptic prophecy by describing the last pope as 'Peter the Roman', who witnesses the destruction of Rome and the Last Judgement.

With Pope Benedict XVI we had reached the penultimate pope. According to the prophecies the next pope would be the last. As Pope Benedict XVI advanced in age and his health declined he chose to act in a manner that has not happened in over 600 years. On 11 February 2013 he resigned as pope and Bishop of Rome. The election of his successor took just 24 hours. The new pope, Francis I, according to the prophecy would be the last and this is where our story begins.

Are the prophecies real, do they actually give insights into future events that will befall the Vatican, and can Pope Francis be identified as the last pope? If Francis is the final pope then according to the prophecy he will oversee the fall of Rome and the destruction of the Catholic Church.

INTRODUCTION

In choosing the current pope there was an opportunity for the Catholic Church to either embrace the destiny Malachy appointed it or try to deny this outcome and forestall its own predicted demise.

CONCLUSION

The interpretations of these prophecies from the 12th century to present day also tell a story of the popes they describe. They follow the custodians of the longest-running organisation in the history of the world, and their place at the centre of 2,000 years of tradition.

And then there is the notion of prophecy itself. Consider for a moment the implications of prophecy on how we perceive time as linear and free will as having some impact on our future. Yet prophecies might have a scientific and psychological underpinning – they may not merely be flights of imagination but something far more interesting.

These are the mysteries that compelled me to explore and write this book, and I hope you enjoy joining me on this journey as we keep one eye on the past and one eye on the future.

Robert Howells

CHAPTER 1

PROPHECY:
AN EYE ON THE FUTURE

WHAT IS PROPHECY?

The common understanding of prophecy is to know and communicate future events. Specific to Christianity it can also describe the revealing of any divine truth but it is generally thought of as the revealing of events that will happen in the future. This is termed a 'revelation' and the role of the prophets in biblical times was to receive and 'reveal' or communicate the will of God.

There are many ways to receive information of a prophetic nature. Some are passively received while others require more work on the part of the seer. The methods employed by seers are not always borne out of natural talents and even the gifted often find a tool or trigger to facilitate their receptiveness.

Prophetic experiences can take the form of visions, images, dreams, voices, journeys of active imagination, or just a sense of inner knowing. Some seers are troubled by flashes of insight that are inflicted upon them without warning, while others strive for results from deep meditation or enter trance and mystical states. There can also be visitations in the form of guides and angels, or through mediums, channels and divination.

The simplest forms of prophecy are premonition and precognition. Precognition is a sense of knowing before you know, and it is often experienced as intuition. We are all prone to spontaneous moments of precognition, such as when someone is staring at you and you turn to face them because you feel, intuitively, that you are being watched. Premonition is to foresee the future as an experience of something separate from your consciousness. There are many examples of this from the biblical prophets and the lives of the saints, who describe visions and portents of future events; by communicating premonitions these become prophecies.

A well-known example of prophecy concerns the Great Fire of London. Three famous seers – Nostradamus, Old Mother Shipton and the astrologer William Lilly – all predicted that a fire would engulf London in 1666. Astrologer Lilly was so accurate in his divination that he was able to name the actual day the fire would start and as a result was arrested and dragged before Parliament accused of having caused it himself. He managed to prove otherwise and was set free.

The above example was not a matter of coincidence or luck, nor were the seers attempting to gain fame or credibility; they were simply communicating as an inevitable fact what had been revealed to them through divination or vision. We can take this as evidence, and there are a multitude of examples in history, that it is somehow possible to receive details of events that have not yet happened. Humans, it would seem to suggest, are capable of seeing the future.

Mother Shipton, mentioned above, was a 16th-century English prophetess who made a number of very accurate predictions concerning what appears to be the 20th century and the Second World War, including:

Carriages without horses shall go. Around the world thoughts shall fly, in the twinkling of an eye. Underwater men shall walk, women will dress like men and trousers wear, and cut off all their locks of hair. When pictures look alive with movements free. When ships, like fishes, swim beneath the sea. When men, outstripping birds, can soar the sky, then half the world, deep-drenched in blood, shall die.

Another example of accuracy in prophecy can be found in the *Prophecy of the Popes* as attributed to St Malachy. The 244th pope is identified as 'the rake' and the corresponding pope that was appointed was Innocent XII, whose family name was 'Rastrello', the Italian for 'rake'. This occurred a century after the prophecies were published so this was not a matter of twisting the text to suit the pope. Nor was the election likely to have been contrived to suit the prophecy, as the conclave that elected Innocent XII was a five-month long battle. It is extremely doubtful that some form of collusion caused the prophecy to be fulfilled – aside from that, what were the chances of someone with the surname 'rake' being present among the cardinals in the first place?

It would seem on this and many other occasions that the prophecies came true. 'Rake' is such an unambiguous and specific word that it could not have been made to fit anyone else present in that conclave and yet, as so often happens with biblical prophecy, it was only recognised as being accurate with hindsight.

We think of prophecy as a phenomenon of biblical times and equate it with the teachings of the Old Testament. At that time prophecy was an integral part of religious life, with prophets believing, or at least claiming, that their messages came directly from God. However, the origin of communicating with angelic realms has its roots in far earlier civilisations.

DIVINATION AND THE EARLY FORMS OF PREDICTION

The development of spirituality is a natural stage in evolution that initially flourished in all early cultures across the world. As each culture developed they eventually sought a way to understand their place in the scheme of their creator. From antiquity the ability to petition the Gods for inspiration and direction has accompanied many forms of faith and mysticism. To early man the elements of luck would be attributed to the gods and every act of chance was considered an act of divinity, spirit or magical power. Major events, such as the eruption of volcanoes, crop failures or the sudden eclipse of the sun, were seen as admonishment from the gods, which would drive fear into the subjects. For primitive people to understand how to appease the gods and avoid this wrath required that they develop some form of communication or interpretation of the signs they considered were being created for their benefit.

To achieve this they developed tools that they believed made it possible to know something of fate and to be able to learn the future from those outside of time. The value of seers and diviners was recognised and those who were naturally mystical took up this role within the tribe. They developed tools and methods to learn the will of their gods and to try to make decisions based on insights into the future.

To this end prophecy and divination were integral tools to the spiritual development of many ancient cultures, albeit sometimes in a crude and simplified form. Many of the tools developed are still in use today, from the rune stones of the Norse to the *I Ching* of the Chinese.

THE TOOLS OF DIVINATION

From the earliest forms of divination a shaman or seer would interpret the signs and symbols for the tribe. This role continued as cultures became more advanced and the great civilisations began to rise. Babylon, located in what is now southern Iraq, is considered to be one of the first advanced civilisations. In the ruins of its temples can be found the remains of magical bowls that were used to divine portents of the future by staring into the water they contained and allowing images to form in the mind.

In classical times the Romans employed divinatory tools such as dice; the ability to read signs and portents was part of everyday life. No longer was the power of the seer limited to the domain of the priesthood, but the tools and methods employed to receive information became prevalent among the wider population. Today we have a wide range of tools in common use, such as automatic writing, crystal balls, concave mirrors, palmistry, phrenology, face reading and tarot cards.

By the 2nd century the Germanic tribes of northern Europe developed a system of runes as a set of sigils on wooden fragments, bones or stones. These were drawn from a bag and placed in an order that could be interpreted by a reader. The runes presented composite icons in a fashion that could be linked together and read as a story. This ability to draw a story from simple images or sigils appears in many of the 'reading' methods of divination that followed.

Many of these divinatory tools were viewed by the Church as belonging to the realm of the 'dark arts', although some can be found to have more intuitive leanings than anything sinister. Numerology, for example, is the act of transposing letters into numbers to broadly identify a personality type. Similar to this is palmistry, which is one of the oldest known forms of character reading through divination.

Astrology

Throughout history astrology has been the most widespread and persistent form of divining the future. We find evidence for its tools and records of revelation from across the world, dating back to the earliest civilisations. In ancient China, India and the Middle East different forms of astrology were developed, and continue to this day. As trade and war brought cultures into contact, astrology was adopted and adapted by different civilisations as a means of discovering the cycles of influence on their world.

For primitive man the heavens were filled with random wonders that were beyond reach. Over time man learned their movements and imposed his own consciousness on the scattered stars and came to understand the cycles of the moon and planets. The primitive mind would have linked these celestial bodies to their archetypes, the totems of their dreams and attributed to them the power of influence over individuals and events. Once the passage of the planets across the night sky was mapped out, astrologers would correlate their location in the sky with the enquirer's time and place of birth.

From this a birth chart would be created and studied to examine the relationships of the planets, the sun and the moon, and their place among the constellations to build a picture of subtle influences on the reader. Not limited to individuals, the chart can also be created for geographic locations or even entire countries as astrologers believed the celestial globe mirrored the terrestrial one.

The symbols of astrology are found throughout the Bible. In the Book of Revelation a scroll is opened to reveal the faces of four animals surrounding a throne: that of a lion, ox, eagle and human. These are often mistaken as representing the four gospel authors, Matthew, Mark, Luke and John, but the same imagery appears in the Old Testament Book of Ezekiel and so predates the

New Testament. Ezekiel is famous for its lurid description of a fiery winged throne descending from the sky, which initially would seem difficult to interpret. However, Ezekiel also mentions the faces of these animals and man, and these give a clue to the true nature of what is being described. The origin of these characters is that they can be traced back to Babylonian astrology, where they represent signs of the zodiac.

The Old Testament has many more veiled references to the use of astronomy and astrology as a key to understanding a particular event. When the court astrologers of Herod the Great informed him that the King of the Jews had been born in Bethlehem he ordered the execution of all young male children. Another account describes how an angel appeared to Jacob in a dream and instructed him to escape with his family to Egypt (Matthew 2:16). There are many other examples of astrology in the Bible but I think one of the most misinterpreted is that of the star in the east that heralds the birth of Jesus, as recognised by the magi. The magi are said to be from the East and to have 'seen his star in the East' (Matthew 2:1). Contrary to popular belief the magi do not physically follow the star. As they were from the East and they saw a star to the east they would have been going in the wrong direction. Also, as it is impossible for an astronomical body to illustrate a specific location on Earth the size of a barn, it can only be a reference to the astrologers of the age. The magi had used astrology to work out the date and location for the birth of a coming messianic figure.

There are many today who claim to have divined the future through astrology, and even more that are happy to believe them. According to a poll conducted by the Opinion Dynamics Corporation in the USA in 2004 nearly a third of the population believed the daily horoscopes they read in newspapers and magazines. Even in these enlightened times, such a vague attempt to summarise the astrological influence for what was then a population of 292 million people in twelve short paragraphs still holds sway over the masses. However, we cannot easily dismiss astrology that is more specific to the individual as there are many examples of its correct application throughout history such as the example of William Lilly predicting the Great Fire of London mentioned above.

Card reading

A late addition to divination was the use of cards to read the future. Divination through cards is usually done using a tarot deck, which has such arcane images that it is often associated with the occult, but in truth these highly symbolic cards are based on archetypal figures, many of which are Christian in origin. A number of what are known as the 'major arcana' depict scenes from the Bible such as the Last Judgement, and specific Christian images such as the pope card. The cards are certainly not orthodox, though, as they contain heretical figures such as a female pope and a high priestess.

Tarot is a system that combines the archetypal influence of astrology with the interpreting of sigils seen in runes. Tarot is a complex system of cartomancy that first appeared during the Middle Ages in Western Europe. It is used by randomly selecting and placing cards in a sequence, to be interpreted in a form of narrative inspired by the images and their attributes. The narrative created tends to be highly personal to the subject of the reading and works best when applied to specific questions and considerations for the future. It can sometimes provide an array of options that the questioner may not have realised existed.

The use of tarot to read the future only works on a general level in terms of specifying times. For a more accurate identification of specific dates it would make more sense to use a standard deck of playing cards. A simple system can be devised with the four suits being the four seasons and the fifty-two cards representing the weeks of the year. To identify days the jacks are counted as eleven, queens as twelve and kings as thirteen so that the total of the cards is 364, with two jokers as a point each to represent both a standard year and a leap year. The inherent ability to use playing cards in this manner would imply that divination had some influence in their creation.

To perform cartomancy requires the reader to enter a state of mind susceptible to the symbols on the cards. To achieve this I have witnessed tarot readers enter trance states and produce readings, after which they have no recollection of what they have said. The appearance of this is initially unsettling as it could be construed as a temporary state of schizophrenia or even possession. In reality they have entered a different level of consciousness, which they are unaware of in everyday life. One possible reason this method is seen to work is that the visually rich nature of tarot cards lends itself to overwhelming the conscious mind, thus allowing discreet connections in the unconscious to come through. The results of these interactions would be triggered in part by the reader having an empathic response to the enquirer which invokes the application of the unconsciousness in divination.

This will be explored further in the next chapter, but the tarot remains an example of a comprehensive oracle capable of answering any type of enquiry. As the origins of the tarot are lost in time, for a better study of the evolution of a divinatory system we must look to the Far East and the development of the *I Ching*.

The *I Ching*

One of the earliest known oracles based on a divinatory tool is the *I Ching*, or *Book of Changes*, which dates from around 1000 BC. As the Chinese culture evolved their tools for divination evolved with them and in some cases, such as the *I Ching*, became fully realised systems of philosophy.

The Chinese system of *I Ching* works by casting three coins twice to provide a formation of six broken or unbroken lines called a hexagram. This system is likely to have derived from the simplest form of divination: the 'yes' or 'no' outcome that is the most basic form of answer to any enquiry. Prior to coins, the same reading could be achieved through the use of bones. This primitive, yet effective, method is to draw a line in the sand and scatter a handful of bones onto it. If more bones land on the left of the line the answer is 'no', and more on the right signifies a 'yes'. It was understood that the perfectly random throw of an I Ching coin would allow the gods an opportunity to influence the outcome and provide an answer.

This idea of an 'absolute' good or bad outcome is primitive in that it puts limits on something that has the potential to be infinite. It portrays a simple black and white view of life that lacks the scope of ambiguity that we have today, but can still provide a simple answer. Over time this black and white approach broadened to include more psychological and religious experience and was developed to reveal information that reflected a broader spectrum of consciousness. This also required more awareness on the part of the reader as they had to communicate more complex symbols and patterns.

Eventually the use of the *I Ching* developed beyond the simple binary 'yes' or 'no' coin throw to the generation of hexagrams that resolved to 64 possible outcomes. Early explanations for the hexagrams consisted of a few lines of text but are now often rendered as many pages of information that are to be contemplated at length. The text of these explanations is filled with insights and definitions that almost need another level of divination if a clear answer is to be found. Through the development of the *I Ching* the simple duality of the coin throw has expanded to reveal a philosophy and wisdom that encompasses all aspects of life.

When the *I Ching* ceased to be based purely on the chance of a coin throw and required interpretation it became an oracle. In the first instance the response can be mechanical, drawing on written explanations for the outcome of the divination. In the case of the *I Ching*, the reader draws upon these written interpretations to create an inspired narrative that reveals something to the enquirer. The value of the reader here is that they open a gateway through the unconscious to reach for a divinely inspired response.

Oracles

The contacting of spirits or other entities usually requires the medium to enter a different level of consciousness such as a trance state. These trance states were sometimes induced or contrived to assist the oracle or channel becoming open to accessing information, through their unconscious, from a higher realm. The ancients experienced accessing these other realms as breaking through the veil of life and death to contact the spirits of their elders on the other side. Some oracles spontaneously trigger an image in the mind, but the most famous examples of the ancient oracles are those that were 'received' as a voice that either spoke directly from the mouth of the receiver, or relayed a message to be communicated by them.

The most famous example of an oracle from this time comes from Ancient Greece. Greece had many oracles, such as the one at Delphi, and these were so central to the religion of the people that they were considered a destination for pilgrimage. The oracle at Delphi was consulted by royalty, politicians and priests, who were in awe of the accuracy of the messages revealed to them. The oracle of Delphi was used by the Ancient Greeks to learn the will of the god Apollo, who would speak through the priestess, sitting in a state of rapture above a vent in the earth. The gases that rose up from the vent are thought to be one of the factors that induced the state of mind required for the oracle to work, but it is not important whether the fumes or other psychoactive agents triggered the revelations. The question here is whether or not the information came from within the unconscious of the prophet or whether the event triggered access to a divine source.

The hearing of voices has continued in many guises since Ancient Greece and took hold in the West during the 19th century as mediumship. We now think of this as clairvoyance but this term is encumbered by the perceptions and the associated scams that plagued spiritualism in the late 19th century. Spiritualism had emerged as a reaction to the industrial age, which threatened to sweep aside faith and with it the answers to the deeper questions of the afterlife. A fear of death or the search for comfort by the bereaved created a psychological void that was filled by the art of contacting entities from the afterlife. Mediums claimed to be able to contact the dead relatives of the bereaved in a practice that was not unlike the summoning of spirits seen in the Old Testament, although it was prone to fraud. As the unscrupulous preyed on the loss of the bereaved, a small industry grew up around the fabrication of contacting entities from the afterlife. The actions and voices of those recently departed loved ones were often exposed as trickery, causing the notion of spirit contact to again fall from favour.

Another means to contact the dead appeared at this time, in the form of the 19th-century parlour game Ouija. We now have a surfeit of horror films to warn us of the dangers of 'meddling' in such matters, but, for the record, from my own limited experience of using such a board, I learned that the 'spirits' I seemed to be in contact with are no wiser in death than they were in life. I did get a coherent response, though, so we cannot discount it completely.

The modern counterpart to spiritualism is called 'channelling' and is an internalised visitation where information is heard, often to be written down later. This method was employed by the most notorious of Western occultists, Aleister Crowley, in the transcribing of his *Book of the Law*. Crowley claimed to have written the book by invoking a discarnate spirit that narrated a book to him from the corner of the room. That the spirit in question, supposedly an ancient Egyptian war god, was prone to quoting medieval monk Rabelais, whose work Crowley often emulated, perhaps says more about the true source of the revelation than the paranormal pretence that surrounds it.

Crowley was drawing on the traditions of witchcraft and magic, so punishable under the Inquisition, which involved the ability to contact entities and receive information from beings beyond the physical realm. This has always been portrayed as the summoning of demons in the propaganda of inquisition (see *Malleus Maleficarum*, published in Germany, 1487) but in the key texts, such as the *Book of Abramelin* (14th century), we discover they actually sought contact with angelic beings or the voice of the Holy Spirit. The Abramelin workings link back to the Judaic practices of the time of Solomon. They include instruction on binding demons in the same manner that Solomon bound Asmodeus to build his temple as recorded in the myths of Judaism.

Fabled necromancer John Dee (1527–1609), undertook the same charge in 16th century. He used what he considered a scientific approach to contact the spirits in other realms. Ink drawings exist of him and his pupil, Edward Kelly, working together in a graveyard in London to summon an apparition with which he intended to converse. Over time he compiled a 'language of the angels' called Enochian, which he claimed to have received in spiritual reverie. Enochian looks like an extrapolation of Hebrew characters, as employed by the cabalists of the Western magical tradition. Dee also used a scrying mirror, a dish lined with black concave glass, which has survived and is on display in the British Museum in London. These ideas can be found in earlier occult works such as the writings of Cornelius Agrippa (1486–1535) and the Arabic grimoire Picatrix dating back to the 12th century.

It is wrong to discard oracles as being mired in the occult as they can also be found at the root of Christianity, where they were common features within the temples of the time. The oracle was to be consulted as an authority on spiritual matters, as it was believed they could reveal the will of Yahweh. Some were in the form of individuals who would receive and communicate information from higher sources directly, while others would employ various forms of divination.

Although the West has relegated the art of mediumship and its associated paraphernalia to the realms of the paranormal, the value of meeting entities has prevailed in many cultures. Many spiritual traditions have evolved beyond simply listening to the spirits and have taken the notion one step further by partnering with them as 'spirit guides'. These spirit guides often take on symbolic appearances, such as the 'wise old man' figure, and in psychological terms equate with the transpersonal idea of the higher self, or the 'Atman' – a term borrowed from Hinduism, meaning the *true self* – communicating to the ego.

Divination and prophecy through self-enquiry

The unconscious of the individual is a tool in its own right for divination and self-enquiry. As the individual delves into their unconscious to find a way to receive information they move away from the tools of divination and towards the experience of prophecy. There are many examples of prediction or prophecy from within the individual and these have run parallel through history with the use of divination. The internal ability to enact divination might draw on an external source for information but differs from other tools of prediction by being fully realised by the prophet themself. It is possible to spontaneously experience this in everyday life through imagination and intuition.

Imagination

The common act of applying one's imagination to an issue or situation can evoke some image of the future. In the creative imagination the urge to discover what might transpire in the future could trigger a sudden witnessing in the mind's eye of such events. We can daydream through imagination into the future. This can be seen in the works of science fiction writers such as Jules Verne and his predictions of the future.

Verne was imaginative enough to write in detail about tanks and submarines before they were invented. His view of a future war came to pass during the First World War as tanks began to replace cavalry on the battlefield and early submarines were introduced. To make this leap of imagination Verne extrapolated on current advances in science and technology in the late 19th century and used this to predict the transport and weapons of the 20th century. He made educated guesses, but these drew on existing inventions in the same way that the *I Ching* readers compiled a narrative from an existing text. In the gap between the known and the unknown the imagination reached towards the future.

There are many examples of actual science drawing from science fiction film and literature, creating a tradition of self-fulfilling prophecy as ideas have been adopted and used by fans of the medium. An example of this is the dramatic use of the countdown sequence that marks the launch of every space mission by NASA. The counting down from numbers ten to one to such dramatic effect was inspired by its use in a German movie from 1929 called *Women in the Moon*.

Beyond technology we can also observe patterns in nature and our environment to predict trends. These can be as basic as interpreting omens such as 'red sky at night, shepherds' delight' to expect a sunny day or the more complex science of modern weather forecasting. As to which is more accurate, I would say that was debatable, but the latter is certainly a lot more expensive.

Intuition and inspiration

Intuition is the gaining of knowledge without learning. It requires a more spontaneous approach to interpreting signs than imagination and often comes fully formed, whereas logic and imagination can require a number of steps to arrive at an answer. Interpretations in early divination and prophecy stemmed from intuition and inspiration.

Inspiration is being able to jump from one notion to a completely new notion, and is almost entirely responsible for our progress as a species. Sometimes inspiration is driven by external forces, such as in response to changes in our environment; at other times it can be purely aesthetic, as in artistic creation. If a scientist has a flash of inspiration, a 'eureka' moment, it is generally a shortcut to information that would have been reached by a linear process but would have taken a longer time to discover. The experience is akin to jumping to the answer without having to go through a long process of working it out.

That we can be inspired is evidence of an innate ability to consider our situation and imagine something new from it. This is how we solve problems. In that moment of inspiration we imagine a future that may or may not come into being. This is not yet a form of prophecy but it is not so far from it. The new ideas that appear to us enter into our awareness from the outside. Within us this link is made via the unconscious and this is first encountered by our awareness through dreams.

The dream state

In parallel to the development of tools for divination, the content of dreams would have been understood as a window to new information. Many dreams are merely compilations of recent events and current concerns as the mind assimilates the detritus of our everyday life. Others can be vivid and rich with symbolic images and messages from our psyche, as explored in the works of Jung and a multitude of psychoanalysts since. The unconscious is a rich soil from which a great understanding of our own psychological make-up can spring forth and there is even a theory that we are dreaming all of the time but that these dreams are hidden by the light of awareness when we are awake.

Of the dreams that are visionary in their scope, some can be spontaneously prophetic without any intention from the subject. This passive method of prophecy is probably the most available but least remembered. The little films that take place in the cinema of our synapses may leave us with a sense of knowing, sometimes foreboding, as if we have witnessed a ghost that haunts us from our future.

The first religions and cultures, such as the Aborigines, would mine their dreams for imagery and often construct totems or symbolic animals that can be recognised as archetypal. Their dreams were a clear channel to the unconscious and the most basic means of personal divination. The crossover between dreams and prophecy occurs many times in the Bible, and was seen as an important form of communication between man and the divine in the Old Testament. The story we learn from childhood is of the pharaoh's dream of seven lean cattle, which Joseph interprets as an impending seven years of famine.

There are a number of dream states that can be experienced within the normal range of brainwave activity experienced during sleep. A more refined and controlled version of dreams can be attained through lucid dreaming. Lucid dreams are different in quality to normal dreams as they appear vividly real and are very immersive. They can be mistaken for reality and to suddenly wake from one can be very disorientating as the residual sense of place can remain. An example of this happens when you are waking from a dream where you are walking and your leg instinctively spasms from a sudden sense of falling.

The boundary between dreams and awareness is a place where we experience waking visions. These are the moments when we rise or descend through levels of consciousness towards sleep or becoming awake. There is a point in this process where we are on the cusp of consciousness and unconsciousness and the mind is free to conjure images that span both states. In our near-waking state we may see an image or scene as if it were real. These images can also bring insights and information that we had not previously known while fully awake.

The visionary artist and poet William Blake wrote: 'I assert that all my visions appear to me infinitely more perfect and more organised than anything seen by the mortal eye.'

The quality of dreams
There is a flow of energy through consciousness that gives more power to certain images and experiences over others. These are the ones that have the most impact and remain in memory long after the event. In terms of psychological energy, the quality of dreams could be mapped to a three-tier scale.

The first level is the basic fantasy of a daydream that we conjure while awake. These daydreams are concoctions of our creative imagination and carry very little psychic energy.

The next tier is the common dream state, which ranges from watching a film that is streaming into the mind from another place entirely, to an altogether more vivid and engaging experience. On reflection these would seem to hold a lot more energy, powered by the unconscious mind and the symbols that it communicates through. Dreams draw their energy from the well of our unconscious so they can become completely immersive, to the extent for lucid dreams that they can appear as part of our reality, fully realised and integrated into our experience of the world.

The third level is the vision as experienced by the prophets. This is brighter than a dream because it has not just the psyche of the individual to power it, but possibly an external source of power from the form that is being communicated with. In the case of prophecy such as Malachy's, which touches upon the entire papacy and history of the Catholic Church, this prophecy is powered by that energy.

Visions

Whereas dreams and divination generally offer something of the 'quality' of possible events, they rarely describe the actual event in detail. Visions can be similar in that they can have a mood or an atmosphere that reveals a sense of what is coming through symbolic language. However, they can also veer towards revealing specific details of actual events at a specific time in the future. For example, there are a number of recorded cases of individuals, including St Malachy, predicting the exact nature and timing of their own death.

Visions also have a different quality to dreams in that they often give the impression of having been imposed upon the viewer, as if from some external power, and can therefore be quite sudden and shocking in their onset. It can also be said that dreams and visualisation exist within the realms of the unconscious, and they are mostly personal. By contrast visions are transpersonal: they bring realisations beyond our own capability to imagine or understand.

Many accounts of visions describe them as coming from somewhere external, as a gift delivered from afar to reveal events in other places or points in time. From a Christian perspective, according to the *History of Prophecy* (Palmer, London, 1862), 'prophecy is like an arrow from God shot into the grazing beast of man.'

Traditionally the onset of a vision was induced through lack of sleep or starvation. The desert or other extreme environments are regular settings associated with saints who were in the thrall of apocalyptic visions, but these were not flights of fancy caused by dehydration or some other chemical imbalance. Just as Jesus was tempted by the devil while in the desert (Matthew 4:1), it is not necessarily a simple case of hallucination but may actually be to do with breaking down certain psychological barriers that ordinarily protect us from such experiences.

In tribal cultures psychoactive drugs are used to trigger visionary religious experiences, as with peyote use by the shamans of the Native American Indians and the Huichol religions of Mexico. During ritual gatherings the hallucinogenic substance takes the role of a sacrament that propels the shaman into deeper levels of consciousness and overwhelms them with revelatory visions. This is a world away from the social drug use during the late 1960s, where visions were considered a pleasant side effect.

BARRIERS TO INTERPRETATION

We cannot assume that all the information we receive is valid or real. The talent has always been in discerning and interpreting the wider truth of these communications. Rarely does the message come so clearly as in Constantine's vision of a cross in the sky accompanied by the phrase, 'By this sign you will conquer', which he interpreted as a sign that he would win the battle on the following day. The symbols of this vision carry their own power and relevance that Constantine recognised and understood.

Symbols have an energy derived from their cultural, historic, religious and personal meaning. The context in which they appear allows the diviner to read them as meaningful based on this energy. Surprisingly, the same can be said for a random scattering of tea leaves in a cup, as even this can be used by seers or diviners to project images onto. The chance of a specific symbol appearing or of the tea leaves forming a specific shape is open to abstraction and interpretation.

The writings of Nostradamus are so shrouded in cryptic and symbolic language that there could never be a single clear interpretation. Many of these cannot be reduced through abstraction to reach a pure conclusion.

It seems counter-intuitive for random patterns to reveal insights and this can expose the enquirer to the risk of finding relevance where there is none. Even the patterns of a Rorschach test can readily be imbued with any meaning we wish to project onto them. These are known as simulacra, where the ability of the mind draws recognisable images where none exists. We do this every time we look at the stars and subject them to a 'join the dots' process in an attempt to constellate patterns in the night sky. Without assimilating these into a meaningful reflection of our human condition, such as giving them archetypal attributes, they would be reduced to their meaningless nature of a random collection of lights in a void.

The standpoint that all divination is fabricated because we invent the interpretation is a flawed approach to understanding what is taking place. With astrology as an example, we have identified our archetypes, our psychological influences as classical forms, and can see them reflected in the outer world by projecting them onto the celestial bodies of the universe. Through astrology we can then attempt to measure their influence on our lives via our unconscious. This was drawn from those early astrologers who witnessed their tribes cower in fear as an eclipse blackened the sun and were petitioned to explain what such events meant. Lacking the body of knowledge available today they would have had to trawl their own psychology to find an answer that resonated with the tribe. In doing so they found the connection between the archetype and the tribal soul.

THE CHALLENGE OF READINGS

Ancient astrologers faced the same risk inherent in all forms of divination and prophecy: that the individual whose role it is to read or relay the information received must do so with the correct interpretation. It is not enough just to be able to produce a tarot deck and let someone draw cards from it while taking a wild guess at the meaning of what they choose. If they were to produce the image of a falling tower, for example, they might decide this meant impending disaster. The tower can signify disaster but it can also be seen as the chance for a new beginning following the collapse of the old. There are plenty of books to assist in the explanation of that symbol but, in that moment, with that individual and their specific issue, the intuitive approach – not the learned one – must be sought.

This is where the real talent of the reader lies – in their ability to read the energetic value of a sign and determine the connection with the situation at hand. If that happens, there is no risk that they may not be able to differentiate between a vision and a mirage.

We are complex in our view of the world and we tend to make complex systems but these sometimes betray our spontaneity.

If a reader brings too much knowledge they risk stifling their intuition and distorting the interpretation. Divination may fail due to the reader having issues which they project onto the content. Through this the energetic meaning of the divination or vision is contaminated with their own psychosis.

It is a known issue in psychotherapy that there are a multitude of dream analysis books that attempt to explain every facet of a sleep encounter within the cinema of our unconscious. These are loathed by psychotherapists as they often override that pure first impression from the analysand with some cultural or historical explanation. Visions in particular can contain a pure fount of unconscious information prior to interpretation.

The analysis of dreams should always begin with a personal interpretation, and take the form of free association with the symbol or event. It is good practice not to let the mind follow threads of ideas but to keep returning to the original symbol to find another direct association until you have one that feels energised. It is the energised aspect of this psychic material that is important as it contains information that has not come from your conscious mind.

Having received a pure vision or dream symbol, the issue then for the individual is not only to interpret the message but to interpret whether the information is just aimed at them or if it is intended to spread to a wider audience. This is a particular challenge when information is received of a religious nature as the urge for the recipient is often to rush out and spread the 'good news'. It is likely that many who divine new revelations from the Bible or other religious sources are confusing a personal revelation that relates specifically to them with something more universally applicable and therefore they feel compelled to share it as a wider truth. This frequently occurs around ideas of the End Times and interpretations of the Book of Revelation.

History has witnessed many examples of seers predicting an actual date for the apocalypse that has failed to materialise. These seers were convinced that in some way they had divined knowledge of the apocalypse and were compelled to share this with others. I have seen an example of this first-hand in recent years. While in Philadelphia in May 2011, I saw a row of black vans painted to promote the message of Harold Camping, a Christian radio DJ who claimed the rapture would come on the 21 May of that year and the end of the world would shortly follow. Camping claimed to have worked out the actual date of the apocalypse by studying the Bible. Sadly for his followers, some of whom had spent money they could ill-afford on a billboard campaign for the event, he failed to mention that he had previously published a book claiming the apocalypse would take place in 1994 and then had to move the date to 2011 when this failed to materialise. When nothing happened in May 2011 he claimed his calculations were out and moved the date again, to October of that same year. He has since admitted he was wrong to try to work out the date, ignoring the warning in the gospels: 'But of that day and hour knoweth no man, no, not the angels of heaven, but my Father only.' (Matthew 24:36).

Current scepticism for such announcements is not surprising as we were given to expect something of an apocalyptic event to mark the end of the 20th century. The two-millennia mark passed without cataclysm, while many churches in England, and presumably elsewhere, devoted their billboards to the kind of 'repent now or be damned' emotional blackmail that is driving people away from the Church.

Christianity is not the only religion that is failing to deliver a spectacular End Time event for all. If you are reading this book the much-vaunted events of December 2012, as projected onto the Mayan calendar, are likely to have passed without incident and those who were so vocal regarding this impending doom are either silent or making excuses such as claiming it was a 'spiritual' and not 'physical' upheaval. Evidence for or against this will be harder to prove on both sides.

WHOSE VOICE?

A deeper issue with accepting prophecy and the results of all forms of divination is to be sure that it comes from a credible source. To be open to prophecy is to allow the personality to drop away and be sublimated beneath something else. Into the void comes a voice that might belong to an angel or demon, or even be a manifestation of schizophrenia.

Possession in early religion gave rise to the idea that an evil spirit could use an individual to lead others astray and there are examples in the Bible of prophecies that are intended to be destructive or false. In Acts (16:16–18) a women fortune teller who is possessed by a spirit follows Paul, announcing that he is a servant of God. Although the spirit in her is correct in what it reveals, it troubles him and he casts it out. He had intuitively understood that although the message was correct, the spirit that was communicating it was not to be trusted.

There are also warnings against false spirits that speak through prophets, for example: 'Regard not them that have familiar spirits' (Leviticus 19:31). There is even an account of a spirit impersonating a physical form in Samuel (28:3–20), when it is summoned to prophesise and appears in the form of Samuel but is discovered to be false.

Another issue is that, although information can be received by channelling or other means, the ego of the person receiving can filter the information and distort it to their own view. This can be entirely unconscious and unintended but, like dream interpretation, the ego can misinterpret what is received prior to communicating it.

FALSE PROPHETS

In some cases the actual personality of the prophet is corrupt. Matthew (7:15) warns us to 'Beware of the false prophets, who come to you in sheep's clothing, but inwardly are ravenous wolves.' Deuteronomy (13:1–5) also has stern warnings against false prophets, stating:

> If there arise among you a prophet, or a dreamer of dreams, and giveth thee a sign or a wonder, And the sign or the wonder come to pass, whereof he spake unto thee, saying, Let us go after other gods, which thou hast not known, and let us serve them; Thou shalt not hearken unto the words of that prophet, or that dreamer of dreams . . . And that prophet, or that dreamer of dreams, shall be put to death.

There is also one poignant incident in the Bible of an accurate communication being wilfully ignored. Pontius Pilate's wife was inspired by a dream to warn her husband not to crucify Jesus because she had 'suffered many things in a dream' (Matthew 27:19) but he chose not to listen.

It was difficult in biblical times to discern the voice of an angel from the voice of the devil, and if there is a warning to be had from these examples it is not to be manipulated by prophecy. To hear and believe it, if you feel so compelled, but we cannot ever really know in absolute terms that the vision and the voice has our best interest at heart. There is a balance to be found when examining prophecy and the Bible offers good advice on this, stating in Thessalonians (5:19–21): 'Quench not the Spirit, do not treat prophecies with contempt. Prove [test] all things; hold fast that which is good.'

With such a potential for misuse the Catholic Church is careful not to authenticate or give credibility in any way to prophecies outside of the Bible. It will neither judge them to be true or false but does seem to tolerate them and take an interest in many of the more famous ones. Various popes have often requested that the prophetic writings of some saints are circulated to a wider audience.

Aside from the obvious risks and failings highlighted above, there is no rule cast in stone that all prophets have to be correct all of the time. The clarity with which information is received can vary, not just from vision to vision but within a single vision. From the ambiguity of language and the risk of misinterpreting symbols, to the difficulty of trying to record a semi-conscious experience once fully awake. In many cases the prophecies are recounted to a scribe on whom we depend to keep an accurate record. Then there is our inherent ability when writing or recounting stories to embellish them with imagination, at the risk of distorting the original message. It is worth noting that a good discipline for creative artists of all kinds is to try to 'get out of the way' of the material that is coming through them.

CONCLUSION

We have seen how prophecy is prevalent across all cultures, and how far it has developed through the ages. There are wonders in what can be revealed but also risks. And we have touched upon the psychological processes and implications of what it means to see into the future.

What is apparent from the multitude of tools available is that anything can be used to divine some form of new information. Tools of divination were developed as a means to summon the gods to influence chance and reveal the future. These tools also provided patterns on which to project unconscious knowledge to make it conscious and act as jumping-off points for the mind to connect to knowledge from beyond the sphere of consciousness. How well the diviner is attuned to this part of their unconscious and how clearly they can allow it to come through, circumnavigating their ego, determines the clarity of what they receive.

Some have been very successful at this leap into the unknown. There are enough historic examples of prophecy being accurate to confirm that the future is available in the present. The existence of prophecy, if accepted, could be more of a revelation than the actual information the prophets reveal as it changes so much of what we understand of time. Our experience of time is linear and our perception of events is that they follow on from each other in an orderly fashion. The real world for us is only manifest in the present moment and from this entrenched point of view we are always in the 'now'. The past has dissolved and future has yet to be formed. A future that is happening now, in some other realm, gives the impression that events are pre-ordained and the stories of our lives are written with every choice already mapped out in full. Prophecy seems to imply that our destiny is completely fixed and all reality is bound to fate. It would seem to counteract any ideas of free will that we have.

All that remains is to ask the difficult question.

How is this possible?

CHAPTER 2

THE SCIENCE OF PROPHECY

INTRODUCTION

Predicting the future should be impossible. Common sense dictates that we cannot know events that have not happened yet. We view time as the cord of a necklace along which events are strung like beads. But as science and psychology begin to explore the possibility of non-local influence, our necklace begins to unravel, allowing the essence of these events to scatter back and forth through time. For these future events to visit the present something unexpected must happen to the physics of time. In simple terms, either the prophet sees space and time fold back on itself, or their awareness separates from their physical self and projects itself into the future.

Aside from the scientific aspects, prophecy holds many interesting ramifications for religion, science, philosophy and psychology. To understand these ramifications we must first attempt to unravel the mysteries of time, which, as prophecy suggests, cannot be as simple as past, present and future.

TIME

Seemingly, for prophecy to work, events in the future have already happened or are happening right now. If the future is available now then reality is a pre-ordained series of events that can be browsed like the pages of a story, and that story has already been written. From this we might deduce that the universe is mechanistic and existence follows a predetermined path, like the movement of cogs in a clock. In a pre-ordained reality all outcomes are inevitable: fate rules and there is no place for free will in this model of reality. Our freedom of choice as individuals to divert the course of history is in question. The implication for physics in this model is that if the future is another place that is real it opens the universe to the idea of time travel.

The theory of physical time travel can quickly be discarded as it is fraught with paradoxes. For example, if time travel were possible I could travel into the future and bring back this book to give to my publisher without ever having written it. How the book came into existence is like a Zen *koan* that cannot easily be answered. Of course, our understanding of the rules of time travel are somewhat limited but there is likely to be a boundary at some deep level of physics that would prevent the book, or anything else, coming into being in such a manner. This barrier would probably prevent any physical interchange between different points in time so that projecting matter through time would be impossible. At these levels of existence physics is not bound by the laws of Newton. For example, at the level of quantum physics there are hypothetical particles called tachyons that appear to travel back in time.

We can conclude that prophecy is not time travel in the physical sense, and as such does not alter the laws of physics. However, through some gateway in time, dreams or visions can become a vehicle for time travel that extends consciousness into the future.

THE PSYCHOLOGY OF SEEING THE FUTURE

It might seem strange to view prophecy and divination from a psychological perspective but psychology has developed a language that allows us to break down how the consciousness works and explain how some of its functions may relate to mystical experiences. There are existing models of consciousness that allow for the past and the future to inform upon the present.

Self-awareness is measured in terms of 'illumination' or light cast on who we are. This 'I' of awareness is like a spotlight within the mind surrounded by the dark of our unconscious. At the edges it fades into the dark of a deep sleep of our personal unknown. On this gradient of grey awareness at the edge of the spotlight the ego has less and less power, allowing content from the dark to intercede. We can examine what comes through or by some means of self-enquiry we may move the spotlight to explore more of this unconscious landscape. By expanding our awareness into the depths of our lower unconscious we can heal the wounds from our past. This is one of the methods used by psychiatrists to help patients uncover trauma that impacts on their everyday lives.

In transpersonal psychology it is recognised that it is also possible to rise up through higher levels of consciousness towards enlightenment. Those who have fully expanded the spotlight into all areas of their unconscious and have knowledge of their entire self are considered 'enlightened'. They have no shadows of the unknown lurking in their psyche. Transpersonal psychologists struggle to understand the shadows in terms of lower and higher consciousness and use the religious tools of contemplation and meditation to experience these different states of being. The divinatory nature of consciousness becomes apparent when we consider it in relation to time.

The middle level of consciousness is where we occupy the present. This is where everyday awareness of the 'I' – of who we are when we are awake – occurs.

The lower unconscious is where the disassociated aspects of our past reside, often needing to be redeemed or healed. The higher levels of consciousness hold our potential and challenge us to evolve and find meaning.

THE LOWER UNCONSCIOUS

There is a saying in psychology: 'That which we are unconscious of rules us.' The lower unconscious contains the aspects of our psychology that formed in the past: usually as unmet needs or emotional wounding. These repressed and unresolved issues seep into our everyday consciousness trying to influence us into meeting their needs. The past haunts the present and, if left unresolved, can divert our energies into narcissistic and regressive activities as a way to avoid the feelings we would rather repress, such as shame and rage. Exploring the unconscious and redeeming the past can lead to an experience of grace and reveal higher functions such as compassion and forgiveness.

To assimilate such content requires humility and therein exists a risk. The ego strives to claim the spirit, and other unconscious material, as its own. This process may have given rise to the Gnostic concept of the 'Demiurge' or half-creator of the world. The demiurge symbolises the ego trying to claim creation as its own instead of seeing it as an act of co-creation at the behest of grace. Inflation of the ego occurs when we pretend to own something that is divine in its origin.

HIGHER CONSCIOUSNESS

Just as the lower unconscious level is bound in the past, so the higher levels are concerned with potential, and with the future. The domain of higher consciousness, or the 'higher self', is preoccupied with purpose and meaning which relate to our potential. Like the lower unconscious, the higher aspect of our unconscious also occasionally calls for our attention by erupting into the light of our everyday awareness.

These eruptions may take the form of spontaneous prophecy. Sometimes, as with the visionary artist and poet William Blake, the receiving of visions is not in any way contrived or summoned. Blake received flashes of insight and intuition that would occur at any time. It would seem that many of the saints were prone to this form of prophecy and certainly the Bible is alive with such visions.

Messages can come from higher consciousness as dreams, visions or inner voices and are likely to be the same means as described by the biblical prophets. Being open to these levels can trigger mystical experiences as it is here, on the cusp of awareness, that we can open to receive information about the future. The symbolism we see in divination speaks directly to this level as the higher states of consciousness tend to distil language down to a simplified form. Poetry is an example of this as it communicates with a very economic use of language from an elevated level of awareness. If we continue to rise in consciousness language simplifies further and is reduced to symbols that are rich in layers of meaning. We see the same archetypal images reflected in divinatory tools such as runes, tarot and other oracles that the higher self can interpret for us.

The ego may also attempt to claim this activity but the creativity that comes through the higher self is an act of co-creation. Anyone who searches for the absolute source of original ideas can only conclude that at least a part of that spark came from outside of them. The nature of the higher self can be seen in the lives of the saints and prophets as their singular devotion to be in service of a higher cause allowed spirit to pour through them.

The grey areas of awareness that allow us to remain awake but open to the higher and lower levels of consciousness are not a figment of psychology: they can be measured as electrical frequencies of the brain. While fully conscious the human mind has an electrical frequency of 15–30 Hz called the *beta* state. Below this is the *alpha* brainwave state at 9–14 Hz. This is half of what we experience when awake and is the state of deep relaxation that can be reached through light mediation and prayer. It can also be used to facilitate visualisation and guided meditations.

Deeper into the darkness still is the *theta* state at 4–8 Hz. This is a deeply relaxed state in which we can experience flashes of insight and dream-like imagery. It is the deepest level of consciousness, where it is possible to have visions while remaining awake. The deepest level is *delta* at 1–3Hz, which is deep sleep.

RECEIVING PROPHECY

As prophecies are often visual it is likely that they occurred during the theta brainwave state, when the mind is both susceptible to visual information and the subject is conscious enough to remember or relate their experiences. In religious practice there are a number of methods that can induce a shift in consciousness towards the theta state. The visual receptiveness can be triggered by starvation, dehydration and other extreme experiences such as pain. The many temptations that appeared to St Anthony and to Jesus could have been caused by such suffering as these events took place in the desert during times of fasting.

Meditative and trance states can also be used and are marked by physical withdrawal as awareness turns inwards. A shaman, saint or mystic will often sit and stare into a fire to synchronise the mind with what is called a 'frequency-following effect'. Pulsing light, such as a fire flickering at any one of these frequencies, if contemplated, would induce that frequency in the mind. This is the theory that underpins all technology used in 'mind-machines' that trigger meditative states in subjects.

While these methods open the mind to receiving prophecies they do not answer the question of how a window into time can exist. For this we must look at the other side of the equation: the science of time and space.

THE ELASTICITY OF TIME

The idea of eternity in religion holds that there is a place of 'no time' beyond the human experience and that everything is happening at once. This would allow events to come together, with time and space folding back on itself, which allows two points to meet. This could only happen outside our current dimension, in a place we call the fourth dimension.

If our consciousness could reach beyond the boundaries of the third dimension it would no longer be subject to time and space. In religious terms the soul and the afterlife must reside somewhere. Some basic theological questions have raised this issue over the centuries: for example, what is the shape and weight of the soul, and where does it reside? The higher realms and heaven are also in question; the ancients placed these among the physical stars but our explorations into space have disproved this. These forms may reside in consciousness alone, but consciousness itself has been recorded as being able to separate from the physical mind and travel to other realms in documented cases of 'astral projection'. It is possible that an astral plane exists where the soul resides so that it remains within the body and yet cannot be found in physical form.

Scientists have long considered the presence of other dimensions that may interact with our own laws of physics. The universe itself appears to be expanding without getting bigger, which requires some curvature through another dimension. With this in mind it may be possible for information, images and the like to traverse dimensions, evading the binds of time. Scientists now posit that there are many dimensions beyond our own and seem to find mathematical evidence for new ones every few years. The impact of these on our own cannot be proven or easily discredited, but it might be experienced as an elastic perception of time passing or jumping.

DREAM TIME

From our experience of dreams we know that consciousness is not bound by the same rules of time as our physical life. The dreams and visions that occur in the cinema of the mind illustrate the elasticity of time. They give an experience of time being relative, capable of being compressed or elongated compared to the steady flow of events in waking life. An example of this is that it is possible to be asleep for a few moments, after the alarm has started waking you, and in that short space of time to dream what feels like hours of content. The effect is to wake up remembering a lot of detailed information and events from the dream only to discover it passed in the blink of an eye.

In those moments not only has our unconscious compressed its experience of time but there can be an emotional impact from the dream that lingers into waking life, proving that we have fully experienced the internal vision, not just imagined a series of scenes that give the impression of a long dream. It is possible to achieve this sense of timelessness through meditative practices but in meditation it would seem to be a matter of perception and not the physics of time that is distorting.

The science of measuring time is to count the intervals of seconds, minutes, hours, etc. This counting reduces time to a sequence of numbers and these are taken to be devoid of any further purpose. However, numbers feature in divination and religion as having meaning and this has become part of our perception.

TIME AND NUMBER

Time is fathomed through counting and our consciousness has integrated this into our language. An example of which is the saying that a person's 'time is up', meaning they have come to the end of their life, or that 'their number was up'.

Number is already an abstraction: it is not the truth of what is being measured, as by counting we apply a symbolic reference to describe the quantity of the subject, without commenting on its qualities. From this initial state of simple representation numbers begin to accrue energy as we give meaning to them.

People can be very superstitious and will use rituals and traditions to support irrational beliefs about numbers. For example, some will choose lottery numbers by attaching personal significance to random numbers, such as the date of birth or age of a family member. This is not prophecy or divination but a basic guessing technique; no more than a game, but the numbers are seen to have some meaning.

In the primitive mind there were few numbers and these were each assigned meanings. Beyond these few numbers were the 'many', which in biblical scripture is usually given as the number 40. In the primitive mind the 'many' would have taken on archetypal status as an attempt to quantify the unknown. Over time our capacity to imagine numbers has grown exponentially, pushing the elusive 'many' towards an infinite number. In mathematics today the search for pi is a continuation of the quest to quantify the archetypal 'many'. Pi remains for mathematicians the dark outside the cave that is haunted with the abstract and mythic. The 'many' was always the 'here be monsters' of ancient seafaring maps.

While our grasp of number theory has grown, the more balanced view of numbers has diminished, since the exploration of the 'many' has led to a greater sense that we have control over many aspects of numbers. The ego, which claims ownership of mathematics as a science, chooses to ignore the beauty of numbers and the depth of meaning that can be found in them that originates in a more mystical place. Contemplation of any cathedral or sacred place will often reveal a divine proportion in the architecture that can elicit an emotional response. This is an application of the harmonics of numbers that can affect the individual directly on many levels, and illustrates that we understand numbers to be something more than integers for counting.

There are also many numerical references in the Bible, such as the mention of a 70-year period described in Daniel. Some are veiled references to astrological events – in this case, 70 years is the length of time of the procession of the zodiac. Another form of divination at play in the Bible is the method of assigning Hebrew letters with numeric values, called gematria. These values are then compiled into words that have meaning based upon their total numeric value and the values of the components. Many of the numbers present in the Bible, including the number of the beast in the Book of Revelation, being 666, are likely to stem from the cabalistic method of divining meaning in this way.

The Greek word for number, *arithmos*, is the source of both rhythm and arithmetic. In the philosophy of the *I Ching* the universe has an underlying rhythm that can be interpreted in number form. The dynamic flow of this rhythm is mathematical but considered to denote a rhythm of events in life. These life events can be considered points of energy in our timeline, like energised pearls on a necklace of moments.

Unfortunately, since the Age of Reason mathematic theory has attempted to remove the divine aspect of numbers, reducing them from meaningful principles to mere integers of counting. In experimentation and all forms of measurement numbers are a constant factor that can be reproduced endlessly to provide a fixed foundation. For divination the opposite is true.

Like science, the art of divination depends on experimentation but its aim is to achieve the exact opposite of a scientific outcome. The divinatory approach is based on valuing the exception that occurs when repeating an experiment, or not to repeat the experiment at all.

Basic scientific experimentation is a measure of everything that is not subject to change. Accuracy is measured through repetition as this reduces chance to an acceptable minimum, but it cannot eradicate it completely. At the cutting edge of science many experiments are now considered a success if they can be replicated two out of three times, which is a poor average from which to draw a conclusion. The empirical pinnacle is not fully enforced and if we discounted all findings that could not be replicated every time, without fail, there would be a lot less considered 'known' within the scientific community. That divine intruder, chance, impacts on these experiments, reducing the outcomes to a 'best guess'.

That's not to say modern science is wrong in its findings – it just illustrates the truth it upholds is more of a grey scale of probability than the black and white of absolutes.

The same 'chance' our scientists strive to exclude is the quality that we seek in understanding divination. Experiments in divination measure chance as complementary to the findings. The simplest way to keep chance in play is by only conducting the experiment once. The results are based upon a single unique outcome. Whereas the origin of scientific thinking is the prediction of outcomes based upon a scientist's next direct action, the beginning of an oracle is the same but the action is indirect, as in an unconscious act that influences the experiment.

SYNCHRONICITY

One of the key realisations in quantum theory is that the viewer influences the outcome of the experiment. The implication of this is difficult to grasp as it implies that the physical, external world that we experience is co-created. From this we can surmise that reality is part objective external experience and part subjective influence. In terms of divination we have to take some responsibility for the results, as these external tools are partly of our own creation.

This idea has been around a long time in psychology where events that are linked to us are described as *synchronistic*. The development of the psychological aspect of divination has its roots in synchronicity. Any event that happens without cause can be described as a synchronicity, a *deus ex machina* that ties together events into meaningful coincidences. The stark realisation of understanding synchronicity is that the universe colludes with the individual to create reality. It mirrors our consciousness in the world.

Jung's writings on synchronicity advocate the 'relevance' of external events and environments to our psychological situation. The Chinese consider reality to be 'sympathetic' in the same way that Jung saw it as 'synchronistic'. As the *I Ching* became more than a tool for divination, it developed into a fully fledged philosophical outlook on reality. To read the *I Ching* or other forms of divination is to increase the likelihood of a synchronistic event taking place.

To remain in an elevated state of consciousness we may find an unexpected relevance in some external aspects of life. Looking back on life events one can often get a sense of why something happened when it did. It may have been difficult at the time but often some life lesson, some level of meaning, can be deduced as if the universe had presented a lesson for us to learn.

Anyone who has successfully worked the *I Ching* or tarot cannot help but be moved by the appropriateness of the results. There appears to be a non-local effect at work. I have had direct experience of this, just as we have all had déjà vu and moments of synchronicity.

Another example of synchronicity can be seen in Robert Louis Stevenson's *The Strange Case of Dr Jekyll and Mr Hyde*. The author conceived the story in a dream but in hindsight it can be seen as a fictionalised account that clearly illustrates the idea of schizophrenia. At the same time, in a different part of the world, Freud was formulating his theory on schizophrenia, but this was not published until four years after *Jekyll and Hyde*. It would appear non-local influence was in play as Freud and Stevenson shared a synchronistic event.

It is possible to recognise a meaningful coincidence in life where our inner psychological condition has drawn a synchronistic event into our environment. As these are synonymous and more frequently experienced at higher states of consciousness, it is possible to interpret them as evidence that you are 'on the right or wrong path'. This does not mean the entire experience is limited to being a product of our own intellect. If a higher power chose to communicate with us, the most appropriate method would be through our lives and the outer limits of our consciousness.

The key to understanding prophecy and divination is that it is activated in the consciousness of the individual. But if prophecy were a function of the mind then why are so few predisposed to experiencing it? The answer might be that to access future events a trigger of some kind might be required. A tool or a trance state is often employed by the seer to bring about the experience of the future.

From this state of mind or via some form of divinatory device the prophet can witness something of the past and future from a source which can be tapped into remotely. The information that comes to them from another time and place has to enter into the conscious mind of the prophet – by examining divination we can try to understand how we are able to draw into consciousness information from both within and beyond the prophet's own psyche.

REMOTE VIEWING

A psychological discipline that is visual in its results and can be seen to have insights into the process of prophecy is remote viewing.

Remote viewing was explored at length by the US security and military agencies during the 1970s and 1980s as a means of spying. They had discovered that certain individuals could be given a set of map reference coordinates and these would trigger a connection between the viewer and a remote location. The viewer then describes in words or images what they see in that location. The remote view would manifest as a visual image or a set of inferences in the mind of the viewer. Sometimes the location would be seen at a different point in time.

The importance of the trigger for this event being numerical coordinates should not be overlooked. Map reference numbers are complex and they hold great meaning, especially for trained soldiers who learn to survive by navigating maps in strange lands.

The US military put forward a scientific explanation for this method: the target location was a 'matrix' and by knowing its coordinates it was possible to attune the mind to reading the signal this matrix was transmitting and follow these signals back to the source. The source would manifest as a visual image, in the mind of the viewer, who would translate this into images expressed through automatic drawing. It is as if the information bypasses the conscious mind and transmits directly through the automatic nervous response system. Interpretation is applied after the image has been rendered.

The structure of this matrix was a model of space and time seen in terms of 'fields' made up of points that interact with each other and the points on this matrix were seen as items of information.

Surprisingly, the challenge for the remote viewers was not in obtaining images and insights into a location but in preventing their conscious mind from interfering in the process and distorting the results based upon their own predisposition, the environment or projected material from the unconscious of the person issuing the coordinates.

The model of treating locations as points in a field of space and time is entirely appropriate to the question of seeing the future. From such diverse sources of shamanism as the *I Ching* and Jungian psychology, points in time are thought of in terms of a matrix of synchronistic events. Synchronistic events have no 'before' or 'after' but form remote connections and can be found in religious teachings such as the notion of karma. The points are linked by association.

THE MATRIX MODEL

Although we live through time in a linear fashion, our thought associations are non-linear as we group our memories by content and not by their context. A sunny day from childhood is remembered among other sunny days and not the days that preceded or followed it. The information is organised in a way that can be easily accessed, like an online search engine, but author and philosopher Jorge Louis Borges argued that any two states of mind that are the same are actually a single event, even if they take place years apart.

If events are points in the field of time and are linked together they form a matrix. The matrix model can be applied in both physics and psychology, and as the two are both forms of energy they can interact where there is synchronicity between points. Physicist David Bohm argued that there is an implicit order that connects consciousness to the brain. The shape of the grid would be archetypal in itself as it forms an underlying template for both time and psychological energies where these can become synchronised. This is not a unified theory of physics but a unified architecture, the grid that underpins all forms of energy. Events are arranged into a pattern, a field or grid, constrained by nature's urge to reduce energy into geometric forms. The link between the fields of time and consciousness is that they interact at the quantum level and will influence the physical world.

In psychology Jung perceived the archetypes as existing on a matrix of points that are energised. Each node on this matrix is both relevant to time and to psychological events that link to that moment. The points amass energy, like the Higgs boson particle hunted by the physicists of Cern, which is seen as behaving like a field of 'gravitational pull', giving mass to some particles and not to others. Energy is now seen as substance in physics and these energetic processes reduce to specific patterns like those produced by magnets, or archetypes in psychology.

Being energised, these archetypes interact with the points around them. That they interact at all is described in physics by the Schrödinger 'cat model', where reality is influenced by the viewer. In Schrödinger's model the cat is neither alive nor dead until it is viewed. The act of viewing influences the outcome and concludes the ambiguity that physical space and time are not fixed but in flux. In physics this is seen in the experience of light, which can be measured as either a wave or particle and will take either form depending on how it is measured. As light is able to behave as two different states, perhaps time can exist in both a linear and field form.

The dual nature of time allows us to experience it in a linear fashion, a straight line of events, but it also behaves as an energetic field where events can have influence sideways, making prophecy possible. The interaction between the linear and field forms of time takes place in the higher levels of consciousness, where it dynamically creates a dream of non-local information.

Using the field model of time is a viable explanation of how prophecy might work. The receiving of non-local information from other points in time has been shown many times by the sages and seers of all ages. The question that remains is not one of science or psychology, but of free will.

FREE WILL

The philosophical debate of free will versus destiny has raged throughout history. Knowledge of the future that is available in the present directly challenges our concept of free will and evokes superstitious ideas of fate. Should a prophecy contain images of actual events with real people carrying out real actions in the future then every aspect of that vision would be fixed in time: the event must happen at a predetermined moment in time and those that are present would have led inevitable lives that lead up to that point; they would be drawn towards that moment as if every choice they ever made was already set in stone.

The issue can be explored using astrology as an example. Astrologers would have us believe that the position of the planets at the time of our birth would dictate a map of our lives as if it were set from that point onwards. If an astrologer was to tell you that, according to the positions of the planets, you will get run over by a bus tomorrow, you might take the precaution of not crossing any roads, or even not leaving the house should you put great trust in astrology. It would seem irrational and superstitious to others, but assuming a bus did not detour through your house you will have defied the future and exerted your free will over the situation.

Modern forms of prediction are often portrayed as open to change, as if our own free will has the power to redirect our destiny away from a predestined event. There is often an attempt to give people choice by reducing the outcome from a fixed event in time to a possibility. In this case astrology would only map the life of cowards, people who have never chosen to act through their own free will and are moving towards whatever conclusion fate has in store for them by default.

CHANGING THE FUTURE

It is possible to argue that, as the prophet is receiving a snapshot of the future that is travelling back to them, what happens between now and that point remains under our control. The issue with this is that the closer we get to a fixed point, the less free will we can exercise around it.

Another option for having the ability to change the future draws upon the idea that all outcomes exist somewhere, allowing for prophecy to be averted as we can potentially move into another reality. This requires multiple universes, or a 'multiverse' model to underpin the physics of the universe.

The theory of a multiverse postulates that every possible outcome of an event must exist somewhere. These would take the form of multiple realities that are breeding at a rate of billions to cover every eventuality of random acts. This would also allow for any kind of prophecy to come true somewhere as they are all possible outcomes but the number of parallel universes would be infinite, which seems wasteful – and nature is rarely wasteful.

Philosophically, this endless quantum variation is countered by the notion that if every possible reality exists then in one of those universes there is only one 'real' universe and the others exist only as mathematical theory. Common sense – mine at least – would dictate that while all these universes exist as 'possibilities', there is only one that actually does exist: the one we inhabit. The conclusion we can draw from this is that the multiverse theory remains just a theory and we occupy that single universe: a unique instance of reality and all else remains a mathematical abstract of what might have been.

In contrast to this, it is entirely possible that the prophet sees a potential future, energetically in the making, that has not, and might not, come to fruition.

THE FUNNEL

In any situation there is a network of relations. In his *An Experiment with Time*, J W Dunne proposes a second dimension of time that consciousness can tap into, which signifies potential. It gives rise to the idea that although we are moving through linear time there is a 'meta' level that encompasses all time as a single event. We can picture this as a funnel projecting from now into the future, getting wider as it gets further away from the present moment, while our linear experience is a cord that runs through the centre. The further ahead we look, the wider the funnel gets and the more possibilities come into play. The open end of the funnel has infinite possibilities but is reduced down to a specific outcome in the present moment. The potential here is that the cord is flexible enough that we could steer it to shift the path within meta-time and change the future.

It is possible to view the cords as sharing influence with others, which brings to mind an image of them woven together into the matrix of time as explained above. If in the future a node on the matrix is changed by our actions the energy from this reverberates outwards and rewrites the vision that was seen in the first place. The event is undone and the prophecy changes at the source, but we would never know.

The funnel model supports what many would like to think: that prophecy is a window to only one possible future. It is often said that prophecy and divination in all its forms has an element of uncertainty and that the future is one possible outcome and can be used as a warning of events that can be averted. This may be seen as weakening the case for prophecy but there is some value to this idea – and not just to calm the nerves of those who uphold the notion of free will.

DIVERTING THE COURSE OF HISTORY

Some researchers, such as Nostradamus' biographer Manly P Hall, believe that there are events in history that can be changed or delayed, and that if this happens it has an effect on events that were to follow, sometimes causing them not to come into being. By this reckoning it is possible to divert the course of history, and to maintain free will in a mechanistic universe.

In recent history there is an example of a prophecy that was loaded with potential but did not come into being. In 1909 Pope Pius X spontaneously entered a trance. He closed his eyes and remained still for a short time. When he opened his eyes again he recounted a vision in which he saw a pope escaping the Vatican and fleeing Rome by clambering over the dead bodies of cardinals. Pius later added more details, claiming that the pope would share his name and, although forced into hiding, he would later die a cruel death. The potential for this to happen came with the German occupation of Rome during the Second World War. Pope Pius XII had, prior to the war, signed a concordat of peace with Adolf Hitler, but had become critical of Hitler and was under pressure to speak out against him. Had he cancelled the concordat with Hitler and made a stand against him the occupation would have likely turned into a bloody siege with the exact outcome predicted by Pius X.

Both the prediction of the demise of this namesake and the carnage surrounding the Vatican would appear to have been averted. Of course, it is possible that this will happen at some point in the future anyway, but it illustrates what appears to have been a possible future. There are also many examples of prophecies that only partially came true in parts, and examples of these will be given in a later context.

With the science and psychology of prophecy considered, if not concluded upon, the next step in our investigation is to look at prophecy in the context of Christianity. The Bible contains hundreds of predictions, many of which came to fruition within the time of the gospels, and others, such as the Apocalypse of St John, are yet to happen. The tenets of Christianity are underpinned by prophecy and yet since biblical times the Catholic Church turned its back on the visions and revelations of those within the Church. However, some prophecies cannot be ignored.

CHAPTER 3

PROPHECY IN CHRISTIANITY

Where there is no vision, the people perish.

Proverbs 29:18

INTRODUCTION

In Christianity prophecy is considered knowledge from God, via Himself or angels working on His behalf. For many it is the gift of the Holy Spirit revealing the divine will or teachings from the highest source conferred through grace. According to the great psychologist Carl Jung any wisdom revealed to us that is not of our own creation is spirit incarnate; it comes from a projected part of our unconscious that can allow an autonomous personality to replace our ego, or, in religious terms, the prophet is possessed of the Holy Spirit. The Holy Spirit is often represented by a dove artistically and is considered the 'breath of god', which brings wisdom and inspiration to those who follow Jesus. As the emissary of God's will, it can communicate it to people through inspiration.

Receiving prophecy in the form of a voice would seem incongruous as language has evolved so far over time. As the voice of prophecy tends to speak the language of the prophet, be it Hebrew, Aramaic, Latin, French or any other language, this may give rise to the notion that the voice is not the Holy Spirit or some external force but the murmuring of our own unconscious. According to the epistle of Corinthians prophecy manifests differently according to who is receiving it and is therefore a personalised experience:

> But the manifestation of the Spirit is given to every man to profit withal. For to one is given by the Spirit the word of wisdom; to another the word of knowledge by the same Spirit; To another faith by the same Spirit; to another the gifts of healing by the same Spirit; To another the working of miracles; to another prophecy; to another discerning of spirits; to another divers kinds of tongues; to another the interpretation of tongues: But all these worketh that one and the selfsame Spirit, dividing to every man severally as he will.
>
> 1 Corinthians 12:7–11

The words that the prophet hears are not always descriptive of future events, as in Christian writings prophecy and revelation are often interchangeable. As such the term prophecy can also be used to describe revealed information that forms the basis of many tenets of Christianity – such as the Ten Commandments, as given to Moses by God. One of the most famous visions of the Old Testament was had by Jacob when he witnessed the ladder connecting the earth to the heavens with angels ascending and descending. This was not a prophetic vision, in terms of showing the future, but more a revealing of a symbolic truth to Jacob.

OLD TESTAMENT PROPHECY

The orthodox Catholic view is that all authentic prophecy is the word of God communicated through the seer, who acts as a vessel and has no ability to prophesise themself. They are messengers of God's revelation because only God can know the future. Regardless of the ambivalent view of the Church, mystical and prophetic experiences have always played a central role in shaping Christianity. Prophecy was an integral part of religious life in biblical times and over 100 prophecies in the Old Testament alone attest to that. During that era all temples had an oracle of some form and these oracles were consulted as it was believed they could reveal the will of God.

The Old Testament describes bands of prophets roaming the land (called the 'nabi') claiming to be conduits of divine knowledge of the future and the revelations of God. Their communications were proven to be accurate as the majority of biblical prophecies are simple to understand and were often fulfilled almost immediately after being revealed. A famous example is the prophecy of the flood which is announced in Genesis 6, with the deluge occurring as predicted in Genesis 7:21. Others are far more complex and some are yet to find fruition such as the 'great tribulation' of the apocalypse described in Revelation 6–22. Much of the Book of Revelation is devoted to describing worldwide destruction in great detail through a myriad of causes, including war, famine and pestilence.

Many of the events in the New Testament are foretold in the Old Testament, giving them credibility at the time they occurred. The Old Testament is steeped in prophecy and prophets are often directly referred to, including Mary, the sister of Moses, who is referred to as a 'prophetess'. In terms of foretelling the arrival of Jesus, as mentioned above, both Balaam and Daniel prophesise the coming of a Messiah figure. The Book of Daniel contains many historical events of its time and prophecies relating to the near future. It is written that Daniel 'had understanding in all visions and dreams'. Daniel also accurately predicted the destruction of the Temple of Jerusalem, which came to pass in AD 70.

The same prophecy regarding the destruction of the temple was gifted to Ezekiel but he also learned of the eventual building of a new temple in Jerusalem. Ezekiel received warnings to communicate to the people regarding the will of God and the future, such as the temple being destroyed due to pagan worship. It would seem this prophecy was avoidable but the people failed to take heed. The Book of Ezekiel also contains much of the basis for the Jewish mystical tradition of the Cabala, but he is also recognised as a prophet in Judaism, Christianity and Islam. It begins with the priest receiving a series of fantastical visions of God. These were followed by the appearance of God in physical form. When God spoke, Ezekiel experienced a spirit entering him and was commanded to go and be a prophet among the peoples of Israel.

The Old Testament prophets were revered as messengers of God, bringing revelations of hidden teachings as well as the future. They would gather in towns and cities to address the public and proclaim their experiences. The gatherings were sizeable, as in Kings 1:18:4 we read that Obadiah took 100 prophets and hid them in a cave where he fed them bread and water.

The teachings of the prophets commanded the highest respect and continued to be a major influence in the New Testament.

NEW TESTAMENT PROPHECY

The importance of the prophets as teachers continued into the New Testament as described in Revelation: 'worship God: for the testimony of Jesus is the spirit of prophecy' (Revelation 19:10).

Jesus was recognised as a prophet as well as a teacher, and in Mark 8:27 he describes himself as a reincarnation of one of the Old Testament prophets. In the gospel of Mark Jesus predicts the coming of the kingdom of God: 'And he said unto them, Verily I say unto you, That there be some of them that stand here, which shall not taste of death, till they have seen the kingdom of God come with power' (Mark 9:1).

From the New Testament it is clear that Jesus understood the importance of prophecy. He often prophesised during his ministry and told the disciples at the last supper that 'one of you will betray me' (John 13:21), explaining that he was doing this so that 'when it does happen you will believe that I am who I am' (John 13:19). Later Jesus also prophesised that Peter would disown him three times before sunrise and both events happen as predicted.

In Paul's famous speech of Corinthians 13 he states that prophecy must be used with charity or it fails. He goes on to say that as a child he saw clearly, but as an adult he only sees in part. Paul admits to speaking partly as prophecy and partly from knowledge, as if the coming of knowledge and the development of the rational mind, like the tree of knowledge of good and evil in Genesis (2:17), has impeded his relationship with God. He uses the phrase 'through a glass, darkly' which many assume means a shrouded window that partly obscures his view of the kingdom heaven but it is equally likely to be an acknowledgement that it is an imperfect mirror through which his perception of himself is a distorted reflection.

The entire address by Paul is a fascinating piece of insight into the mind of someone of that era, and he concludes by saying that faith, hope and charity abide but charity is the greatest of these. Many recent translations of the Bible have replaced 'charity' with the word 'love' but this undermines the meaning of the scripture.

True charity is altruistic and can only be in service of others. It is beyond the ego and self gratification and cannot be directed towards one's self.

POST-BIBLICAL PROPHECY

With so much stock put in prophesising one wonders why it is not a part of modern Judaism, Christianity or Islam. It was certainly depended upon to identify the coming Messiah as predicted in the Old Testament, but since biblical times the acceptance of prophecy has declined.

Prophecy was still paramount to Christians in the early centuries that followed the time of the New Testament. Leading figures in early Christianity were recognised for their prophecies, such as Ignatius of Antioch in AD 100, Justin Martyr (AD 160), Polycarp of Smyrna (AD 150) and Iranaeus (AD 150).

Commentaries have survived from this time and the *Didache* (*Teaching of the Twelve Apostles*), dating from the 1st and 2nd centuries AD is one of the oldest forms of Christian doctrine. In part it describes travelling prophets and how to judge if they are false or not. If they are found to be true it instructs the reader to feed and care for them. During the 2nd century, *The Shepherd of Hermas* document describes prophecy in Rome at this time and is similar to the *Didache* in that it explains how to test false prophets.

During the latter part of the 2nd century prophecy rapidly declined from use in the burgeoning Catholic Church. A possible cause was the sense that it held a power that was beyond the control of the Church. For a pope to have supreme power it would not have been favourable to have prophets roaming the land speaking directly from the mind of God. Certainly, later in the history of the Church prophecy was frowned upon and rarely taken seriously.

Another possibility was that prophecy had ceased to be a method of receiving information from a divine source. A 3rd-century revival of prophecy came in the form of the Montanists led by founder Montanus. These were a religious order given to ecstatic visions and reverie. These were rejected by the Catholic Church and branded false prophets, having been judged as allowing themselves to be 'carried away by the spirit'. In the centuries that followed, other than a few well-publicised saints, the visions and voices of the future fall away to darkness and silence.

By the 4th century the Apostolic Constitutions make clear that prophecy is 'superfluous' and that those who possess such gifts 'are warned not to exalt them over the Church rulers'. This denotes a clear change in how the Catholic Church viewed prophecy. It had decided to defend itself from such influence, and from this point frowned upon any utterance that might undermine its leadership. The prophetic order of the Church was relegated to lower roles and made to keep silent over matters of import.

The recognised authority on prophecy in Catholic history was Cardinal Thomas Cajetan (1469–1534), who is credited in the *Catholic Encyclopaedia* as writing the often-quoted 'no credence is to be publicly given to him who says he has privately received a mission from God, unless he confirms it by a miracle,' so setting the bar high for all would-be prophets to gain any acceptance within the Church. Eventually, to protect itself from any interference from prophecy the Catholic Church passed the edict that no prophecy could be judged true or false, but it also adopted the stance that true prophecy cannot contradict biblical scripture or the doctrines of the Church.

While the act of listening for a voice of divine wisdom has not been upheld by the Catholic Church, it was impossible for Catholicism to completely eradicate this tradition from its ranks. Visions and prophecies from the Bible and the lives of the saints are an integral part of Catholicism and St Malachy takes his place among this tradition. However, apart from when the occasional saint that has felt compelled to publish their experiences, the tradition has been relegated to smaller groups such as the evangelists.

Outside of the Church the search for divine opinion has not declined but has moved into more acceptable methods of divination. As we have seen, these techniques of divination exist to energise the unconscious into receiving or revealing knowledge that the conscious mind is unaware of, which can provide the kind of personal revelation that we saw in Corinthians earlier.

SAINTS AND SEERS

As prophecy declined within the Church there were those beyond the walls of Rome who took up the torch, although some of them found it unwillingly thrust upon them as they were overwhelmed by voices or visions. A number of the saints in particular were compelled to share the guidance they received.

In their quest to know the divine first-hand, many saints seemed to care little for the trappings of religion as they experienced rapture and heard for themselves the voice of what they thought to be the Holy Spirit. Some that were divinely inspired found that their calling came from an inner voice which gave them direction and the strength to achieve great things. St Francis of Assisi (1182–1226), founder of the order that bears his name, witnessed a painting of Jesus come to life and command him to put the house of God in order. It is worth noting that although St Francis was a great and pious man he was also devoted to fasting for long periods of time, which is known to induce hallucinations. The vision did, however, compel him to do great works. He petitioned Pope Innocent III to sanction his order but the pope was initially reticent. That night the pope had a dream in which he saw the Lateran Basilica about to collapse when a man ran to take the weight of it on his shoulders. Innocent recognised that man as Francis and took it to be a sign of his importance to the Church and sanctioned the creation of the Franciscan Order. Towards the end of his life St Francis had a vision while praying on Mount Verna. In his vision he saw an angel and an image of the crucifixion. Following this event, which greatly moved him, he developed the signs of stigmata on his hands and feet and the wound in his side echoing the lance that had pierced Jesus on the cross. His life and work are the inspiration for the chosen name of the current pope.

Another famous saint who is entirely relevant to our story is St Hildegard von Bingen (1098–1179). Hildegard was a Benedictine nun who was prone to visions from the age of three but chose to keep them secret. At the age of 42 she had a vision and was instructed to make her experience public. In this vision God commanded her to: 'Write what you see and hear. Tell the people how to enter the Kingdom of Salvation.'

St Hildegard described her experience of receiving visions as the Holy Ghost descended into her from above and filled her with visions which she would record on wax tablets. She compiled 26 visions into a book called *Scivias* (*Know the Ways of the Lord*). The book took ten years to complete, and explores the mysticism of God, creation and redemption. The *Scivias* is accompanied by her own illustrations and interpretation as a commentary inspired by the visions. It includes many prophecies, such as: 'Some countries will prefer their own Church rulers to the Pope' and 'The German Empire will be divided', both of which history has proven correct.

Hildegard also wrote extensively about the End Times, a theme that recurs throughout prophecy. Other notable figures who predicted the End Times include St Hilarion (291–371),

St Ephrem in the 4th century, Bede the Venerable and St Odile in the 8th century, and St Giovanni Bosco (1815–88).

Even a number of popes are reported to have been subjected to visions. These are not always welcome: they can well up at inopportune moments and also contain unpleasant revelations. On 13 October 1884, Leo XIII (pope from 1879 to 1903) collapsed in one of the Vatican private chapels. He was unconscious for a number of minutes and when he awoke he recounted a vision of the coming 20th century. He stated that he had seen how evil would peak in power. Pius X (1903–14) had a similar experience when he fell into a trance and witnessed a vision of a future pope fleeing the Vatican over the bodies of cardinals. Pius XII (1939–58) returned from a vision to warn that mankind would face the darkest days since the deluge.

NOSTRADAMUS

The greatest known prophet could never be described as a saint, although he was Catholic and did much to heal the sick. He was the great seer Michel de Nostra Dame (1503–66), better known as Nostradamus. This French physician and seer outlined over 100 prophecies in the form of cryptic quatrains in his published works *The Prophecies* (1555) and *Centuries and Presages* (1550).

The family of Nostradamus were Jewish in origin but his father had converted to Catholicism, and he is included here as he is not only a leading example of a modern prophet but also because he made a number of predictions regarding the papacy and the end of the world. Many question the accuracy of these prophecies or even if it is possible to interpret the writings that he left to us, but none can doubt the historical record of the numerous predictions he made that came true during his lifetime. He predicted

Catherine de Medici would outlive her three sons, which she did, and the death of King Henry II of France was predicted during a 'duel' and that his eye would be pierced. This came to pass during a friendly jousting competition when a shard of his opponent's lance splintered through the king's helmet, pierced the eye and entered his brain, killing him instantly.

Nostradamus also saw further into the future and was summoning images of inventions such as the submarine and tank, describing them as 'metal fish with death coming from their mouths' and 'moving fortresses'. His descriptions are crude because there was no logical way for Nostradamus to arrive at an understanding of these vehicles in the 16th century.

His legacy is a series of quatrains that make predictions for the centuries to come. Nostradamus saw the rise of an Antichrist and a great schism that would split the Church. Like St Hildegard, he also commented on popes, stating that one would be murdered.

The importance of Nostradamus cannot be underestimated when considering prophecy. Unfortunately, today his writings are often subjected to the extremes of cynicism or unquestioning belief through convoluted interpretation. His detractors will often claim that important events from our current era were not foretold, but it is worth noting that what we consider of great importance in the present may one day be considered to have no lasting importance to the path humanity treads. What the newspapers would have us believe is history in the making can only be recognised retrospectively in terms of its true import.

Many consider Nostradamus' talents for prediction to have been a natural gift that he was endowed with from birth, but on closer inspection it seems he may have had help from the same source as those Old Testament prophets. He was born in France and was devout Catholic for most of his life, but his ancestors were of the biblical tribe of Issachar, mentioned in Chronicles

1:12:32 as people who 'have knowledge of the times, to know what Israel ought to do'. The Issachar were a tribe of prophets. Over the centuries some of the tribe migrated to southern Europe and Nostradamus would have been a descendant of this tribe.

As such biographer Manly P Hall (in *Sages and Seers*) claims Nostradamus inherited a library of ancient texts from the Issachar and these supported his natural talent for visions. Prophecy via astrology was certainly one of the tools he employed to assist in the receiving of prophecies. The visions Nostradamus saw were so terrible that he avowed to protect mankind from them. Aside from the cryptic nature of his writings, he was witnessed making a fire of a pile of documents late in his life. It was assumed that these papers were his prophecies in an unencrypted form but in truth it is more likely that this was the library of his forefathers, the means to see into the future.

We will return to Nostradamus in a later chapter as his presence in history might have had a direct influence on the prophecies attributed to St Malachy, which were first made public just after Nostradamus' death.

VISION AND VISITATION

Since the High Middle Ages a number of visitations have occurred of angels or biblical figures appearing in person to communicate their message. There were many similar accounts of this in the Old Testament and some in the New Testament as angels would manifest to explain the will of God. In recent times visitations have taken the form of the Virgin Mary apparition. Marian visions often give direct instructions by dictating a specific course of action or work to be done, such as where to build a church (Le Laus, France in 1664), or cast a medal of gold with specific designs

(Paris, France in 1830 to Catherine Labouré). Many of these visitations continue the tradition of revealing information through warnings and prophecies. Although never openly acknowledged, these are seen as immensely important within the Catholic Church and the information received will sometimes be treated as highly influential and kept under lock and key within the Vatican.

It is possible that some of these events were hoaxes or a product of hallucination, or that something else was happening but cultural leanings might paint them with a Catholic veneer. The sites at which they appeared became new destinations for pilgrimage; the effect of pilgrimage bringing wealth was well known and in some cases exploited through the relics trade during the High Middle Ages.

These visitations seem predisposed to make prophecies; unlike most forms of prophecy, Virgin Mary visitations tend to be very specific in the information they impart. That they choose a child in the middle of nowhere instead of a pope or world leader presents similar problems to UFO witness accounts, though none of these concerns need devalue the quality of the information provided by the 'vision'. The phenomenon of Virgin Mary apparitions are difficult to dismiss as hoaxes or imaginary as Our Lady often appears to groups for prolonged periods of time.

Early accounts of these visits can be found in a collection of stories dating from the early 15th century called *Miracles of the Blessed Virgin Mary* by Johannes Herolt. These are mostly anecdotal evidence and have no specific dates or named sources but they illustrate that the phenomena was becoming more common place and popular among Catholics.

One of the challenges in evaluating these prophecies is that the records of them were often created long after the event. In Walsingham, England, in 1061, Lady Richeldis is reported as having had three visions of the Virgin Mary in the home where Jesus grew up. Under specific instruction she funded the construction of a replica, which became a shrine. Unfortunately the earliest written account of this event dates from the 14th century, so its credibility is in doubt. The same issue surrounds the visitation of Our Lady of Guadalupe, which occurred in 1531. The first written account of this event dates from 29 years later.

An important example can be found in the accounts of La Salette, France in 1846. This sets a blueprint for later visions – in the nature of the vision and the fact that it appears to children to communicate prophecies. This visitation was witnessed by a young shepherdess and a boy and their account describes the vision of a bright light and then a lady, though they never specifically identify her as Mary. The vision imparts a prophecy of famine, with a specific mention of crops failing, including potatoes. The prophecies came true and each of the crops that the vision specifically mentioned failed in the years that followed. That the vision only appeared to children, as is often the case, seems to indicate that children are pre-disposed to visualising such paranormal events. This would corroborate Paul's speech in Corinthians, mentioned earlier, that as a child he saw clearly, but as an adult he could only see in part.

Later events, although famous, also raise questions of authenticity. In Lourdes, France, in 1858, a vision appeared to Bernadette Soubirous. The decision to identify the vision as the Virgin Mary was made by an adult, who concluded this without actually seeing the apparition, not the child who witnessed the event. Bernadette, the only person who actually saw and heard the vision, was attended by audiences that numbered in the thousands, waiting to hear her account of what had been imparted. Unfortunately the written accounts from her revelations are sketchy and sometimes contradictory.

FÁTIMA

The most famous of these events is the appearance of the Virgin Mary in Fátima, Portugal in 1917. A figure described as 'brighter than the sun' appeared to three children and imparted three secrets to them in the form of prophecies. The visitations continued for six months, drawing ever-increasing crowds of witnesses until an estimated audience of 70,000 people were in attendance – but for the most part only the children could see or hear the events. Other witnesses claim to have seen phenomena, such as a ball of glowing light, but nothing resembling a figure. The visions concluded with a 'dance of the sun' but the accounts of the audience, though all involved the sun in some form, differ in their description of the event.

The first of the Fátima prophecies was of an image of hell with people trapped in fire among demons. The second prediction stated that, although the First World War would end, if people did not mend their ways a second war would occur, far worse than the first. Over 20 years later the outbreak of the Second World War would seem to fulfil this prediction.

The third prophecy was initially withheld and was rumoured to be about the End Times. It was decided that it would only to be revealed by the pope after 1960. The Vatican had a change of heart and reneged on the 1960 release date, holding back until the year 2000. Sister Lúcia, who witnessed the vision and recorded the secret, stated in her memoirs that the final prophecy began with the words: 'In Portugal, the dogma of the Faith will always be preserved.' The version eventually released by the Vatican has no such beginning and is clearly not the same message.

There are clues to the actual nature of the third secret. Sister Lúcia also wrote articles for a number of Catholic publications, referring enquirers to chapters 8–13 in the Book of Revelation.

This recounts the opening of the seven seals and the rise of the Red Dragon during the apocalypse. Pope Benedict XVI, in 1984 when he was still Cardinal Ratzinger, also confirmed that the third secret of Fátima dealt with the End Times. In the same year Ratzinger stated in the Pauline Catholic magazine *Jesus*, 'It adds nothing to what Christians must know respecting what is stated in the Book of Revelation.' Pope John Paul II had also been reported as commenting on the third secret of Fátima: 'If you read that the oceans will inundate continents, and millions of people will die suddenly in a few minutes, once this is known, then in reality it is not necessary to insist on the publication of this secret.'

ESCHATOLOGY

When considering prophecy from both a Christian and secular standpoint the overwhelmingly negative nature of the majority of predictions cannot be ignored. From plagues and famines to wars and great cataclysms, the bringers of prophecy are generally the harbingers of doom. As a result of this and scripture, many Christians in the West have an expectation of an impending event, in some cases tied to the millennium or a New Age variation, but fixated on the End Times and the promise of apocalypse.

The term apocalypse comes from the Greek word *apokalyptein*, meaning 'uncover' or 'reveal'. The 'revealing' in biblical terms is often of God's will or a prophecy of cataclysm and coming events. Christianity, Islam and Judaism all revere apocalyptic scripture. Buddhism, Hinduism, Maya and Zoroastrianism also see history in terms of cycles of creation and destruction. The apocalyptic tradition as a visionary form occurs in many religions and comes under the heading 'eschatology'.

For Christians the key source of eschatology is the Book of Revelation, the short, final book of the New Testament. Revelation is a visionary and highly symbolic journey through three stages of the past, present and future as predicted by St John of Patmos. The future aspect of the text is a revelation drawn from prophecy.

Calvin warns us that studying the apocalypse would make us insane but it remains the most enigmatic of the Bible texts. Visions can be frightening to experience and one imagines that when St John was overwhelmed with the abstract nightmare of the apocalypse he would have suffered some form of psychological breakdown.

During the apocalypse Christ returns to judge the people and this is the source of the Catholic belief in the Second Coming. There is a Golden Age, to last for a thousand years, and that will be followed by a period of rule by Satan, the Antichrist. This culminates with a final battle, followed by the Last Judgement and ultimately, the end of the world.

At the centre of the Book of Revelation is the opening of seven seals, which describe the events of the end of the world. Each seal is opened to release some cataclysmic event such as plague, wars or famine to ravage the earth, and the outcome of the disaster is usually measured in numbers of dead. As war and famine have been constant features of recent decades it is difficult to know if these events are already underway.

THE VISIONS OF ST MALACHY

The writings attributed to St Malachy form an important part of the tradition of prophesising and of eschatology. He has secured a place among the ranks of saints and seers listed above, and numerous other prophets in Catholic history that were compelled to make known their visions and experiences of future events. Malachy made predictions throughout his life but none are as famous as the 'prophecies of the succession of the popes'.

According to legend, nearly a thousand years ago the Archbishop of Armagh in Ireland, later canonised as St Malachy, had a vision in which he saw every future pope from medieval times to the present day. Although there are no contemporary accounts of Malachy making this specific prophecy, in the 19th century Father Cucherat wrote that the prophecies were the result of visions Malachy had received in 1139–40. Unfortunately Cucherat gives no source for this information but he describes Malachy as having had a vision in which the remaining popes were paraded before him until the last.

We do not know what it was like for Malachy to have spontaneously experienced the entire history of the popes from then until now. He must have known of the importance of his vision, and of the truth that set it apart from normal dreams. It is possible that he sat in reverie, reciting them from the trance-like theta state of a waking dream as one of his monks hurriedly transcribed them. The language used in the prophecies lends itself well to the idea that they were taken from visual experiences.

Cucherat maintains that Malachy presented the prophecies as a gift to Pope Innocent II during his stay in Rome from 1139 to 1140 to console him on his difficult reign with the knowledge that the papacy would endure for centuries to come. This would no doubt have appeased the troubled pope but now those centuries have passed and, according the prophecy, the reign of the popes is coming to an end. At the time of writing this the list of popes has just reached its conclusion, with Benedict XVI having resigned and Pope Francis having been elected. The concluding paragraph of the prophecies tells us that the next pope will be the last and he will witness the destruction of Rome and the final judgement of all. This final statement is in keeping with the apocalyptic theme that runs through Christian eschatology.

Apart from taking solace from knowing there were many popes to follow, Innocent II would have recognised the influence that these prophecies could have on the papal elections and would have prevented them being circulated publicly. It would appear they were secreted in the Vatican archives, where they remained until they were rediscovered and published in the 16th century. On their release, some 400 years after being written, questions were raised as to whether Malachy was the true author or if they were a recent creation. Regardless of questions over the authorship, the importance of the predictions lies in their accuracy.

The prophecies of the popes have remained a topic of fascination during the centuries since their publication. The reason for this ongoing interest is that they accurately identify many of the popes that have been elected. Often it is not realised until after the pope is in place how accurate the prophecy has been. This is not an attempt to interpret them to fit the incumbent pope, but in this sense these prophecies follow the Old Testament tradition of being prophecies after the fact – sometimes they can only be understood in the light of events that have already taken place.

As the Catholic Church refuses to pronounce on the accuracy of the prophecies it remains for the individual to decide how credible Malachy's prophecies are in terms of their source, content and authorship.

In this case it would seem that either the Holy Spirit revealed to Malachy the future of the popes or his own fervent and devout consciousness somehow drew images of the popes from the future. Such was Malachy's devotion to God and the good works of the Church that he almost embodied the archetype of a 'Good Catholic'. Such a figure would carry the collective spirit of the age, or 'zeitgeist'.

This is the point where divinatory or prophetic gift can move from being a personal projection to become something more social, reflecting the zeitgeist. Receiving information for an entire group such as the Catholic Church is based on 'shared fate': the interdependence of the group. This would usually be triggered when a collective concern builds within the psychological energy of a group, a tension such as the traumatic times of the Church in the High Middle Ages. Malachy would have been steeped in the issues facing the Church and perfectly attuned to the matrix of the popes and the individual signals they send out through time. In his role as a nexus, or archetype for the fears of the Church, he would have been collectively summoned as the archetype of the perfect Catholic.

That Malachy was completely immersed in the Catholic mindset is beyond doubt. Malachy's visions display a collective power entrenched in the faith in the same manner that the above-mentioned children would witness a phenomenon and later describe this as an apparition of the Virgin Mary. The manifestation of the Catholic group mind carries something of the spirit of Catholicism needed by those present and such apparitions provide a response to the need of the group through prophecy.

PROPHECY TODAY

Today there are no prophecies coming from within the Catholic Church, but other Christian groups have upheld this tradition. The evangelical ministries continue to value prophecy and see it the highest form of religious experience.

The methods used by evangelical orders involve prayer and meditation, and actively waiting on God with an open heart.

The prophets among these congregations have a strong desire to align with the divine forces, and focused expectation while listening and petitioning God to reveal His will. Believers who follow these methods can sometimes succumb to seizures or speaking in tongues prior to having an experience of revelation. The phenomenon of speaking in tongues was first mentioned in Corinthians 14, 'For he that speaketh in an unknown tongue speaketh not unto men, but unto God: for no man understandeth him; howbeit in the spirit he speaketh mysteries.' The act of speaking in tongues can, but not always, precede the receiving of prophecy or some revealed knowledge.

The evangelists believe that all true prophecy exists to clarify existing scripture; they have identified a need for prophecy in the modern world as it fulfils a different role to teaching. Teaching is seen as a means to explain scripture for the mind to understand, whereas prophecy or revelation has the ability to speak directly to the heart. The prophecies that these groups advocate as being true are only accepted if they fall into a clearly defined parameter. As Corinthians 14:3 goes on to say, it is preferred to prophesise and to 'speaketh unto men to bring edification, and exhortation, and comfort'.

As evidenced by the Old Testament prophets, Jesus and the saints that followed, it would seem possible to communicate with a divine source of revelation. But there are many issues with prophecy – for every prophecy that seems correct there are hundreds that make no sense or come to nothing. It is still possible to find books from as recently as 20 years ago that claim the world would be buried under ice by the year 2000 or that some other cataclysm should have befallen us by now.

CONCLUSION

To explore Malachy is a religious undertaking. The context of his writings requires us to travel within the confines of the Catholic faith and its long tradition of prophets that date back to the Old Testament. His words are woven into a tapestry that reaches back to the origins of the Christian churches. Malachy would have been acutely aware that so many of the teachings in Christianity were first made known through revelation. These were truths that the Holy Spirit sought to convey through those it selected as emissaries as well as disseminating coming events. From the wise and devout to innocent children who relay the words of angels, we are compelled to accept that by being so attuned to the divine they became vessels of communication, giving a voice to the realms beyond our own. Many became sainted, so faithful and spiritual were their characters.

And yet the prophet often stands alone. The Catholic Church has refused to pronounce on any prophecy revealed after the Bible was compiled; although the visions and revelations may be circulated and speculated upon endlessly among the higher ranks of the Church, no conclusions can be drawn. So the visions that pour into these holy men and women go unrequited as they can never be accepted or allowed to influence the Church in any way. The pope himself must choose to ignore them, regardless of how divinely inspired they may seem. Malachy was canonised for a great many good deeds but his most Christian quality, the gift for prophecy that resonates back to the Old Testament, remains unrecognised and denigrated as his least influential attribute.

A final thought on prophecy was inspired by George Orwell's *1984*, which itself is an excellent study in the revision and fabrication of history. Towards the end of the book Winston Smith is presented with drink by his captor, O'Brien, and asked if he would like to toast the future. Smith responds that he would prefer to toast the past, and his captor agrees, proclaiming that the past is more important. It is an interesting challenge to the prophets who seem obsessed with divining the future when a clear window on the past might be of greater use. So the past is where we begin.

CHAPTER 4

THE HISTORY OF THE POPES TO MALACHY

INTRODUCTION

M alachy's *Prophecy of the Popes* defines the Catholic Church through the succession of popes from the 13th century to the present day. Aside from the final prophecy, which recounts the last days of the papacy, every prediction describes either a pope, the context of the pope or the challenges they will face. The final chastisement is explained in terms of how the pope will experience it with no wider reference than the fate of Rome. The prophecies do not concern themselves with the fate of the Catholic Church or its congregation, beyond what happens to the pope. As other prophets and prophecies saw their remit as a broad canvas incorporating all aspects of faith, Malachy's vision is very specific. It would appear that through Malachy's eyes the pope and the Catholic Church are synonymous.

With so much emphasis to be placed on the role of the pope we must understand a little of what the title signifies.

THE POPE

The title 'Pope' comes from the word 'papa', meaning 'father', and this is the most commonly used of the nine formal titles for the head of the Roman Catholic Church. The other eight titles are the Bishop of Rome, Vicar of Christ, Successor of the Prince of Apostles, Supreme Pontiff of the Universal Church, Primate of Italy, Archbishop and Metropolitan of the Roman Province, Sovereign of the State of Vatican City and Servant of the Servants of God.

The titles 'Supreme Pontiff' and 'Servant of the Servants of God' may seem at odds with each other but go some way to explain the diverse functions the role now requires. Certainly 'service' would be more in keeping with the life of Jesus but at the same time the pope is now required to act as a ruler, a statesman and a politician as well as a spiritual leader.

The many titles of the pope reflect the multi-faceted nature of the role as head of the worldwide congregation, upholder of the apostolic teachings and head of the Vatican State. In person he is addressed as 'Your Holiness' or 'Holy Father'.

HIERARCHY

Over time the structure of authority within the Church has become fixed and the pope now holds supreme power over the spiritual and physical aspects of the Church. As Bishop of Rome he is considered the direct successor to St Peter. Within the Vatican, the pope is also head of the Roman Curia, which manages the administrative duties of the Vatican. It is within his authority to appoint other bishops and these are considered successors to the apostles. They form the College of Bishops and are responsible for the running of the Catholic Church.

Each bishop is also responsible for a diocese, a geographic region that would usually contain a number of individual parishes. The main church in a diocese is usually the cathedral. If the population or scale of a single diocese is larger than usual there might be an archbishop, with other bishops appointed to support him.

Beneath the bishops are priests, who are responsible for individual parishes. Originally there would have been one priest to a church, but due to the decline in congregations there are sometimes clusters of churches that are managed by a single priest. Priests speak directly to the flock, or parishioners, perform civil duties such as weddings and funerals, hear confession and hold mass. They work at a community level and are often supported by deacons. The role of deacon was once exclusively for trainee priests but has since widened to include those who have no calling to priesthood. Only at the rank of deacon may a member of the Church hierarchy be married.

BECOMING POPE

When an individual feels he is called to become a priest he must make a life-long commitment to celibacy, devotion and service. Usually he will take the advice of a local priest and pray to God for guidance on how best to serve his faith. If he decides to be a priest he will then apply to a seminary, a theological college, for training to join the priesthood. The candidate will be expected to study all aspects of the faith in a process that can take up to two years. He will then spend at least a year assisting within a parish as he trains to be a deacon. Once qualified as a deacon the candidate will serve for at least six months before being ordained as a priest. Priests take vows of celibacy, poverty and obedience to their bishop. Celibacy as a vow was inspired by the passage in Matthew 19:12 where Jesus pronounces on the divine union of marriage: he tells the disciples that it is adultery for a man to divorce and re-marry unless the wife has been unfaithful. The disciples state that it would be better not to marry in that case and Jesus responds by stating: 'For there are eunuchs who have been eunuchs from birth, and there are eunuchs who have been made so by men, and there are eunuchs who have made themselves eunuchs for the kingdom of heaven.' As there is no actual mention of celibacy, but the Catholic Church has interpreted it so, this has often been made an issue of contention.

Once installed as a priest, progress through the Church is at the discretion of the local bishop and the pope. The likelihood for many is that they will not be promoted for many years, if at all, so they remain as priests for life. The next stage is that they are ordained as bishops, priests or deacons. Ordination means incorporating an individual into an order. For those not wishing to be ordained but who still choose to devote their life to God, they will often join holy orders. Monastic orders are an example of this, where the members believe a community is the best environment to practise their spiritual life.

The pope or bishops may appoint other bishops, priests or deacons but only the pope can appoint bishops to the College of Cardinals. These are usually the more senior bishops. Cardinals can remain as bishops, overseeing a diocese, or they can take an administrative role in the Vatican. It is a select group from the College of Cardinals who gather to elect a new pope. Technically they can appoint anyone as the pope but it is now common for them only to promote someone from within their own ranks.

RECORDED HISTORY

The Catholic Church began in humble circumstances and barely survived the first few centuries as the apostolic succession eventually took root in St Peter's early Christian community in Rome. The centuries that followed were fraught with challenges that had great effect upon Malachy's time and the popes of the second millennium after Christ.

As the papacy has developed as an organisation over the last 2,000 years, the parallel history of its spiritual development seems strangely absent. Unlike the biographies of the saints, the lives of the popes are often bereft of any record of their mystical leanings other than their daily spiritual practice. The inspirational aspects of the popes are seemingly ignored with the overall spiritual evolution of the papacy overlooked in favour of scandal and political machinations.

It is true that in those formative years there was a transformation from a spiritual organisation to political one and so the history of the popes is often measured in political events. The pope has played a central role in many of the great military, political, cultural and scientific upheavals over the centuries. The involvement of popes in such matters has seen them accused of acting beyond their remit, or in some cases, such as the Second World War, not acting at all.

Matters of faith, it must be remembered, are rarely considered by historians, who are far more interested in the machinations of the popes. So while the journey through the last two millennia of Catholic history may seem materialistic, this is more the fault of historians than a true reflection of the popes' lack of spirituality or faith. To some extent the Catholic Church has only itself to blame for how history remembers it. While critics and historians have certainly focused on the scandals and intrigues, the Vatican's own published encyclopaedias of papal history have erred on the side of political history. This constant focus on the outward events and the actions of each pope and not their inner progress has left those viewing the Church from outside with a picture of an organisation where religion is a fixed set of rules instead of a living, breathing way of life.

But these histories should not detract from the core purpose of the papacy: the spiritual mission that has made the Catholic Church one of the longest standing institutions in the world. The structures of Rome were built with wealth and intrigue, as some may accuse the Church, but they were also built on faith.

Such a vibrant history often detracts from the mystical elements guiding the spiritual development of the Church. The role of the pope is also to translate and convey the mystical aspects of Christianity into everyday ways of living that can easily be communicated to an audience of lay people – people who, in the early days, were often illiterate and uneducated. The challenge over time has been to expand upon those simple messages, as the audience became learned, philosophical and scientific.

THE FIRST POPE

The papal succession is traced back to the apostle St Peter. He is considered the first 'Bishop of Rome', after which all popes follow in his footsteps. Tradition has it that St Peter left Jerusalem and came to Rome, where he circulated among the many Christian communities that had already sprung up there. Eventually Peter was martyred and entombed on the site where the Vatican currently stands. As there is no mention of him being in Rome in the New Testament the accounts of St Peter's travels are pieced together from fragments of historical evidence.

The importance of Peter to Jesus and his place among the apostles is not in question, as Jesus spoke highly of him on a number of occasions. The Gospel of John records that Jesus repeatedly requests that Peter (called Peter or Simon Bar Jona – Son of John) 'Feed my lambs, feed my sheep' – as if Jesus was instructing Peter to teach on his behalf.

In Rome during the 1st century Christians were not a single body but a collection of individual communities and factions, each with their own leader. It has been argued that there was no single Christian leader in Rome at this time, so St Peter could not have been the head of the Christian Church. However, his prominence in scripture and as a witness to the teachings of Jesus would have made him something of an authority to all Christians – if not politically, then certainly their natural spiritual leader. In this sense it is possible to recognise Peter as the leading influence of the Christian Church in Rome, and therefore the first pope.

Rome was settled upon as the seat of power as both St Peter and St Paul died there. It is considered the 'apostolic see', 'see' meaning seat because it was the location of the bishop. 'Cathedra' also means chair, hence the use of the term cathedral today to denote where a bishop is situated. The most important 'see' is that which belonged to St Peter as it is located where his throne would have been if such a thing existed. The bishops that followed St Peter are considered an extension of the apostles, so Rome became the 'apostolic see', and the highest position within the Church was to occupy this seat as head of the Church, overseeing all other bishops. The title for this role was the 'father' or 'papa', which became 'pope'.

St Peter had been confided in by Jesus, who referred to him as his 'rock'. Peter had claimed that he was ready to go with Jesus to prison and even to death but Jesus accurately prophesised during the Last Supper that Peter would deny knowing him three times before dawn. Even with this in mind Jesus continued to describe Peter as his 'rock' (Matthew 16:18), so it would seem that it was not a test to fail but one of character building. Later Peter denied knowing Christ three times as Jesus had predicted, but following the resurrection he became a devout teacher of the message that Jesus had shared with him and in the decades that he lived after the death of Jesus he would have been considered the expert on the teachings of Jesus.

A Christian community existed in Rome during that 1st century and letters surviving from that period show that they knew and venerated Peter.

St Peter was believed to have been martyred in Rome, probably in AD 70. There exists a graveyard in an underground section of Rome called the Sacred Grottos. It was here in 1952 that a 1st-century tomb was found, with devotional inscriptions naming Peter. There is also a 2nd-century shrine devoted to Peter nearby. It is not conclusive that the tomb is his but it does add further weight to the argument that his final days were spent in Rome.

There are a number of issues with the tomb, as with many relics dating from this period. A number of sites in and around Rome have been cited as Peter's final resting place and the Vatican has been reticent in choosing a specific one, having accepted a number of different corpses in different locations over the centuries. As the holy sites are often dependent on the donations of pilgrims I doubt carbon dating will be applied to the various remains any time soon.

During his time in Rome Peter would have been recognised as an authority on spiritual matters by the small Christian communities that were springing up in the city. Christianity at the time was still under the threat of Roman persecution, so faith was very much kept a private matter. There were no public gatherings for services and this time is often thought of within the Church as a period of 'simple' Christianity. Having been so close to the time and the source of its teachings, the new religion should have been closer to the essence of what Jesus brought to the world. Some groups have since attempted to return to those times of simple faith but the world has moved on.

THE CATHOLIC CHURCH TO THE TIME OF ST MALACHY

The role of pope has existed for nearly 2,000 years as the head of the Roman Catholic Church. While most countries during that time were ruled by succession and benefited from the continuity that brought, the popes were always elected. As so many of the popes were at an advanced age when they were elected, it made for short reigns and constant change.

For the first 300 years Christianity was persecuted by Rome and the succession of popes had little or no power; there is no clear record of them in the histories. At that time Christianity in Rome was not a single structured organisation but a number of small groups meeting in secret that would have considered themselves part of a greater whole. It is likely there was no central figure of leadership unless St Peter appointed a disciple of his own.

The issues facing these groups would have been about making decisions regarding which texts to follow from the Old and New Testaments, as well as the Hebrew scriptures. They would also have debated which dates were to be accepted as points of historic events and the focus of days to worship. The Church was forming, and the date of when to celebrate Easter, or which of the gospel authors were closest to the truth, would have been considered at length at gatherings known as synods.

Prior to the 3rd century there was very little instruction on how a pope should behave. Many were thought to have been married until this practice was outlawed in the synod of AD 305. Even at this time the persecution of Christians continued, but as they proved to be no military or political threat they were able to continue practising in private without too much interference.

Then in 312 Constantine became emperor of the Roman Empire. He was tolerant of Christians and was a major influence on the coalescing of the Church into a single body. Partly influenced by his Christian mother, St Helena, Constantine facilitated the stabilising of the Church.

The most successful action was to instigate the Council of Nicaea, located in northern Turkey, in AD 324. It required the attendance of over 250 bishops from all over the world to decide and agree upon many of the fundamental tenets of the Catholic Church that are with us today, and quell the fragmentation that threatened to the shatter the early Church.

Constantine's legacy was to allow the Christian Church to take shape and become public. Those scattered groups rose up from the catacombs of Rome without fear of persecution and began to openly share their beliefs. And with their new-found freedom came a certain amount of power.

By the 5th century Italy was at the mercy of invading forces from Western Europe. The Visigoths led by King Alaric swept back and forth across the Italian states and eventually pillaged Rome. The Vandals followed and in the 6th century the Germanic Lombards seized control of much of northern Italy. They threatened to invade Rome and were only kept in check by increasing amounts of bribery. Over time many converted to Christianity, but their final defeat was at the hands of the military power that had risen in central Europe in the form of Charlemagne, king of the Franks, during the 8th century. Charlemagne's influence was key for the tribes of Germany and the papacy as he supported Pope Hadrian's attempts to reform the Church across Europe.

It was Charlemagne who established Roman rule across Western Europe and set the primacy of the pope in the Church. He also invaded and took possession of the lands that were occupied by the Lombards and donated them to the pope. In AD 800 the pope repaid Charlemagne by crowning him emperor of Europe.

After Charlemagne heresies continued to challenge the authority of the Church in the form of alternative Christian sects. These groups continued to attract converts until their popularity peaked in the Middle Ages, when the Catholic Church brought down a persecution of its own with the hammer of the inquisition.

Charlemagne had protected the pope from his enemies both within and outside Rome. Challengers to Pope Leo's primacy had seen him imprisoned for adultery and perjury. The pope's oath to reform his ways was witnessed by Charlemagne, who had now manoeuvred himself into a very influential position. Two days after witnessing the oath Pope Leo crowned Charlemagne emperor.

Charlemagne was not necessarily a religious man but he understood the political and social importance of religion. By the 9th century his empire spanned most of northern Europe. He had stitched together this patchwork of countries, cultures and tribes through the positioning of archbishops, bishops and priests to connect the communities. Their role was to educate and lead the masses but also to ensure that they conformed to Charlemagne's rule.

The archbishops were powerful figures and at times would challenge the authority of Pope Nicholas I. Nicholas had a strong opinion of the pope's supremacy over the archbishops and stood his ground on a number of occasions.

By the time John VIII (872–82) took to the throne of St Peter, political intrigue and in-fighting within the Church had reached a nadir. He was reputedly poisoned and clubbed to death by one of his own staff. There followed a spate of short-lived popes and many that were no more than political puppets. This state of disarray would last for almost a century as many popes were either murdered or manipulated by political interests. It was as if the papacy was descending into madness – eventually matters came to a head when the corpse of Pope Formosa was exhumed and put on trial by his rival and successor Stephen VI. Stephen himself eventually met a brutal end, but not before he had had Formosa's corpse mutilated and thrown into the Tiber.

At the close of the 9th century the papacy had reached an all-time low and in the nine years between 896 and 904 nine different popes reigned. This was in part due to the assassination of a number of the popes, which had become a regular occurrence as rivals attempted to depose the pontiff. During this time Pope Stephen VII was imprisoned and died at the hands of a fellow inmate and Pope Sergius III was thought to be responsible for ordering the assassination of at least one other pope during his rise to power. He also had a son, by his mistress, who grew up to become Pope John XI. When Pope John XII (955–64) came to power he immersed himself in debauchery, installing a brothel at the Church of St John Lateran in AD 955. He was said to have died of a stroke during the throes of an adulterous liaison. In the same year Pope Benedict V eloped to Constantinople with a young woman, returning to Rome later, only to be murdered by a jealous husband.

It was not until the 11th century that stability and reason were sought to curb the excesses of the papacy. When Pope Benedict VIII came to power in 1012 the tide was turning against sexual relations among the clergy and other practices that were bringing the Church into disarray, although some of the more flagrant abuses of power remained. In a grand act of nepotism after Benedict's death, his family were powerful enough to see that he was replaced by his younger brother, who was not even a priest. Pope John XIX was followed by his nephew Benedict IX, heaping more scandal upon the Church. Eventually he was deposed by Clement II, who had the support of Emperor Henry III. Clement moved to outlaw the selling of offices, to prevent further popes being installed by the powerful families of Rome.

Clement was followed by Pope Leo IX, another reformer who continued Clement's work by further legislating against simony – the selling of offices – and sexual relations for the clergy. He was well liked and travelled Europe to once again exert influence over the Christian countries.

The reforms continued and by the late 11th century much of what we now consider to be Catholicism was in place. The rules for the papal elections were set, marriage was forbidden and the appointing of popes could not be a matter of wealth. This was true for much of Europe, though not the case in Ireland, which was in decline at this stage and finding itself increasingly cut off from the radical developments taking place in the rest of the Church.

In 1089 Urban II created a curia, giving more power and influence to the cardinals. He had created an inner circle of advisers to the pope. The role of cardinal was taking shape: already they alone chose a new pope and eventually they would run the administration of the Vatican and limit the election of further popes to those from within their own ranks.

Urban II also instigated the First Crusade to capture the Holy Land for the Christians. He held a synod in France to drum up support and finance the campaign; politically it united the West under the banner of Rome against a common enemy. In 1099 the armies of the West, under the command of European nobles, slaughtered their way to occupying Jerusalem. Urban II died shortly after.

His successor, Pope Pascal II, supported Germany's Henry V, but Henry marched on Rome and demanded to be crowned emperor. Unhappy with Pascal's response, Henry kidnapped him and forced him to conduct the ceremony. As soon as Henry's troops retreated, Pascal renounced his own actions and returned to Rome with the intention of abdicating, but he died before he got there.

In 1119 Callistus was crowned pope in Vienna. An excellent diplomat, he resolved the issue of Henry V and, as a direct result of Henry's earlier insistence that he could appoint his own bishops, Callistus created the template for 'concordats'. These are formal agreements drawn up between the pope and a ruler clarifying that only the Church has the power of investiture over bishops, therefore separating Church and state. The concordat continues to be used today and was notoriously invoked in recent years as an agreement between the pope and Adolf Hitler.

By the 12th century European nations became defined by their emerging kings and rulers, distancing themselves from the control of the emperor. Hereditary power was on the rise and brought stability to the leadership of countries. The Church of the second millennium had also transformed completely from the small Christian groups that had met in secret a thousand years before.

Even among the popes the first thousand years were a fluid and sometimes barbaric time. The role was also fraught with challenges as historically the pope was required to be as much a politician as a spiritual leader. In the centuries preceding Malachy the papacy had often been in turmoil as the powers of the pope had been fought over. Such disagreements would sometimes delay the election for years at a time, adding to the turmoil within the Church.

THE TIME OF MALACHY

By the time of St Malachy the power of the Catholic Church over its subjects was at a peak. It controlled all aspects of life for the members of the congregation by controlling education and learning, while holding influence over kings and heads of state, who were eager to keep in favour. But those who meddle in politics rarely come away unscathed and for a time the influence went both ways, with kings and nobles contriving to create popes for political ends.

Just prior to Malachy the crusades had begun, and would continue for nearly 500 years. The Catholic Church had rallied Europe, finding support from kings and nobles in the fight to stem the tide of Islam that had been spreading west since the 7th century. Spain had fallen to Islam in the 8th century and by the 11th century Christian Europe was under siege on all sides. Islam was a more robust faith than previous pagan beliefs had been and proved impervious to missionaries, who were often imprisoned or killed for preaching Christianity in Islamic countries.

The crusades to reclaim parts of Europe and liberate the Holy Land captured not just Jerusalem but the imaginations of the people across Europe. It gave the Catholic Church a single enemy and a purpose the people could identify with. Donations of land and money poured in to support the crusades and the power of the Church grew exponentially, to the point where it became more powerful than any king or country. The pope could influence politics in any country and was becoming feared and respected as a necessary ally to kings.

It was also a time of gothic cathedrals: towering symphonies of geometry, stone and glass stood above every other building as landmarks that could be seen for miles around, always visible as a reminder of the ever-present God and power of the Church. However, such wonders and the progressive nature of the Church, which saw the influence of Catholicism spread across mainland Europe as a single force, had not reached Ireland.

The 12th century was also the age of St Bernard of Clairvaux, whose writings were widely circulated to meet the demands of the rising number of theologians and scholars. The study of canonical law had become popular and education was ever widening its catchment of the populace. As Europe moved towards scholasticism, with the rise of education and study of widely circulated religious texts and thinkers such as St Bernard and St Anselm, Ireland was at risk of being left behind, mired in religious turmoil. It had become a place where faith was either in decline or distorted to suit the political ends of local rulers.

Then into this milieu St Malachy was born.

CHAPTER 5

THE LIFE OF ST MALACHY

INTRODUCTION

A t the geographic extremity of Western Europe Ireland had avoided the majority of the turbulent upheavals that had reshaped European civilisation since the fall of the Roman Empire. As the barbarian hordes raged across Europe after the sacking of Rome in the 5th century, Ireland became one of the last bastions of the Catholic faith in Europe.

CATHOLICISM IN IRELAND

The full conversion of Ireland to Catholicism is attributed to the mission of St Patrick, who had laid the foundation for organising the Church, although compared to mainland Europe the influence of pagan religions in Ireland was still very much in force.

Although St Patrick had 'converted' Ireland his influence had only gone as far as developing the existing beliefs of the people towards the start of a Christian path. The influence and inspiration of St Patrick remains a strong symbol to the Irish Catholics and instigated some of their traditions.

St Patrick was born in the west of England and at 16 was kidnapped by Irish pirates and forced into a life of servitude in Ireland. After six years, guided by what he believed to be an angel, he escaped his captors and returned home to eventually train as a priest. Inspired by a visionary dream, once ordained he returned to Ireland as a missionary. He became the Bishop of Ireland in AD 435 and advocated the setting up of monasteries throughout the land. His biographers claim that he was responsible for the building of over 700 churches, and appointing hundreds of bishops and thousands of priests. During his life he was said to have performed over a thousand miracles, including raising many people from the dead. In less than 30 years Ireland had gone from being almost entirely pagan to mostly Catholic. While prophecy is very much a part of the Catholic faith, in Ireland there is a long tradition of saints displaying talents such as performing miracles and seeing the future. The emphasis on this particular aspect of the faith stems particularly from the legends surrounding St Patrick.

St Patrick is quoted in *The Life and Acts of St. Patrick* as saying, 'The Lord hath given to me, though humble, the power of working miracles among a barbarous people.' He also made a number of predictions, including that Dublin, at the time a small village, would become a great city and that the people of Ireland would be spared from Judgement Day by being destroyed by a deluge prior to this.

After his death in AD 461 St Patrick's influence waned and the country reverted to a hybrid of pagan and Christian beliefs. There followed other saints and bishops who upheld the cause of Catholicism, and the primary ones are referred to as the 'twelve apostles of Ireland'. The structure of the Church was corrupt, though, with bishops being appointed not by Rome or even elected, but by hereditary succession within the Irish clans.

The Catholic Church had influenced the rebuilding of much of Europe during the 6th and 7th centuries and was responsible for establishing many of its colleges and forms of education at that time. This gave the Church a great influence over many aspects of life and culture that are still with us today and highly prevalent among Irish Catholics.

Removed from mainland Europe, Ireland continued to uphold the faith, building abbeys and monasteries and creating the strong Irish tradition of training and despatching missionaries across the world. An old Irish priest once told me: 'Ireland never invaded anywhere by force, but it invaded many countries by stealth with its missionaries.' In the 6th and 7th centuries the missionaries sailed forth and spread Christianity back through Europe, re-establishing it as the dominant religion.

By the early 9th century the Viking invaders had begun their campaigns against Ireland and these targeted the monasteries and churches and slowly stripped away the power and wealth of the local Church. Libraries were burned and monasteries looted. It seemed for a time that Ireland would fall into a Dark Age of its own. Forays by the Vikings into the country continued to undermine Christianity, and for a time it seemed that the situations in Ireland and Europe would be reversed.

Meanwhile, the rest of Europe had revived and the barbarian hordes had dissipated or been absorbed into the societies that they had once preyed upon.

Whereas the remoteness of the country had originally protected it from the hordes of barbarians that had swept across Europe after the fall of Rome, the later invasions by the Vikings had once again secluded Ireland, although this time it was from the developments being made in Europe, stymieing Catholic control of the country.

Ireland was slow to follow Rome, but during the 11th century some of the Viking invaders began to convert to Christianity and settle, while the remaining force were finally defeated at the battle of Clontarf on Good Friday 1014. There followed a terminal decline in their harassment of the Irish peoples and those Vikings that remained converted to Christianity.

Many historians from this period (Lanfranc and Anselm, for example) agree that Ireland was at a low cultural and spiritual ebb by the 11th century. Malachy is portrayed by his biographer, St Bernard of Clairvaux, as 'a sheep among wolves but a sheep who converted them'. Ireland at the time of Malachy consisted of many different tribal territories and, whether from the reports of Malachy or by his own invention, on a number of occasions St Bernard describes the people of Ireland as 'barbarous' and 'uncultured'. St Bernard continues to denigrate the people of Ireland as if to contrast how saintly Malachy was by comparison. He calls them a 'rude people' although he himself never set foot in Ireland.

St Bernard's vehement reaction is echoed by other Christian historians such as Giraldus, who described the Irish people as 'a filthy race, a race sunk in vice . . . ignorant of the rudiments of faith'. This Christian view that the Irish as a people were devoid of faith is likely to be due to the unorthodox practices that were widespread. The Irish nation prior to the arrival of St Patrick did not exist in a spiritual vacuum, so it was likely that the Catholic historians of the time could not accept that the Irish had kept the tenets of their older religious beliefs. Even after St Patrick had walked among them they were reluctant to completely abandon the traditions of their prior religion and had chosen to merge these with the faith of St Patrick. The result was a form of pagan Christianity, at a time when the Catholic Church was heavily persecuting those who deviated from accepted practice.

The negative descriptions also ignore the respect Ireland garnered for its centres of education. The scholarly tradition continued to flourish and Ireland was considered a seat of learning in Europe for many centuries. There were many scholars of renown in Ireland and this continued into the 11th century with colleges such as those at Armagh and Kildare. Great works were produced during these times, such as the beautifully illustrated manuscripts filled with coloured images and striking calligraphy.

With such famous and well-respected academics and learning centres, European nobles and even kings would travel to spend time in the care of the learned professors. As Catholicism provided the majority of education available by the High Middle Ages the Church controlled many aspects of people's lives, including how they viewed the world.

Nonetheless, Rome had all but turned its back on Ireland: there were many Irish bishops but they had no authority in the eyes of Rome and were not recognised as being able to perform officially the sacraments such as ordination. In some cases the bishop would be the head of a local clan, not ordained by other bishops or by Rome but appointed by hereditary succession. This was entirely unorthodox and unacceptable to Rome. By the time Malachy took up the mantle, Ireland's position was quite removed from the jurisdiction of the Catholic Church. The powers of the bishops were sanctified and their jurisdiction was limited to their own means. This allowed for a high degree of variance in practices across the country. Morality was lax and the religious practices such as confession were not upheld.

A great reformation subsequently swept the country and by the 13th century Ireland was organised into dioceses in line with the rest of Europe, with each having a bishop and a cathedral as the seat of power, supported by a clergy. A strict adherence to the sacraments was reinstated to bring the Irish Church back in line with the orthodox view. The cause of this sudden rediscovery of faith in the Catholic Church and subsequent conversion and uniting of the disparate factions that had fragmented Ireland was due, in great part, to one man.

MALACHY O'MARE

For centuries St Malachy was known primarily as a leading reformer of the Catholic Church in Ireland. His devotion to God and the Catholic Church was inspirational as he sought to unite the many bishoprics that were scattered across his home country.

Through Malachy's influence Ireland would once again be a beacon of Catholic faith and community.

Early life

Malachy was born into the O'Mare family near Armagh, Northern Ireland in 1095. The name Malachy is a Latin version of the Gaelic 'Maolmhaodhoc' and his mother was of the O'Hanratty family. Both parents were strong Catholics but his father, a teacher, died when Malachy was eight years old, leaving him in the care of his mother, who St Bernard accords with great respect for raising him so well alone. She sought support through her faith and worked hard to provide the moral and spiritual upbringing that would benefit her son so greatly in later life.

Malachy was described as meek and subdued, lovable and gracious to all, a model child but in some ways like an old man, without playfulness. His father's death must have taken something of his childhood away, as often is the case when a boy without a father takes on the mantle of 'man of the house'. Part of the friendship of St Bernard and St Malachy may well have been cemented by the common ground they shared of childhood bereavement – St Bernard had experienced a similar situation, having lost his father at an early age.

Rise to recognition

As a teenager Malachy became a disciple of an austere hermit called Imar O'Hagan, who founded the monastery and church of Armagh, and who occupied a bare cell attached to Armagh Cathedral. Malachy would sit at his feet and join him in his silence and severity. At 17 it was his master who taught him humility and the monastic rule. He passed through adolescence studying and gaining wisdom and is described by St Bernard as being pure of heart and well liked.

The use of seminaries as training establishments for priests was already in place during the 13th century so it would seem Malachy was not intending to become a priest. People like O'Hagan were known as 'anchorites' and led the life of an ascetic, often self-imprisoned in a small cell attached to a church, dependent on the support of others for their food and sanitation. He would have appeared to Malachy as the model of a pious figure, living a life devoted to prayer and contemplation. Anchorites were essentially hermits who taught through the bars of a small window. As many would remain incarcerated until death, a morbid custom at the time was for the local priest to administer the last rites to the anchorite before they went in. This would include an enacting of the death scene.

An early role in the church for Malachy was to prepare the dead for burial. His sister would admonish him for seeing that the poor had dignified burials and he called her a 'wretched woman' who could quote scripture but was ignorant of what it meant. Malachy's sister is held up by St Bernard as an example of a sinner in contrast to Malachy's pure spirit. They never healed this sibling rift and many years later, when she had died, Malachy was compelled to spend many hours saying prayers for her, having seen visions of her restless spirit. He also heard voices in dreams telling him about her plight of hunger in the afterlife which made him pity her. Her spirit visited Malachy as a vision three times as he continued to say prayers for her over a period of days. At first she appeared in dark clothes and was unable to enter the church. In the account of the second apparition she wore lighter clothes and could enter the church but not approach the altar. On her third visitation she was dressed in pure white, which Malachy took to be a sign that she had been saved.

The example introduces Malachy's penchant for visions but it is also being presented as evidence of the power of prayer to redeem lost souls.

Ordination

In 1119, at about 25 years old, Malachy was ordained a priest, the lowest age limit for this role, though such rules were not strictly adhered to in Ireland at the time, as St Bernard would have us believe the bishop wanted to set Malachy's obvious talents to work in spreading the word of God among the people. It was soon recognised that Malachy had an ability to speak well and convert people, to remain pious and set a good example to those he was preaching to.

Bishop Gilbert wanted to heal the schism and unite the local factions in Ireland. This would have been the mission he had in mind for Malachy, but although Malachy had the diplomatic skills to achieve the task he lacked the background in theology to carry through his arguments. Deciding he was not qualified for the role, Malachy moved to Lismore and spent the next two years studying under St Malchus.

Malachy returned to Armagh with the intention of reforming the abuses of clergy and reinstating the sacraments to the congregation which had been abandoned in some areas.

Bangor Monastery

In 1123 he was made Abbott of Bangor, a title that had been unused for two centuries, and here he established a new monastery by working with the monks from Imar's community. During the work he swung an axe and accidentally hit a fellow worker's back. The axe crashed down on the spine of the man and was thought to have wounded him so severely that it was expected he would soon die. On inspection, beneath the man's shirt he was found to be unharmed. This is said to be the first of many miracles Malachy performed in his life, though it should be noted that the event, if true, was not the wilful act of Malachy performing a miracle but an example of grace interceding upon him.

Malachy was head of the monastery and under the guidance of Imar. He led by example in teaching the monks how to conduct themselves, but many questioned his ability to administer the business side of such an establishment, as he would often take the revenue that had been collected and dispense it directly to the poor.

During his time in Bangor the region continued to suffer raids and some years later the original monastery as built by Malachy was destroyed by pirates and raiders. At the age of 30 Malachy was promoted to Bishop of Connor, where he continued his programme of reforms by successfully replacing the Celtic liturgy with the Roman liturgy.

His original ordination had been overseen by Archbishop Celsus and in 1129, near to death, the archbishop requested that Malachy succeed him. He sent Malachy his staff – called Bachal Isu, the Staff of Jesus – and a letter appointing him the next Archbishop of Armagh. The Staff of Jesus had come to Ireland as a gift from

St Patrick, who had received it as a gift while visiting the island of Alanensis in the Mediterranean. As St Patrick climbed a hill in prayer he was offered the staff for support. He bequeathed the staff to Ireland, where it was considered an important relic and symbol of power for those that held it. Malachy recognised the staff from a vision he had seen where it was given to him as a symbol of succession.

The appointment of Malachy created a conflict, as tradition had been for hereditary succession and the local clans and self-appointed nobles would not have an outsider take the position. Relatives of Celsus usurped the seat, intercepted and stole the Staff of Jesus, and installed Celsus' cousin, Murtagh, as the archbishop.

To avoid bloodshed Malachy waited for two years before challenging Murtagh. Eventually he was threatened with excommunication if he did not oppose this hereditary archbishop of the local tribes, even though he knew it would anger them. The enemies of Malachy attacked the city of Connor, forcing him to flee to the protection of King Cormack in County Kerry.

In 1134 Murtagh died and was replaced Celsus' brother, Niall. Niall took control of the holy office and schemed to have Malachy killed. On learning of the plot it is said that Malachy prayed and a great storm rose up and destroyed his potential attackers. St Bernard likens this event to Elijah calling down fire from heaven in the Old Testament. This was one example of how God was said to favour Malachy and destroy his enemies. In another account a man who spoke rudely of Malachy had his tongue swell and turn putrid, causing him to vomit for seven days until he died. The ill-will towards Malachy dwindled greatly when a pestilence arose in the city and Malachy prayed for the people to be free of it, after which it immediately ceased.

Niall responded by requesting a meeting with Malachy, who accepted knowing he must risk martyrdom to restore the Church in Ireland. At the meeting Malachy spoke in such a way that he won over the audience and Niall agreed to relinquish the title of archbishop. The Staff of Jesus was still in the possession of Niall and Malachy secured it by purchasing it on behalf of the Catholic Church in Ireland.

Here is not the time or place to consider the veracity of the relic as it served a symbolic purpose well enough. The fate of the Staff of Jesus was that it was eventually destroyed in 1538 on the orders of King Henry VIII of England, so sadly both its power and proof of any credibility are beyond our reach.

Malachy now had the authority to support his words and actions. He spoke so clearly on ecclesiastic matters that St Bernard likened him to the apostles. Malachy sought to spread the word of God by walking the land with his disciples and preaching – in a manner reminiscent of Jesus he took the gospel to the people instead of expecting them to come to him.

As his reputation spread many began to seek his opinion in matters of faith and healing. Local dignitaries, and even one of the kings of Ireland at the time, requested his advice.

Voyages and miracles

Around 1140 Malachy took it upon himself to travel with his followers on a pilgrimage to visit the pope in Rome. The journey took his party via Scotland and England to reach the shores of France. It was on this journey that Malachy first encountered St Bernard of Clairvaux.

By the time of this first meeting, St Bernard had already risen to great prominence in Europe. He was a leading figure in Christianity who commanded great respect across Europe. It must have been an awe-inspiring experience for a humble monk from Ireland to encounter such a legendary figure, but St Bernard saw a kindred spirit in Malachy and the two became close friends.

He wrote a detailed account of this period of Malachy's life that is so filled with miracles that it reads more like a heroic epic of antiquity than a biographical record.

The teachings of St Bernard greatly influenced Malachy throughout his life. Inspired by St Bernard, Malachy introduced the Cistercian Order into Ireland and set to building monasteries. They became great friends but their backgrounds could not have been more different. St Bernard was the son of a nobleman, Tescalin, and was born at Fontaines near Dijon, in France. His mother was a strong religious influence and Bernard undertook a religious life, joining the nearby community at Citeaux. Citeaux was the site of the Cistercian Order founded by Stephen Harding. The order followed the strict observances of the Benedictines, including the banning of luxuries and the move from earnings by taxation to the self-sufficiency of building a farming community.

The *Rule of St Benedict* was written in the 5th century and became the template for all monastic life that followed. The *Rule* dictated how a monk should live, by mapping out his actions throughout the day. This ordered approach of living was self-imposed to reduce the risk of inappropriate or sinful feelings arising, such as pride, but it also gave a structure to the acts of devotion and prayer. Within this framework St Bernard emphasised the fourfold path to spiritual development of 'divine reading', which was a cycle of reading, meditating, prayers and contemplation. This path, which can still be used to great effect today, begat a simple lifestyle, orderly and humble. Part of the rule was a work ethic that the monks would spend a number of hours every day working the land and selling the produce to make a basic living. The remaining food would be donated to the poor. The results of their toil raised funds for the monasteries and surrounding communities and eventually many became successful cottage industries.

Variations of the Benedictines appeared over time and in 1098 the Cistercians were founded by St Robert and St Stephen at the abbey in Citeaux. Under the wise and popular guidance of St Bernard, who took control of the abbey in 1113, it flourished into one of the most successful in Europe.

Using his revival of the monastery at Clairvaux as a template St Bernard drove forward a reformed monasticism that attracted thousands to join his cause. He also became famous for his strong work ethic and his legendary ability to heal the sick, attracting huge crowds to Clairvaux seeking his help and advice. The monasteries became centres for study and teaching, making them one of the few choices for education available. But St Bernard never lost sight of the real purpose of monastic life: to live a deeply spiritual Christian life with like-minded people by taking long periods of contemplation in an environment without temptations or distractions.

For all his wisdom, his sometimes zealous devotion to the Catholic Church saw him condemn heretical groups in Europe, including the Cathars, and promote the Second Crusade in 1145 to retake the Holy Land. He championed the Order of the Knights Templar and authored their code of practice, the *Rule of the Templars*.

By the time of his death there were 400 Cistercian monasteries across Europe and over 700 monks at Clairvaux. He died in 1153 and was considered by then the most powerful religious figure in Europe, second only to the pope.

Having found a friend and mentor in St Bernard, Malachy and his party resumed their pilgrimage to Rome and arrived there in 1139.

In Rome

Malachy remained in Rome for a month and there is little detail in St Bernard's biography of what he did there beyond saying he visited the holy places for prayer. The account of St Malachy's time in Rome goes no further than to provide the brief outline of events.

Catholic historian and author François Cucherat (1812–87) describes in detail Malachy's visit to Rome, claiming that he had many visions while staying in the city. Cucherat claims that during one night Malachy relayed the *Prophecy of the Popes* to one of his monks while in a trance-like state. These consisted of over 100 descriptions of the popes that would succeed the current pope until the end of the papacy. According to Cucherat, Malachy later gifted the prophecies to Pope Innocent II, who was experiencing uncertainty in challenging times. The purpose of this was to assure the troubled pope that the Vatican and the papacy would last another millennium following Innocent's reign. This would be seen to give comfort in the same way that in the Old Testament prophecy shows Abraham the Promised Land that his people would receive and the children he himself would have.

Innocent accepted the document and placed it in the Vatican archives, where it remained undisclosed for four centuries, with access only permitted to high-ranking Church officials.

Cucherat gives no source for the account and we must keep in mind that the prophecies remained hidden in the archive until 1590, and were not published until Arnold de Wyon circulated them in 1595. Critics of the veracity of Malachy's authorship argue that St Bernard also makes no mention of any visions being recorded or of documents being delivered to the pope, and that this is evidence that the prophecies were not Malachy's but forgeries from a later date. We will examine these claims later, but for now we have to consider that St Bernard actually has so little to say on Malachy's time in Rome that we have no idea what was exchanged between the two men. At that time the Vatican kept records of documents being deposited and Malachy is listed as having donated something, but no details of the nature of the document were given. As he had published a number of orthodox and traditionalist Catholic manuscripts it could have been any of these.

Malachy also requested of Pope Innocent II whether he might live at Clairvaux with his good friend St Bernard but the pope declined, deciding that he would be of more use back in Ireland where he could continue his work, but that he might retire to Clairvaux Abbey towards the end of his life. In support of this Innocent bestowed upon him the title of papal legate, or representative, for the whole of Ireland.

Malachy left Rome and returned via Clairvaux, where his entourage stayed on to learn from the monks: they were to be taught in the ways of St Bernard's Cistercians and were to bring these teachings back to Ireland.

Man of Miracles

Like many saints, Malachy was gifted with the power to heal and perform miracles. He would use his powers on his travels to help those who were sick or possessed of evil spirits. The stories of Malachy's miracles are many and varied and they provide some insights into what the saint was thought to be capable of. On his journey to Rome he travelled via York in England, where a monk offered Malachy an old black horse, apologising for the rough condition of the animal. Malachy took the animal on with an open heart and the animal quickly became a refined ride and miraculously turned from black to white. On the same journey, in Ivrea in Italy, he cured his host's dying son.

The entire journey to and from Rome is filled with acts of healing, and as his reputation spread people would bring their sick to visit him from nearby towns. During this time he was said to have healed many, including a paralysed woman who was able to walk home fully restored, a dumb girl who was able to speak again and a woman considered insane was cured. On his return to Ireland Malachy passed through Scotland and is said to have miraculously cured Prince Henry, the son of King David I of Scotland. His method of healing in this case was to instruct the child, 'Trust me, my son, you shall not die this time,' and bless him with holy water. By the following day the prince had recovered fully.

In Ireland Malachy had also gained a reputation as a healer. A man was brought to him with sickness and it was claimed a demon had instructed the man not to listen to Malachy. Using the power of prayer Malachy cured the illness and drove the demon away. There are other accounts of Malachy performing exorcisms. In the city of Coleraine two women were possessed until Malachy drove the demon from one to the other and finally drove it out completely. A man in Lismore had a demon exorcised from him and a child in Leinster the same.

Exorcism seems archaic from the point of view of modern society. Our understanding of the mind has been greatly expanded by research into psychotherapy in the last century. The disturbing notion of demonic possession is now looked upon as schizophrenia or other mental health afflictions, but the examples of Malachy curing mental health issues, cases of insanity and epilepsy are distinct from his exorcisms in that he communicates directly with the spirit that has possessed the individual. There is today in every diocese worldwide an appointed exorcist. Cinema has used the idea of demonic possession for many horror films, but even the original of these, William Friedkin's film *The Exorcist*, based on the book of the same name by William Peter Blatty, has its origins in a real case of the exorcism of a boy during the late 1940s.

Malachy's methods of healing included prayer, physical contact such as touch, blessing water for bathing in, blessing food to be eaten and even using his empty bed after he had left it. In another case Malachy drove out anger from a raging woman by getting her to confess.

The majority of his cures were by prayer alone: either his own or his instruction to the afflicted to pray. The power of prayers in this context must be more than petitioning God to do one's bidding – it must take on some deeper aspect. His prayers were also answered when helping communities: on an island where the locals were starving because the fishermen could find no fish, Malachy knelt on the shore to pray and the fish returned.

His healing powers stretched as far as resurrection, and a story comes down to us of a nobleman who summoned Malachy to save his dying wife. The wife died in the night before Malachy could get there but on arriving the next morning Malachy restored her to life.

As time goes on the accounts become more outrageous and less believable, but they give an insight into what was thought of as miraculous cures at the time. For example, a dumb girl was presented to Malachy in Lismore. He prayed, touched her tongue and spat in her mouth and she went away cured. Another woman who could not speak was instructed to say the Lord's Prayer, which she did and was instantly cured. He is said to have healed cancer by sprinkling blessed water on the patient, and he gave a cup of water he had blessed to a nobleman to take to his wife who was long overdue with child. She drank it and went into labour immediately. It was said that when he tried to bring peace between two rival factions God intervened and flooded the land between them to prevent further conflict.

We cannot know how much control Malachy may have had over his power to heal. Presumably it was a matter of faith that he could perform these miracles and entirely at the discretion of grace that these miracles were achieved. One example of his healing powers is quite telling. Malachy revived a dying man in Antrim long enough to hear his final confession – this raises the question of why he did not heal the man entirely. The answer could be that there were limits to what he was *permitted* to do.

Miracles would not just work through Malachy but also seemed to happen to those around him. He was not without his enemies and even in these matters it seemed that God would intervene on his behalf. According to St Bernard an enemy spoke against Malachy and made up stories to discredit him. Malachy's response was said to be: 'Wretched man, many shall see this finished, but you shall not see it finished.' Almost like a curse, he invoked the wrath of God in a manner that seems out of character, so perhaps St Bernard wrote this to instil fear into those that needed such incentives. When the man returned home a demon set upon him and threw him into a fire to die, but his friends saved him and Malachy was summoned to help and prayed for the man, who opened his eyes and was converted.

Like the relics that were considered to have powers that can be transmitted by touch or contemplation, according to tradition as Malachy cast his magic through a multitude of forms he became a sacred object, an object of power for both spiritual and political ends. In the case of a man in Northern Ireland whose illness was thought to have been caused by demons he crawled into a bed where Malachy had spent the night and was immediately cured. Even after his death visitors to Malachy's tomb claimed to have been healed.

St Malachy lived and achieved a great deal during a time of turmoil in Ireland but the number of miracles attributed to him are difficult to accept from such a distant perspective.

Man of Visions

Having visited Rome, on Malachy's return to Ireland the visions continued. He settled in Bangor and, acting on a design he saw in a vision, he set the monks to work building an oratory. He saw the design after many hours of prayer and adhered to it completely, even though it was an expensive undertaking and the project soon ran out of money. Undeterred, Malachy continued to have his monks dig the foundations and during their excavations they discovered a buried treasure which was used to pay for the oratory.

The visions of Malachy were never the focus of his life. His friend and biographer St Bernard states that Malachy was 'rich in signs and prophecy and revelation' and mentions on numerous occasions that Malachy made prophecies. However, he gives few examples and it was not until the publication, some 400 years later, of the *Prophecy of the Popes* attributed to Malachy that he became famous as a prophet. During his own time far more interest was taken in the prophetic utterances of St Hildegard von Bingen (1098–1179) and others, whereas Malachy was held up as an example of a pious man who could overcome the rage of barbarism with his humble words and actions.

St Bernard does relate how Malachy predicted the exact hour and place of his death and it was not an uncommon form of personal prophecy; Joan of Arc heard the voices of saints instructing her to save France and also discovered the details of her death from a prophetic dream.

One detailed account describes how in the company of bishops they witnessed an altar stone engulfed in fire in the cemetery of St Patrick. Of the group only Malachy understood what it meant and ran to embrace the burning stone. It is clear from the accounts – regardless of whether or not we can assign the *Prophecy of the Popes* to Malachy – that the spirit of prophecy was flowing through him freely.

End of life

In 1148 Malachy left Ireland to visit the new pope, Eugenius III, in France but was continually delayed. Eventually, realising his death was near, Malachy travelled to Clairvaux. Here he was welcomed by his old friend St Bernard. He remained at Clairvaux and died in the arms of St Bernard on 2 November 1148 at the age of 54. He was honoured at Clairvaux with many sermons dedicated to spreading his story and comparing him to Moses or Elijah.

Soon after St Bernard declared him a saint, and this was confirmed by Pope Clement III before the end of the 12th century. St Bernard died five years later, having completed a biography of Malachy. St Malachy's feast day is 3 November, as it was moved a day to avoid clashing with Pentecost. His feast day is celebrated by the Cistercians and throughout Ireland. A mitre and a wooden cup, which Malachy had used during his lifetime, became the saint's relics and were kept at the Abbey of Clairvaux.

Becoming a saint

The pope has the sole authority to make an individual a saint through the process of canonisation. This involves adding the individual's name to the 'canon of saints' and can only happen after the person has died. The title of 'saint' is only given where an individual is thought to be with God, or having led a life that in some way exemplified being a Christian. They also include martyrs, those that were willing to die for their beliefs. The purpose of saints in Christianity is to inspire others and act as icons of veneration and many have been seen as imbued with the power to answer prayers of healing through their relics. Saints whose remains become relics are accorded certain powers but this power is said to represent the Holy Spirit revealing itself through them.

The current route to sainthood requires that an individual's name is proposed and the local bishop undertakes an investigation into their life and death. If the bishop approves, the details are submitted to the Congregation for the Causes of Saints, which consists of theologians and cardinals. If successful, the details are then passed to the pope. At this stage martyrs can be canonised without further deliberation, but other potential saints also need to have performed two miracles in front of witnesses for their sainthood to be finally confirmed.

Saints sometimes are named as patrons of various aspects of life. Some, such as St Valentine being the patron saint of lovers, are in common use, whereas others, such as St Clare of Assisi being the patron saint of television or St Ubaldo the patron saint of dog bites, are not so well known.

THE BIOGRAPHY

Following the death of Malachy St Bernard devoted many hours to compiling a biography of his friend. This detailed work has survived and gives many insights into the life and work of Malachy and brings to light his saintly deeds as he became known as a healer and worker of miracles.

The biography was completed around 1150, two years after Malachy's death, so it can be considered, if not accurate, at least contemporary. The version used throughout this book is the de Backer translation as quoted in *St Bernard of Clairvaux's Life of St Malachy of Armagh* by H J Lawlor.

The biography paints a devout picture of St Malachy on every level. St Bernard certainly knew him well enough to judge his character and he describes Malachy as 'a man truly holy . . . of singular wisdom and virtue'. Unfortunately St Bernard is not one for writing dates and other authors have since toiled to fit the events with known points and places in Malachy's life and Ireland's history. The biography also suffers from painting too perfect a picture of Malachy.

The biographies of saints often exist to serve two purposes. One is to record the life of the saint and their works, the other is for the biography to be used to light the way for others by showing examples of a pious life. St Bernard was instilling the myth of a man who was to be considered one of the great saints of Ireland. In doing so there is no doubt that he embellished the story and may well have elevated a humble life into the kind of heroic epic that older civilisations had cherished. He made Malachy a medieval icon by attributing feats and wonders to him, and went to great lengths to prove how God was always working in favour of his exceedingly pious aims.

There is a long tradition in the writing of saints' biographies of applying varying levels of polish to make the subject shimmer with grace. Bishops would often describe the life of a saint from little or no real evidence from the individual's actual life. Through this they were creating modern icons in an environment that local people could relate to. Malachy underwent the same struggles as his people, the same hardships, and yet he managed to lift up his face to God. The effect of such character, or even caricature, on the lay person was to inspire them further into their religious life. It gave them courage and hope.

This is not the outrageous liberty of historical writing it seems but a simple device to afford Malachy the highest praise. St Bernard recognised Malachy as a humble and saintly kindred spirit in faith if not in personality, concluding that he was 'a true successor to the apostles' when he preached among the people. It is no surprise that immediately after the death of Malachy it was St Bernard who proposed he was to be canonised. Again, this can be seen as an attempt by St Bernard to provide a shining light for those who were seeking to be a 'good Christian' in one of the farthest corners of Europe.

Malachy, it seems, was not held in such high esteem by the pope, who had refused to allow him to join St Bernard's Cistercians. It was possibly a political move intended to stem the power of St Bernard's order by restricting his influence in Ireland, or perhaps the pope wanted to keep Malachy as a direct ally to Rome.

CONCLUSION

For St Bernard, having never visited Ireland, his knowledge of names, peoples and places, and the detail he brings to the life of St Malachy would require Malachy's input, and candidly so. So whether Malachy embellished his story or St Bernard chose to creatively promote his friend as a candidate for sainthood – or if, indeed, the events actually took place – is ultimately for the reader to decide. However, St Bernard is clear throughout that he considered Malachy to be a remarkable man, seemingly capable of miracles and prophecies, but also in his oratorical skills in terms of converting others and mediating between factions.

St Bernard paints him as a perfect Christian, progressive and yet devout, and concerned with the spiritual transformation of mankind. His faith was absolute and his insight into the actions of God revealed to him a clear path of preaching and armed him with a singular mind to argue against heretics and abuses of the Church. Even St Bernard's secretary, Geoffrey, considered Malachy on a par with St Bernard.

I do not doubt that St Bernard wrote the biography of his good friend as both the veneration of a good Christian and to fulfil the political need of creating a saint to convert the heathens of Ireland. It is also unlikely that Malachy's deeds were entirely fabricated. His role in navigating Ireland to a single doctrine of the faith was a great achievement considering the factions that were in play at the time. Malachy was known historically for his work in the reformation of Christianity in Ireland and this assured his place in history.

St Bernard may well have enhanced the life of St Malachy but any embellishments exist to inspire and convert those who read about the saint's life. The wilder aspects and claims in Malachy's name also serve to help the story of Malachy survive to be read by generations to come. For all their inaccuracies and historical dubiousness, the lives of the saints uphold the traditions of Christian writings. We do not teach our children to read using dictionaries.

Since the release of the *Prophecy of the Popes* these have overshadowed the good works of Malachy and outside of Ireland today he is known more for his ability to prophesise than any other achievement. Only in Ireland do they remember why he was made a saint – not for his visions, but for his faith.

CHAPTER 6

THE PROPHECIES – PART I

INTRODUCTION

According to Cucherat, the 19th-century biographer of Malachy, the prophecies were deposited in the Vatican for the edification of the pope and then promptly disappeared from history. It was another 400 years before they reappeared in published form for wider circulation, in a collection of texts by historian Arnold de Wyon.

The release of the prophecies occurs halfway through the list of popes that it predicts and this casts a shadow both back and forth on how the prophecies are read. The prophecies relating to popes prior to publication could have been altered by de Wyon, making corrective changes to suit the popes that had passed. For the popes that follow the release, the risk is that they could have been colluded with or used to influence the appointing of popes.

That the prophecy in its original format has never been released has also caused some to speculate that no original text exists and that the prophecies are a fabrication of the 16th century. We will examine the case for this as we reach the point of publication. The earliest version of the prophecies in circulation has come down to us from Arnold de Wyon's *Lignum Vitae* (published in Italy, 1595). The *Lignum Vitae* consists of two parts and the prophecy is included in the second book. The version I had access to during this study is an original from the British Library in London.

De Wyon states in the *Lignum Vitae* that the version of the prophecies he published was taken from an original list. No explanation is given of how he came by them or if there was any supporting text identifying St Malachy as the author. From de Wyon's version we can ascertain that the original was little more than a list of brief Latin phrases.

As the *Lignum Vitae* was published by de Wyon in 1595 he adds explanations for the popes listed prior to this date. The prophecies are presented as a list of short phrases to which de Wyon has appended the name of the corresponding pope and a brief attempt to explain the link between the pope and the prophecy. Beyond 1592 the short prophetic phrases are set into three columns as a list of unnumbered entries concluding with a paragraph describing a 'Peter the Roman' as part of the final tribulation and judgement.

The first group of prophecies as recorded by de Wyon are as follows:

Ex castro Tyberis, Inimicus expulsus, Ex magnitudine motis, Abbas Suburranus, De rure albo, Ex tetro carcere, Via trans-Tyberina, De Pannonia Thusciæ, Ex ansere custode, Lux in ostio, Sus in cribro, Ensis Laurentii, De schola exiet, De rure bouensi (bovensi), Comes signatus, Canonicus de latere, Avis Ostiensis, Leo Sabinus, Comes Laurentius, Signum

Ostiense, Hierusalem Campanie, Draco depressus, Anguinus vir, Concionatur Gallus, Bonus Comes, Piscator Thuscus, Rosa composita, Ex teloneo liliacei Martini, Ex rosa leonina, Picus inter escas, Ex eremo celsus, Ex undaru bnedictione, Concionator patereus, De fessis Aquitanicis, De sutore osseo, Corvus schismaticus, Frigidus Abbas, De rosa Attrebatensi, De montibus Pammachii, Gallus Vicecomes, Novus de Virgine forti, Decruce Apostilica, Luna Cosmedina, Schisma Barchinoniu, De inferno pregnari, Cubus de mixtione, De meliore sydere, Nauta de ponte nigro, Flagellum Solis, Cervus Sirenæ, Corona veli aurei, Lupa cœlestina, Amator crucis, De modicitate lunæ, Bos pascens, De capra & Albergo, De cervo & Leone, Piscator Minorita, Præcursor Siciliæ, Bos Albanus in portu, De parvo homine, Fructus jovis Juvabit, De craticula Politiana, Leo Florentius, Flos pilei ægri, Hiacynthus medicoru, De corona Montana, Frumentum flocidum, De fide Petri, Esculapii pharmacum, Angelus nemorosus, Medium corpus pilaru, Axis in medietate signi, De rore cæli, Ex antiquitate Urbis, Pia civitas in bello, Crux Romulea,

Each appears with a corresponding pope and explanation but the original was likely to have the above form. At this point de Wyon's book was published and the remainder of the popes were yet to be identified. The remaining prophecies are listed in three columns, fitting neatly across the page so as not to waste paper. There are no gaps or line breaks to indicate that anything has been omitted.

They appear as follows:

Undosus Vir.
Gens perversa.
In tribulatione pacis.
Lilium & rosa.
Jucunditas crucis.
Montium custos.
Sydus Olorum.
De flumine magno.
Bellua insatiabilis.
Pœnitentia gloriosa.
Rastrum in porta.
Flores circumdati.
De bona Religione.
Miles in bello.
Columna excelsa,

Animal rurale.
Rosa Umbriæ.
Ursus velox.
Peregrin Apostolic.
Aquila rapax.
Canis & coluber.
Vir religiosus.
De balneis Ethruriæ.
Crux de cruce.
Lumen in cœlo.
Ignis ardens.
Religio depopulata.
Fides intrepida.
Pastor angelicus.

Pastor & Nauta.
Flos florum.
De medietate Lunæ.
De labore Solis.
Gloria olivæ.
In psecutione,
extrema S.R.E. sedebit
Petrus Romanus,
qui pascet oves in
multis tribulationibus:
quibus transactis civitas
septicollis diruetur,
& Judex tremêdus
judicabit populum suum.
Finis.

THE POPES

There have been 266 popes since St Peter, according to the Catholic Church. St Malachy's prophecies of the popes, beginning in the 12th century, have pronounced on nearly half of these. These prophecies follow the lives of the popes and the meandering route of the Catholic Church like a river that runs through time. It is a river that ebbs and flows, from the quiet lakes of peace to the waterfalls of upheaval and scandal. As this stream of Catholicism wended its way through time there stood on the banks were not fishers of souls but Malachy, our commentator who cast his eye ahead to warn us of what may lie beyond the next bend. Even from our age of cynicism we can look back at Malachy's words and be swept along with the current just as the author was overtaken by divine visions to predict what may befall any given pope.

The *Prophecy of the Popes* begins with Celestine II in 1143 and continues to the present day. The name of the pope is given first, along with the dates of his rule. There follows the prophetic statement, which is translated and interpreted, and finally a short biographic sketch of the pope and his place in the history of the Catholic Church.

We begin with two brief popes who lacked the time to bring stability or implement much change within the Church.

Celestine II (1143–1144)

Prophecy: Ex castro Tyberis
Translation: From a castle on the Tiber
Interpretation: Celestine II was born in Castello, meaning castle, a town on the river Tiber.

Lasting only five months, Celestine cut an intelligent and learned but severe figure. His tenure as pope was too short to really make a difference but his one success was to lift the interdict from France, placed by his predecessor.

During the reign of Celestine II a rival 'antipope', Victor IV, gained support of King Roger of Sicily but Celestine died before he found a solution to the political conflict.

Lucius II (1144–1145)

Prophecy: Inimicus expulsus
Translation: Enemy expelled
Interpretation: Possibly a pun on the pope's surname 'Giaccianimici', meaning 'chased by enemies', but also apt in terms of his demise.

Before becoming pope Lucius was papal legate in Germany and a strong advocate for Innocent II. Lucius had met with King Roger of Sicily on behalf of Pope Innocent but had failed to find terms. As pope he was forced to intervene by leading an army to threaten the usurpers, but he failed against both the supporters of the antipope and the republican Romans. He was outmanoeuvred politically from within and without. Lucius saw no choice but to resort to a military response but was defeated and died shortly after of his wounds. To some within the Church he remains an uncanonised martyr.

Eugene III (1145–1153)

Prophecy: Ex magnitudine motis
Translation: From the great mountain
Interpretation: Eugene's family name was Montemagno, derived from 'mons magnus', Latin for 'great mountain', and he was born in the castle of Gramont, or 'Great mount'. This would suggest Cucherat was right to correct de Wyon.

In response to the threat of King Roger and the antipope Victor IV the cardinals loyal to Lucius quickly appointed a Cistercian monk as the next pope. Seeing that Rome was descending into turmoil after his election Eugene immediately fled the city. Of noble birth, he was influenced by St Bernard of Clairvaux and both men held the other in high esteem. When Eugene instigated the Second Crusade St Bernard roused support across Europe on his behalf but ultimately the campaign failed.

Rome meanwhile was undergoing another civil uprising that targeted the churches, monasteries and palaces. These were looted, and in some cases destroyed, before Eugene could eventually negotiate peace. Eugene remained in France, where he supported theological and philosophical schools and made peace with King Louis. Finally he mustered enough political and military power to give him safe passage back to the Vatican. He would continue to come and go for the remainder of his time but never completely resolved the Roman uprisings that occurred.

Anastasius IV (1153–1154)

Prophecy: Abbas Suburranus
Translation: Suburran abbot
Interpretation: His family name was Suburra/Suburri.

A brief 18-month tenure as pope saw Anastasius negotiate peace between the papacy and Frederick Barbarossa. He also supported the Order of the Knights Hospitallers in the crusades but achieved little else as his time was so short.

Adrian IV (1154–1159)

Prophecy: De rure albo
Translation: Of the field of Albe
Interpretation: He was born in St Albans, England and was Bishop of Alba prior to being pope.

Thought to hail from the county of Hertfordshire in England, Adrian remains to this day the only pope of English origin. During his career he was sent to Norway as papal legate where he excelled in reforming the clergy and was recognised as decisive and strong willed. As pope he was strict, demanding full observance from kings and courtiers alike. His inflexibility caused consternation among European leaders and he found himself at odds with William I of Sicily.

THE 'ANTIPOPES'

The antipopes first occurred as early as the 3rd century AD with Hippolytus and have periodically dogged the Catholic Church to the present day. During the High Middle Ages the struggle for power in Italy between different factions saw a succession of antipopes challenging the power of Rome. Victor IV is the first of a number of 'antipopes' found in Malachy's list. These were born out of schisms within the Catholic Church, often based upon an undercurrent of family power struggles and political motives. The rival popes challenged the appointed pope for power over the Catholic Church but in time their power fell away and they are not officially recognised by the Catholic Church. Victor IV arrived at a time when there was schism between the popes and what remained of the Holy Roman Empire under Frederick Barbarossa. Barbarossa had invaded Italy and been crowned King of Italy in 1155. Victor had been critical of the current pope and had chosen to follow the previous antipope Anacletus II (who is not included in the list of popes).

Intending to control the Catholic Church, Emperor Frederick Barbarossa backed Victor IV over Alexander III, who had been elected. Frederick called a council to decide the legitimate pope but chose to head the council himself and to no surprise declared Victor IV the legitimate candidate. Word spread of the injustice and Pope Victor found that he carried no real power or influence over the cardinals. After Victor died Pascal III, Callistus III and Innocent III followed in quick succession under the patronage of the emperor. Later popes also chose the names Callistus III and Innocent III, cementing the notion that these were not legitimate figures and striking them from the history of the papacy. In 1176 Frederick's armies were finally driven from Italy and without his benefactor Innocent III was forced to flee as well. The true pope Alexander III, who had outlived four antipopes, returned triumphant to take his place in Rome.

At the Third Lateran Council Alexander III declared that a two-thirds majority would be required to elect a pope in future to prevent further schisms occurring.

Emperor Frederick continued his political scheming and had his son marry the daughter of the Sicilian king, who was one of the pope's strongest military allies. This left the Papal States, which covered much of central and northern Italy, undefended and Frederick once again mobilised to invade Rome. As his campaign was gathering force news reached Europe that Saladin had invaded Jerusalem. A third crusade was called and Frederick's armies were diverted to Jerusalem. He died en route, thus at last removing the threat of him subjugating the papacy.

Victor IV (1159–1164), antipope

Prophecy: Ex tetro carcere
Translation: Out of a foul prison
Interpretation: He was a cardinal in the Tullian prison.

Victor came from a powerful Roman family but had few supporters among the cardinals. He was bound up by the politics of the schism and without universal support his tenure achieved little. His inclusion here is of interest as he would not be considered a true pope. The presence of a number of antipopes in the prophecies gives credence to them not being contrived after the event. No Catholic would include them by choice.

Pascal III (1164–1168), antipope

Prophecy: Via trans-Tyberina
Translation: Road across the Tiber
Interpretation: He was formerly the cardinal priest of Santa Maria in Trastevere, which translates as 'St Mary across the Tiber'.

Pascal was an antipope who succeeded Victor IV and took up the conflict with Alexander III but could achieve little else.

Callistus III (1168–1178), antipope

Prophecy: De Pannonia Thusciæ
Translation: From Tusculan Hungary
Interpretation: Pannonia was the Latin name for Hungary. Callistus was Hungarian and the Cardinal Bishop of Tuscany.

Alexander III (1159–1181)

Prophecy: Ex ansere custode
Translation: Former goose custodian
Interpretation: His family coat of arms depicts a goose.

Pope Alexander III fought off many forms of invasion. At one point he was forced to flee Rome, which had been invaded by Frederick I. Frederick held Rome until his defeat at the battle of Legnano in 1176.

Alexander III returned to Rome and immediately instigated the Third Lateran Council, which began in 1179, with the intention of removing political interference from Church affairs, such as the appointment of bishops.

Lucius III (1181–1185)

Prophecy: Lux in ostio
Translation: A light in the door
Interpretation: He was Cardinal of Ostia, meaning 'doors'.

Supported by St Bernard of Clairvaux, Lucius only lasted four months in Rome before being chased out for withholding privileges his predecessors had granted local politicians. He returned before the end of his life but was forced to leave again and finally settled in Verona. His time as pope seemed to be marked by a constant battle of wills with Emperor Frederick I and as both parties stood their ground little progress was made on either side.

Urban III (1185–1187)

Prophecy: Sus in cribro
Translation: Pig in a sieve
Interpretation: An unfortunate epithet, but his family coat of arms displays a pig and his family name Crivelli means 'sieve'.

To avoid interference and influence from Frederick the cardinals engineered a quick election following the death of Lucius.

The presence of Frederick's armies in the Papal States continued to undermine the power of the papacy by holding a political marriage in their own backyard, as it were. Urban hailed from Milan, which had been invaded by Frederick some years before, so the pope followed the embittered path of trying to keep Frederick in check in a succession of political disagreements.

He was also a fervent supporter of the crusades and in particular favoured the Hospitallers. Rumours attributed his death to the shock of hearing the news of the crusader defeat in the battle of Hattin.

Gregory VIII (1187)

Prophecy: Ensis Laurentii
Translation: Sword of Lawrence
Interpretation: He was the cardinal of St Lawrence and his family coat of arms depicts a sword.

During a year when the crusaders were being routed from the Holy Land Gregory was appointed as a viable diplomat. Well educated and respected, he would have been capable of finding peaceful solutions to the challenges made by Frederick at home, while directing his energies and funds to reclaiming Jerusalem. But it was not to be, as Gregory died less than two months after being appointed.

Clement III (1187–1191)

Prophecy: De schola exiet
Translation: From the school
Interpretation: His family name Scolari means 'scholar'.

Roman by birth, Clement was a popular choice with the local people and politicians and he marked a welcome return of the pope to Rome to take up residence there again. A peaceful man, Clement organised the Third Crusade and used this to unite the many factions of Europe with the single purpose of retaking Jerusalem. The great and diverse army swept east but Clement died just prior to the capture of Acre.

Celestine III (1191–1198)

Prophecy: De rure bovensi
Translation: From cattle country
Interpretation: Family name of Bobone, from the word 'bovensis' or 'bovine'.

Elected in his eighty-fifth year, he immediately crowned King Henry VI of Germany as emperor. Lacking the peaceful approach of his predecessor, Celestine supported the king's military campaigns as he fought his way through Italy to claim Sicily. Henry's bloodlust and political machinations (he ordered the imprisonment of Richard the Lionheart) cast a shadow over the reign of Celestine as he continually failed to challenge or curb the violent king's excessive nature.

It was Celestine who agreed to canonise Malachy.

Innocent III (1198–1216)

Prophecy: Comes signatus
Translation: Signatory count
Interpretation: A descendant of the counts of Signy, later called the Segni family.

Pope Celestine III was succeeded by Innocent III. Highly educated and widely published, he seemed perfect for the transition into age of scholasticism. Unfortunately he was responsible for launching the disastrous Fourth Crusade, which resulted in the destruction of Constantinople and divided the Eastern and Western Church. The crusade was intended to retake land from the Muslims in the East but the crusading army travelled via Constantinople and found itself mired in local politics. This resulted in the siege of Constantinople and eventually half of this magnificent, already Christian, city was sacked and burned to the ground.

Innocent also instigated the Albigensian Crusade to eradicate the Christian heretics of Europe by burning them en masse. His single-minded approach saw him excommunicate the entire English nation for adopting the Magna Carta, which put King John in the service of his subjects and not the pope.

Although popular and scholarly in his writings and refinement of canonical law, Innocent is remembered chiefly for his brutal suppression of heretics. He had set in motion the inquisition.

HERESY

The first inquisition set a trend that would cast a shadow over Europe for 500 years. The impact of the inquisition was not only the destruction of rival religions and heretics but it spread a fear that would hold back scientific reasoning for centuries. Through the inquisition the Catholic Church was willing to sacrifice some of Europe's greatest thinkers for speaking out.

By the 14th century the ostentatious power and wealth of the Catholic Church was becoming difficult to reconcile with the humble life and teachings of Jesus. Other variations of Christianity began to spread from Eastern Europe into the West. Among these were the Catharist priests who chose to live and work among the people as Christ would have done, teaching and subsisting on charity. They refused to own possessions and anything they earned above their basic needs they gave to the poor. Unlike the Catholic Church they asked for no taxes and shunned power. The Cathars did not build or own buildings so they held their sermons in fields and barns and were also advanced in terms of equality, accepting women as priests.

As living examples of a Christian way, and by not charging taxes, the Cathars easily attracted and converted many people to their faith. However, this threatened the Catholic Church, which responded by ordering a crusade against them. The Albigensian Crusade against the Cathars in 13th-century southern France saw the death of up to a million people at the hands of armies raised to quell the heresy. One of the last of the Cathar strongholds in the French foothills of the Pyrenees mountains was a castle donated to the Cathar cause called Montsegur. This fell in the siege of 1244 and many of the remaining 200 Cathars who surrendered the hill-top castle were offered mild penances if they converted back to Catholicism. So strong was their faith that it is said that every man, woman and child chose to burn at the stake rather than become a Catholic.

Honorius III (1216–1227)

Prophecy: Canonicus de latere
Translation: Canon from the side
Interpretation: He was canon of St John Lateran.

The primary aim of Honorius was to reclaim the Holy Land. The methods of negotiation he employed were less aggressive than some of his predecessors and he disseminated a call to arms for a crusade across Europe. Money poured in and so did volunteers, though not always of military stock. As many of the European countries had committed their troops to local skirmishes the meagre and untrained force that sailed east were easily repelled.

Honorius realised the importance of strong leadership and an able army in taking the Holy Land, so he spent many years negotiating with King Frederick II of Germany, who had promised to lead an army. The lack of available troops across Europe also compelled him to mediate between European nations to settle their differences and internal struggles – although driven by the need to procure the use of their armies, it was still an achievement that brought peace to great areas of the continent.

Gregory IX (1227–1241)

Prophecy: Avis Ostiensis
Translation: Bird of Ostia
Interpretation: Before becoming pope he was cardinal bishop of Ostia.

A former papal diplomat, steeped in European politics, Gregory was marred from the start by a rigid mindset about Emperor Frederick II. Following his coronation, Gregory immediately ordered Emperor Frederick to make good on his promise of a crusade but the emperor returned after a few days at sea claiming to be ill. Gregory mistrusted the excuse and the ensuing rift between the two ended with the pope excommunicating the emperor. The emperor proved his resolve and undertook the crusade, but the pope refused to support his actions; realising the undertaking was futile the emperor returned to Europe.

In a seeming change of character Frederick attempted to reconnect with the pope but Gregory died before they could resolve their differences.

A lack of tolerance seemed to be a failing of Gregory's term as pope. His hard-line approach saw him support the burning of heretics and the war against the Cathars in southern France. He was also the first pope to formulate the inquisition as a tribunal to try heretics.

Celestine IV (1241)

Prophecy: Leo Sabinus
Translation: Sabine lion
Interpretation: He was the cardinal bishop of Sabina with a lion on his family coat of arms.

Celestine IV survived a mere fifteen days following his appointment as pope.

Innocent IV (1243–1254)

Prophecy: Comes Laurentius
Translation: Count Lawrence
Interpretation: Descended from the counts of Lavangna, he was the cardinal priest of San Lorenzo (St Lawrence).

After 18 months of difficult debate Innocent IV was elected and inherited Gregory IX's feud with Emperor Frederick II, who was now in occupation of the Papal States surrounding Rome. He would have seemed a good choice for resolving the situation as he knew the emperor personally prior to being elected. He opened negotiations with Frederick, who conceded control of the Papal States but reneged on other conditions. As the hostility grew between the two men, Innocent, fearing for his safety, fled to France and the protection of King Louis IX. Here he attempted to have Frederick deposed in Germany but his plan failed, so he ordered a crusade against Frederick. His pre-occupation with the politics of the day stalled any reforms within the Church.

Alexander IV (1254–1261)

Prophecy: Signum Ostiense
Translation: Sign of Ostia
Interpretation: Count of Segni and Cardinal Bishop of Ostia

Like Innocent III and Gregory IX, Alexander was of the noble house of Segni. A spiritual but vain man, he inherited a papacy already mired in the politics of Europe. An attempt to rally the disparate factions into a crusading force failed immediately, only to prove how fragmented Europe was becoming.

Urban IV (1261–1264)

Prophecy: Hierusalem Campanie
Translation: Jerusalem of Champagne
Interpretation: He was made patriarch of Jerusalem in 1255 and was born in Troyes, Champagne.

Urban is described as energetic and astute. He had inherited the debts of his predecessor and immediately focused on finding a way to restore the finances and balance the books going forwards.

It seems he felt indebted to those who had elected him as within a year he thanked the eight cardinals by selecting six new cardinals from their relatives. Of the fourteen cardinals he created, three would later become popes.

During his time as pope he succeeded in influencing the ruling of Sicily, Germany and France but died before his actions fully came to fruition.

Clement IV (1265–1268)

Prophecy: Draco depressus
Translation: Dragon suppressed
Interpretation: His choice of papal coat of arms was an eagle holding a serpent in its claws, the device of the Guelphs, befitting his military background.

Clement had an unlikely journey to the role of pope. He was married, a father, and at one time a soldier before progressing towards a life in the Church. To his great surprise, following the death of Urban IV, he was summoned to the conclave in Perugia where he was informed that he had been elected pope by a unanimous vote based upon his pious nature and ascetic lifestyle. With great reluctance he undertook the task.

His military background did not desert him and he funded the creation of armies to stay his enemies in Europe. A crusade to the

Holy Land would have suited his nature but he deigned to focus his military thinking on matters in Europe by funding the French to wage wars on his behalf.

Gregory X (1271–1276)

Prophecy: Anguinus vir
Translation: Snake man
Interpretation: The Visconti family coat of arms has a serpent eating a boy.

Following the death of Clement IV it was three years before the new pope was elected. This was due to a refusal to compromise between the French and Italian cardinals, who each favoured one of their own countrymen. The conclave in Viterbo became so drawn out that the local dignitaries imprisoned the cardinals in the palace and starved them into choosing a pope.

Gregory was on a pilgrimage to the Holy Land when he was summoned by the Sacred College. At the time he was neither cardinal nor priest, which shows how difficult the decision must have been. During his tenure he crowned Rudolph von Hapsburg as the new emperor and worked towards settling the differences among the warring factions of Italy. He also secured funding and support for a crusade to the Holy Land using combined French and English armies but he died before seeing the plan come to fruition.

Gregory was made a saint in recognition of his virtuous nature and success in maintaining peace.

Innocent V (1276)

Prophecy: Concionatur Gallus
Translation: French preacher
Interpretation: He was of French birth and of the Order of Preachers, and Archbishop of Lyon.

Innocent V survived his coronation by only six months. A professor of theology who had served as an adviser to Gregory X, he is remembered for continuing the previous pope's direction of securing peace among the factions of Italy.

Adrian V (1276)

Prophecy: Bonus Comes
Translation: A good count/companion
Interpretation: The family name was Ottobono, 'bono' meaning 'good', and he was a count of Lavagna.

Adrian proved to be another brief pope as he died one month after being elected. He was the nephew of Innocent IV and another member of the powerful Fiechi family to occupy the Holy See, which raised the issue of nepotism and succession by family.

John XXI (1276–1277)

Prophecy: Piscator Thuscus
Translation: Tuscan fisherman
Interpretation: He was the Cardinal Bishop of Tuscany.

Prior to becoming pope John was a professor of medicine and theology and the author of a key work on logic (*Summulæ logicales*). He had been appointed by Gregory X as personal physician. Once in power he focused his efforts of setting forth a crusade to the Holy Land but in-fighting prevented the army leaving Europe. The pope mediated peace between the military factions but the opportunity had passed.

Diplomatic in nature, John arranged for a synod to be held in Constantinople to unite the two Churches but a proposed military alliance to form a crusading army failed to ignite. He added an apartment to the palace at Viterbo and was using this as an office when the roof collapsed and injured him. He died within a week of his unfortunate accident.

Nicholas III (1277–1280)

Prophecy: Rosa composita
Translation: Composite rose
Interpretation: His family coat of arms has a 'composite' rose.

In spite of the roof falling in on John XXI the papal residence remained at Viterbo. Nicholas was another noble Roman, of the Orsini family. A diplomat of some skill and impartial in his dealings with heads of state, Nicholas was successful in mediating between France and England and secured an Italian province from Rudolf von Hapsburg.

He was considered to have integrity for refusing gifts and yet he saw no problem with promoting members of his family to high, and financially rewarding, office. Nicholas also restored the Vatican as the papal residence and transformed the palace and gardens.

Martin IV (1281–1285)

Prophecy: Ex teloneo liliacei Martini
Translation: From the bank of Martin of the lilies
Interpretation: He was the treasurer of St Martin of Tours under the government whose symbol was a lily.

French by birth and a former chancellor of France appointed by King Louis IX, Martin became the papal legate for France and was perfectly suited to rooting out the corruption that had taken hold there.

His election was unanimous but corrupted by Charles de Anjou, who had imprisoned two opposing cardinals prior to the conclave. Being of French extraction, Martin was so unpopular with Rome's inhabitants that he could not set foot in the city. To escape the scandal of the imprisoned cardinals he fled to Orvieto within the Papal States surrounding Rome.

Due to the political influence on his election Martin was compromised. He repaid the debt by promoting Charles de Anjou to Roman senator but could never be fully accepted by his subjects.

Honorius IV (1285–1287)

Prophecy: Ex rosa leonina
Translation: From the leonine rose
Interpretation: The Savelli family coat of arms displays a rose carried by lions.

Like Honorius III he hailed from the wealthy Savelli family. Honorius IV reigned at a time of peace in Rome. As a Roman he was able to maintain authority over the Papal States with little resistance. His election was immediate following the death of the previous pope to avoid outside influence corrupting the proceedings. Incapacitated by gout, he was unable to walk at the time of taking office.

Honorius published a papal bull against the abuses of governments and urged them to uphold justice and peace. It was aimed primarily at the French occupation of Sicily, which he had supported, and later he went so far as to excommunicate the Sicilian king James of Aragon.

Nicholas IV (1288–1292)

Prophecy: Picus inter escas
Translation: Woodpecker between food
Interpretation: He was born in Escoli, alluding to 'escola' meaning 'to eat'. The town was originally known as Piceni, derived from 'picus'.

The conclave of 1287 was suspended due to the death of a number of electors and reconvened in early 1288 when Nicholas was unanimously appointed.

Lacking the nobility that supported many of the popes at this time, Nicholas nevertheless was well educated and a patron of the arts. In politics it is thought he was influenced by the Colonna family in his decisions and found himself embroiled in the power plays of Europe. He organised and funded a fleet for a crusade into the Holy Land but his call to arms fell on deaf ears. The appetite for such adventures was coming to an end in Europe.

Celestine V (1294)

Prophecy: Ex eremo celsus
Translation: Exalted from the desert
Interpretation: He was a hermit in the desert and forced to take the position of pope.

When Nicolas IV died in 1292 the cardinals spent 20 months deciding the next pope. During this time they received a letter from a hermit called Murrone urging them to make a decision, as he saw that the lack of leadership was putting the Church at risk. The letter proved so popular that the cardinals elected the hermit *in absentia* as the new pope. Murrone begrudgingly accepted, took the title and adopted the name Celestine V. It transpired the hermit had been inspired to write by Charles II, who then became his patron and relocated him to Naples where he could be coerced to do the king's bidding. It soon became clear that Celestine was not fit to be pope as he was all but a willing hostage. He was coerced into doubling the number of cardinals by appointing Charles' favoured friends, but eventually Celestine conceded that he was not up to the task so he committed that rarest of papal actions – he abdicated, intending to return to his life as a hermit. His resignation was seen as a failing by many and even Dante places him in hell where he stands accused of cowardice, but considering his compromised position and lack of political nous it was clearly his only option.

Boniface VIII (1294–1303)

Prophecy: Ex undaru benedictione (de Wyon misspells this as 'bnedictione')

Translation: From the blessing of the waves

Interpretation: The papal coat of arms has two waves diagonally and his first name was Benedict, meaning 'blessed'.

Celestine V was quickly replaced by Boniface VIII, who was a throwback to the more barbarous popes of the first millennium. Boniface concluded that having a previous pope still at large was potentially a threat to his position so he had Celestine incarcerated and the hermit later died in prison. Boniface's actions were another scandal for the Church and caused a prolonged feud between rival Italian families. His response to this was to issue the *Unum Sanctum* papal bull claiming the superiority of the pope over all monarchs and people and that only those who were subjects of the pope could find salvation. It was a clear claim to power over the kings and noble families that were challenging his actions.

Benedict XI (1303–1304)

Prophecy: Concionator patereus

Translation: Preacher from Patara

Interpretation: He was born in Patara and a member of the Order of Preachers.

Following Boniface was a run of French popes beginning with Benedict XI, who, to appease the unpopular French king Philip IV, found himself under increasing pressure to favour the king, who was manoeuvring to control the papacy.

Clement V (1305–1314)

Prophecy: De fessis Aquitanicis

Translation: Ribbon of Aquitaine

Interpretation: His family coat of arms has three bars known as 'fesses' and he was the Archbishop of Bordeaux in Aquitaine.

Clement V remained in France for his entire term as pope. Again the power of the papacy was shifting into the hands of the French monarchy and Rome found itself without a bishop. Too ill to stand up to the king, Clement was coerced into settling in Avignon and supporting the king in his destruction of the Knights Templar. King Philip arrested members of the order under charges of heresy, though it was clear that his intention was to deprive them of their wealth. A letter discovered by Dr Barbara Frale in the Vatican Secret Archives in 2003 (the Chinon Parchment) written by Pope Clement absolves the Templars of any wrongdoing, but the letter was never sent. The primary role of the pope now appeared to be as a political puppet for the French king. He also created more French cardinals, a number of which were his own nephews. The aim of this was to control the papal elections and ensure future popes were French and not Italian.

John XXII (1316–1334)

Prophecy: De sutore osseo

Translation: The cobbler of Osseo

Interpretation: His family name was Ossa and he was the son of a shoe-maker.

After the death of Clement V in France he was replaced by John XXII, the former Bishop of Avignon. This election was to prove the point that the seat of the Catholic Church now resided in France.

John was an energetic 72 year old who lived to be 90 but continued the tradition of nepotism by favouring his family members for promotion within the Church. He fought many of the groups that challenged the orthodox view within the Church and set to right the financial troubles that plagued the Vatican by further taxing its members. By the end of his term he was becoming unpopular and there were also demands for him to reside in Rome, which was falling into unrest.

Nicholas V (1328–1330), antipope

Prophecy: Corvus schismaticus
Translation: Schismatic crow
Interpretation: 'Corvus', meaning 'crow', is likely to be the origin of his family name Corvaro/Corbara. Nicholas was another antipope and as such part of the schism within the Catholic Church at this time.

Benedict XII (1334–1342)

Prophecy: Frigidus Abbas
Translation: Cold abbot
Interpretation: He was an abbot in the monastery of Frontfroid, which is French for 'cold front'.

Thought to be of humble beginnings and seemingly without many political or hereditary entanglements, Benedict would have made a neutral choice for many in the conclave. A Cistercian, he had earned a doctorate in theology at the University of Paris and his nationality ensured the papal seat would remain in Avignon for his entire tenure as pope. He did provide some financial support to Rome to placate the unrest there and also condemned abuses of power within the clergy.

Clement VI (1342–1352)

Prophecy: De rosa Attrebatensi
Translation: The rose of Attrebatensis
Interpretation: He was Bishop of Attrebatensis (Arras).

Another French pope and a Benedictine monk, Clement created an additional group of over 20 French cardinals. He held a jubilee in 1350, which proved very popular as pilgrimage in general was still enjoying a golden age. He also worked to relieve Emperor Louis of Bavaria of the power to appoint bishops and abbots, and to keep the Turks at bay with a minor crusade in 1344 that ended in truce. A rather lavish lifestyle unfortunately took its toll on the papal coffers and resulted in the introduction of further taxation.

To his credit, during the Black Death he issued papal bulls to prevent the murder of Jews, who were being blamed for the pestilence. In 1562 the Protestant Huguenots desecrated his grave and burned his remains.

Innocent VI (1352–1362)
Prophecy: De montibus Pammachii
Translation: Of the mountains of Pammachius
Interpretation: Born at Mont near Limoges, he was a cardinal priest with the title of St Pammachius.

Pope Innocent VI was also forced to remain in self-imposed exile due to the uprisings in Rome. He eventually chose to send a military response to reinstate his control but never managed to return there.

Urban V (1362–1370)
Prophecy: Gallus Vicecomes
Translation: French viscount
Interpretation: He was born of French nobility.

Eventually it was Pope Urban V who was compelled to return and take back the throne of St Peter, but the political situation had changed. The politicians of Rome were not so keen to hand back control to a French pope so Urban returned to Avignon in the latter part of his life.

Gregory XI (1370–1378)
Prophecy: Novus de Virgine forti

Translation: New of the virgin fort
Interpretation: Family name was Beaufort, and he was Cardinal of Ste-Marie La Neuve (St Mary the New).

Gregory XI also intended to return to Rome. He sent a military force ahead to quell the rising dissent before he could safely undertake such a journey. He returned to Rome but, like Urban before him, was eventually forced to leave the city and died in exile.

Urban VI (1378–1389)
Prophecy: De inferno pregnari
Translation: From the pregnant inferno
Interpretation: He was born in the town of Inferno, with the family name Prignano.

This was another quick election, this time spurred on by the unrest in Rome and the risk of Avignon challenging the papacy. Urban hailed from the Kingdom of Naples, which at the time was more aligned with Sicily than northern Italy. Civil unrest continued across Rome and again the pope was forced into exile.

Urban was quick to condemn the cardinals for their wealth but at the same time he promoted four of his nephews to office. He also shunned Avignon and was therefore disliked by many within both France and Italy.

The resulting dissension was seized upon by the French who elected the antipope, Clement VII. The continual vying for power in Rome was distracting from the more pressing developments happening in Europe at that time.

Clement VII (1378–1394), antipope
Prophecy: Decruce Apostilica
Translation: The apostolic cross
Interpretation: He was a cardinal priest of the twelve apostles and being of the house of Geneva had a cross on his coat of arms.

THE GREAT WESTERN SCHISM

Following the death of Gregory, Urban VI (1378–1389) was enthroned in the Vatican. He proved to be another low point for papal history as he soon revealed a violent temper and deeply paranoid personality. Even within the Church, those he worked with accused him of being a demon or the Antichrist. At the time little was understood of mental health issues, so the cardinals eventually had no choice but to annul his election and replace him with Clement VII. Urban responded by electing his own school of cardinals in what became known as the Great Western Schism.

Clement was in a strong political position, with ties to both French and German noble families. It was hoped he would influence the remaining supporters of Urban to change their allegiance to his cause but he failed; he was also rejected by the politicians of Rome and was forced into exile at Avignon.

The two popes exchanged excommunications and a long and violent feud ensued as kings and clergy alike took sides. The cardinals struggled to decide how to resolve the conflict while watching their Church split into factions. Urban, for his part, continued to display signs of serious mental health issues: his response to the challenge was to have those he thought were plotting against him tortured and murdered.

Some argue that Clement should not be included in the list of popes but to this day the Catholic Church has not pronounced one way or the other on the legitimacy of either pope at this time.

Even today there are a number of figures around the world who claim to be the legitimate 'antipope', including a French antipope, who is said to originate with this schism.

Boniface IX (1389–1404)

Prophecy: Cubus de mixtione
Translation: Cube of mixture
Interpretation: Family coat of arms contains cubes in the form of dice.

Boniface came from a poor family of nobles. He was well respected and tactful but uneducated in theology. During his reign he reclaimed control of Rome and fortified the city and Papal States against further attacks. This was an expensive undertaking and it brought criticism from other countries that were being taxed to pay for these improvements. He held two successful jubilees to raise funds and swapped excommunications with his opposite, antipope Clement VII.

Innocent VII (1404–1406)

Prophecy: De meliore sydere
Translation: From a better star
Interpretation: There is a shooting star on his papal coat of arms and his surname is Meliorati, from 'meliore' meaning 'better'.

From humble beginnings, Innocent spent ten years in England, and was known, prior to being elected, for having a good grasp of financial matters. He turned his attention to ending the schism but the continuing uprisings in Rome detracted from this task. His weakness was nepotism and this resulted in a conflict with his own murderous nephew, whom he had promoted. Criticism for this and his failure to end the schism taints his time as pope.

Gregory XII (1406–1415)

Prophecy: Nauta de ponte nigro
Translation: Sailor of the black bridge
Interpretation: He was from Venice and the Church of Negroponte ('black bridge').

Born in Venice and of noble family, Gregory was Bishop of Castillo and Patriarch of Constantinople. Unanimously elected pope as he was seen as a good candidate for ending the schism with the antipopes, his terms of reconcilement were wise indeed. He offered to abdicate if the antipope Benedict XIII would do the same. This would have allowed a new conclave to reinstate a single pope and end the schism, but Benedict refused to comply.

A council was convened to resolve the schism but both popes refused to attend, fearing they would be imprisoned or murdered. The stalemate continued and finally the council, in absence of the popes, appointed a third pope, Alexander V. This simply exacerbated the problem as there were now three popes.

There follows a slew of antipopes led by Clement VII. These are usually excluded from orthodox lists of popes but appear in the prophecies.

The only failing of Gregory was to continue the tradition of nepotism as he promoted four of his nephews to cardinals.

Benedict XIII (1394–1423), antipope

Prophecy: Luna Cosmedina

Translation: Cosmedine moon

Interpretation: The family name was de Luna, and he was Cardinal of Santa Maria in Cosmedin.

Benedict XIII followed Clement VII and the rift continued, with neither side willing to relinquish their position.

Alexander V (1409–1410), antipope

Prophecy: Flagellum Solis

Translation: Whip of the sun

Interpretation: Whip might be a pun on his name, Philarges. He was also Archbishop of Milan Cathedral, which has a famous statue of St Ambrose holding a whip in self-flagellation. His family coat of arms has a rising sun.

When both Gregory and Urban failed to work out a solution to the schism a council convened to resolve the matter and in their absence elected a third pope, Alexander V. Alexander had no support or power other than what the council had conferred upon him and his tenure was short-lived as he died within a year.

John XXIII (1410–1415), antipope

Prophecy: Cervus Sirenæ
Translation: Stag siren
Interpretation: He was the cardinal of St Eustace, who is depicted in art with a stag. He was also from Naples, which has the symbol of a mermaid or siren.

When Alexander died within a year of his election he was replaced by Pope John XXIII and the tragedy of the three popes rumbled on with no clear solution in sight. John proved unpopular and eventually fled in disguise from the Council of Constance. He was arrested, stripped of his position and imprisoned for a year.

Clement VIII (1423–1429), antipope

Prophecy: Schisma Barchinoniu
Translation: Schism of Barcelona
Interpretation: He was the antipope and Canon of Barcelona.

Avignon had developed its own group of cardinals for electing popes in opposition to Rome. Clement was appointed cardinal by Benedict XIII but he was aware of the damage being done to the Church by the schism and in 1429 a delegation from Rome convinced him to abdicate. He died in 1446.

Martin V (1417–1431)

Prophecy: Corona veli aurei

Translation: Crown of the shining veil
Interpretation: The family coat of arms has a crown, and Martin was Cardinal Deacon of Velabro, a name that means 'golden veil'.

When Benedict XIII passed away in 1423 the cardinals could finally elect a single pope. They chose the Italian Otto Colonna, who took the name Martin V.

Martin returned to Rome to restore the Holy See and repair the physical and spiritual damage that had befallen the Vatican in the absence of a pope. He worked to tirelessly organise the Church as an institution worthy of its purpose, but his strong will also made him a formidable pope. He died in 1431.

THE RENAISSANCE

By the time of the Renaissance the Catholic Church was perceived as being corrupted by its power. The popes were elected according to political aims and the background machinations of powerful families such as the Borgias and the Medicis. At the same time the Church was finding itself under threat again from within Europe as advances in art, philosophy and medicine were quickly moving beyond its control and beginning to contradict its authority on matters such as science.

Eugene IV (1431–1447)

Prophecy: Lupa cœlestina
Translation: Heavenly she-wolf
Interpretation: He was a member of the Order of Celestines and Bishop of Sienna, which had a female wolf on its banner.

Felix V (1439–1449), antipope

Prophecy: Amator crucis

Translation: Lover of the cross
Interpretation: The family name is Savoy and it has the symbol of the cross on its coat of arms. Amator might be a pun on his name, Amadeus.

Felix, another antipope, unsuccessfully opposed Eugene IV and at last the Great Western Schism looked to be coming to a close.

Nicholas V (1447–1455)

Prophecy: De modicitate lunæ
Translation: Of the mean moon
Interpretation: Born to poor parents, his place of birth was Luni, or Luna. He also took the symbol of the moon for his papal coat of arms.

Nicholas V saw the end of the schism as the final antipope Felix conceded the role and returned to the mainstream Church as a cardinal. Nicholas attracted thousands of pilgrims to Rome to help restore the finances. The new-found wealth was used to improve the city and bring clean water to its populace, thus securing the support of the mob that had previously driven popes into exile. The threat of republican sympathisers remained, though, and Nicholas survived an assassination attempt.

He also centralised the libraries and greatly added to this by supporting scholars in the translation of many documents, thus cementing the creation of what is today the Vatican Library.

Through the patronage of Nicholas the Vatican was renovated to such a high degree that, from this point on, it became the primary residence of all the popes to follow. His funding of Renaissance artists at the inception of this movement supported an explosion of art and sculpture, much of which was commissioned by leading figures in the Catholic Church.

Much to Nicholas' dismay, in 1453, towards the end of his reign, Constantinople fell to the Turkish Empire.

Callistus III (1455–1458)

Prophecy: Bos pascens
Translation: Ox pasturing
Interpretation: The family coat of arms included a grazing ox.

Callistus III, a Spanish pope, tried and failed to raise a crusading army to reclaim Constantinople. He was also a Borgia and heralded the beginnings of this notorious family's influence on papal elections. He began by making his nephew a cardinal – this nephew would later become Alexander VI.

Pius II (1458–1464)

Prophecy: De capra & Albergo
Translation: From a goat and an inn
Interpretation: He was a former secretary to cardinals Capranico and Albergatus, whose names stem from 'capra', meaning 'goat', and 'alberga', meaning 'tavern'.

Pius II, an intellectual, continued to seek support for a crusade but this also fell on deaf ears.

Paul II (1464–1471)

Prophecy: De cervo & Leone
Translation: From a stag and a lion
Interpretation: He had a commendatory at Cervia and took the cardinal title of St Mark, symbolised by a winged lion.

In spite of being the nephew of Eugene IV, Paul had achieved a high level of religious education and risen through the Church on his own merits. He was a collector of art and supporter of universities, but openly hostile to pagans and heretics. He funded the building of the Venetian Palace and support for the poor of Rome.

Sixtus IV (1471–1484)

Prophecy: Piscator Minorita
Translation: Minorite fisherman
Interpretation: He was the son of a fisherman and a Franciscan, who are also known as Minorites.

Sixtus was a learned man who showed all the signs of being well equipped to be pope, but once in power he became the puppet of his Machiavellian nephew. His nepotism stands as the papacy's darkest example of such practice. He made six of his nephews cardinals and sold titles and privileges to generate wealth. This wealth he spent mostly on those he favoured, although he did invest heavily in the Vatican Library and continued the city improvements, including the building of many churches and the famous Sistine Chapel, which is named after him. Both the Sistine Chapel and the Vatican Library would be contenders if a contemporary shortlist for the Seven Wonders of the World was ever drawn up, but Sixtus' radical building programme emptied the Vatican coffers once again.

Under the influence of his nephews Sixtus made many political errors, including the instigation the Spanish Inquisition. It would seem he left the politics to his nephews, concerning himself only with the Turkish Empire, which was expanding into Europe from the south and the east.

Innocent VIII (1484–1492)

Prophecy: Præcursor Siciliæ
Translation: Sicilian precursor
Interpretation: He lived in Sicily and was known as 'John the Baptist', the precursor of Jesus.

Pope Innocent VIII continued selling offices and favours to try to clear the debts he had inherited from Sixtus. This corrupt activity did not go unnoticed and dissension was growing among the bishops and those who were not based in Rome – the taxes being levied on their countrymen were being lavished upon Rome and its inhabitants, along with favours to friends and families of the pope.

Innocent continued to support the Spanish Inquisition and authored a papal bull granting Tomás de Torquemada control of this order. It was a sign of the darkness to come.

INDULGENCIES AND CORRUPTION

The position of wealth, power and influence sometimes made the role of pope attractive to those who sought to fulfil their own desires. Popes could make strong political allies so it was in the interest of kings and emperors to maintain good relations. This uneasy alliance saw the balance of power swing back and forth between the two sides throughout the centuries. Financially the Church has always been dependent on donations, be it wealth or land, and this could be used to support other activities such as crusades to reclaim the East.

The donations were originally separate from any spiritual activity and not in any way a measure of the individual in terms of their piety, until the use of indulgencies became popular.

Indulgencies began in a harmless manner as a way that priests could offer something of salvation and prayers to Catholics who had performed a penance of some kind. The intention was to give hope to those who had transgressed in some way, such as criminals, and to offer a means for them to make amends and find peace. As the practice grew in popularity it became possible to make small financial donations for indulgencies. This quickly became a corrupt method of obtaining money from rich and poor alike, as the threat of eternal damnation would empty the coffers of those who sought to buy salvation. Corruption at a local level within the Church was always difficult to police as donations were already the main source of income. Now land and wealth could easily be donated in lieu of favours or pardons.

As the practice became widespread some accused the Church of becoming a tax on people's souls and getting rich off the proceeds. The situation got worse when it was decided that members of the Church were in a position to grant pardons on behalf of God.

As this trend grew, the opposite was also happening within the Church. The Franciscan order of monks founded in the 13th century had taken Jesus at his word and taken a vow of poverty, renouncing wealth and worldly goods to live on the charitable donations of others. They asked for no tax and provided no paid services. But the greed of the Church was such that it could bear no such criticism, and in 1415 a Catholic priest, Father Jan Hus was denounced as a heretic and burned at the stake for arguing against the sale of indulgencies.

Alexander VI (1492–1503)

Prophecy: Bos Albanus in portu
Translation: Bull in Alba Port
Interpretation: He was Cardinal Bishop of Alba and Porto and had a bull in his coat of arms.

Innocent was followed by Alexander VI, another Borgia, and the most legendary of the decadent popes. Legends abound of his sexual depravity and he was known to have fathered nine children in total by different woman, two of these while he was pope. Unlike previous popes who had shown discretion, Alexander made no such concession about his children. He continued the practice of promoting members of his own family to high-ranking positions within the Church. One of his sons, Cesare, was so corrupt that he became the inspiration for Machiavelli's *The Prince*. Alexander's death in 1503 was rumoured to have been by poison – he had certainly made a lot of enemies, but it was more likely to have been through illness.

Pius III (1503)

Prophecy: De parvo homine
Translation: From a small man
Interpretation: The family name was Piccolomini, 'piccolo' meaning small man.

Pius III took his title from his uncle Pius II. He only lasted three weeks due to illness, although rumours circulated that he was poisoned.

Julius II (1503–1513)

Prophecy: Fructus jovis Juvabit
Translation: Fruit helped by Jupiter
Interpretation: The family name was Rovere, meaning 'oak tree'; the tree and its fruit were consecrated to Jupiter in antiquity.

The corruption continued and the next pope was decided by bribery more than any kind of democratic vote. Julius II had a military background and struck fear into those around him. He was a formidable politician and military strategist but chose warfare over negotiation as his primary approach to conflict. In spite of his rigged election he published a papal bull banning papal elections by bribery. He also managed to balance the books again after the previous popes had squandered the treasury. Other than conquest, he had a penchant for art and commissioned Raphael and Michelangelo, whom he tasked with painting the ceiling of the Sistine Chapel.

Leo X (1513–1521)

Prophecy: De craticula Politiana
Translation: From a Politian gridiron

Interpretation: His educator and mentor was the distinguished humanist and scholar, Angelo Politiano. The 'gridiron' is the motto that evidently refers to St Lawrence, who was martyred on a gridiron. This is a rather obtuse reference to Leo's father Lorenzo (Lawrence) the Magnificent.

Leo X also displayed cultural leanings, enjoying the company of artists and writers, and was better suited to politics than theology. He signed a concordat with the French king, Francis I, to stave off an invasion of the Papal States, but in doing so rescinded the rule that prevented monarchies appointing bishops. Considering he was of the Medici family, his time as pope was relatively scandal-free compared to his recent predecessors, although some poor political decisions made him so unpopular among the cardinals that they plotted to assassinate him. The plot was discovered and Leo had the ringleader executed; he ensured no further threats would emerge by populating the College of Cardinals with friends and allies.

REFORMATION

Into this political arena came a German preacher from the Augustinian monastic order called Luther. Luther was gaining support as a critic of the Catholic Church based on a doctrine that only God can save people through grace, and this grace cannot be bought. The wealth of donations pouring into the Vatican and the crimes of simony (selling masses and pardons), bribery and donations to gain indulgencies had been a major source of revenue for the Church. These were being sold as if they somehow bought a place in heaven. In 1517 Luther famously nailed his *Ninety-Five Theses* to the door of Wittenberg Cathedral in Germany. It was a scathing collection of judgements against the Church – some aimed directly at the pope.

Threatened with excommunication for questioning the authority of the pope, Luther dug in his heels and set himself in the role of Church reformer. He criticised the taxation by the Church that was being squandered on what he saw as extravagances not in keeping with a Christian way of life. Many of the points made were entirely valid, but in his zealous rhetoric he failed to see that some of what was happening had a spiritual dimension that served a purpose for the masses. For example, Luther criticised pilgrims being drawn to Rome because he saw this as a way to bring in revenue. While this was the case, many of the pilgrims would undergo a spiritual experience on the journey, which is in the nature of pilgrimage.

The printing press had been invented in Germany 100 years earlier and Luther's words found swift circulation as the dissemination of ideas was now beyond the control of just monks and scribes.

Luther was also responsible for a German translation of the New Testament, which had previously been under the control of the Church. To disseminate the Bible in the vernacular empowered the public by allowing them direct access to scripture instead of having to listen to the interpretations passed down to them from priests. Christians who adopted this new-found freedom and supported Luther became known as Protestants, from the word 'protest'. The inevitable excommunication took place and Luther was seen by many as a heretic, but his words would echo around the Vatican for decades to come and are still relevant today.

Adrian VI (1522–1523)

Prophecy: Leo Florentius
Translation: Florens lion
Interpretation: The family name was Florens, and his coat of arms included a lion.

Adrian VI, a Dutch pope, lasted only a year and he was to be the last non-Italian pope for over 450 years.

Clement VII (1523–1534)

Prophecy: Flos pilei ægri
Translation: Flower of the pill of the sick
Interpretation: From the Medici family, his coat of arms had medicinal balls, one bearing the image of a lily.

The Medici Clement VII, through a combination of bad decisions and sheer bad luck, witnessed the sack of Rome and a plague that greatly impacted on the population. He also seemed incapable of diplomacy and excommunicated Henry VIII, who had requested an annulment to his marriage to Catherine of Aragon after she failed to provide an heir. The king responded by appointing himself the head of the Church of England and promptly seized the wealth and property of the Catholic Church throughout the realm.

During his short reign Clement failed on all fronts, be it uniting Europe against the advancing Turks or quashing the Lutheran movement in Germany.

Paul III (1534–1549)

Prophecy: Hiacynthus medicoru
Translation: Hyacinth of the medics
Interpretation: His papal coat of arms has six hyacinths and he was cardinal of St Cosmus and Damianus, who were physicians.

When Paul III took the throne of St Peter the Church was besieged, both spiritually by the Lutherans and physically by the Turks encroaching upon southern Italy.

Paul was a mature member of the Church and proved far more proactive and strategic than Clement. He supported the continuation of the Renaissance works of art and architecture as well as funded the rebuilding of the Sapienza University of Rome. Sadly, he was also guilty of nepotism and promoted two nephews as soon as he took office.

In 1536 he proposed to reform the Church in answer to some of the issues raised by Luther and set up a commission to decide the matter. The commission's response was to restate that the will of the pope was absolute and implied that anything that opposed this will was heresy. The result was a new inquisition organised by the newly formed Holy Office. Paul also supported other emerging religious orders, including the Jesuits, who applied themselves to education via a number of new universities they set up across Europe.

THE COUNCIL OF TRENT

Over the years the council passed through the hands of a number of popes. During the reign of Paul III it managed to find an answer to Luther's accusation that only by the grace of God could people be saved. Eventually the council's response was that, although God alone granted grace, the route to achieving this was through co-creation with the individual. To some extent this made sense, in that an individual would need to be open to grace in the first place, and that by applying themselves to good works they might achieve a state of being that allowed for grace. It also meant the Church could continue to accept gifts, donations and taxes.

THE COUNTER-REFORMATION

The 16th century saw the counter-reformation, which included changes to ecclesiastical structures and the formation of new orders to stem the tide of Protestantism. One such order, the Jesuits, founded by the Spaniard St Ignatius Loyola, can be seen as an attempt to reform the Church from the inside by taking up the cause of the lay person. He published his 'Spiritual Exercises', which were instructions on daily prayer and devotion for members of the Catholic Church. He also founded the Jesuits, who were teachers giving direction to individuals, especially nobles who were becoming increasingly disenfranchised and disconnected from their religion. He reconnected people to spiritual practice by emphasising the work of the individual as part of the work of the Church.

Julius III (1550–1555)

Prophecy: De corona Montana
Translation: From the crown of the mountain
Interpretation: The family name was 'del Monte', meaning mountain. His coat of arms has palm leaf laurels as coronets.

With the passing of Paul III the council had been suspended, but his successor Julius III attempted to reinstate it. Julius seemed ill at ease with his role and spent much of his time on personal pursuits and entertainments. He made little headway in attempting to reform the Church and died before he could really make an impact.

Marcellus II (1555)

Prophecy: Frumentum flocidum
Translation: Flaccid wheat
Interpretation: He was a short-lived pope with ears of wheat on his coat of arms.

Paul was replaced by Pope Marcellus, who kept his own name as pope, and was an altogether wiser man. He understood the accusations against the Church and was willing to cut his personal expenditure and share the money with the poor. He was also strongly opposed to the nepotism that had tainted the reputation of the Church and he could potentially have been a great pope had he not died after a mere 22 days as pontiff.

Paul IV (1555–1559)

Prophecy: De fide Petri

Translation: From the faith of Peter

Interpretation: His middle name was 'Peter' and his family name Carafa means 'dear faith'.

Paul IV was highly devout and seemed a worthy pope, but the power of the role was too much for him and he became autocratic and fanatical. These traits can be useful in a religious leader but make for a poor politician. Paul's view of the world bordered on paranoia and he began to persecute as heretics anyone he saw as a threat to the Church. He was a strong advocate for the inquisition and the creator of the *Index of Forbidden Books*, which made clear his attempts at censorship. At the time of his death he was so hated in Rome that an angry mob threw a statue of him in the Tiber.

Pius IV (1559–1565)

Prophecy: Esculapii pharmacum

Translation: Aesculapius' pharmacy

Interpretation: He was a member of the Medici family, whose coat of arms had medicinal balls, and had studied to be a physician at Bologna.

Pius IV followed and immediately set about undoing some of the more extreme rules laid down by Paul IV. He also brokered peace with the heads of European royal families and sought justice against those within the Church who had abused their power.

Pius V (1566–1572)

Prophecy: Angelus nemorosus

Translation: Angel of the grove

Interpretation: Pius' middle name was Michael, after the archangel, and he hailed from the village of Bosco, which means grove.

Pius V was a former officer of the inquisition and brought with him the same austere outlook to the role. His intolerant nature saw him exile many Jews from Rome and ban prostitutes from the city. He also advocated censorship and actively hunted heretics, causing him to excommunicate Elizabeth I, the ruling monarch of England. Pius rallied support to drive the Turks from the Mediterranean. Though an austere pope, he was revered by members of the Church and was canonised in the 18th century.

Gregory XIII (1572–1585)

Prophecy: Medium corpus pilaru
Translation: The half body of the balls
Interpretation: His coat of arms contained half a dragon's body and he was appointed cardinal by Pope Pius IV, whose coat of arms had medicinal balls on it and Pius IV was pope for only half as long as Gregory – this explanation feels like a stretch but there is an alternative interpretation that the 'half ball' of the body is a joint, which is a pun on the family name Boncompagni: 'compagni' comes from 'compago' and translates from Latin as 'joint'.

Gregory XIII followed Pius and in some respects continued the work the previous pope had undertaken. He sought a military solution to negotiations with countries and groups that rejected Catholicism. In France the power of the Protestant Huguenots was perceived as a serious threat to King Charles IX when his sister married a Protestant. In the days that followed the wedding the leaders of the French Protestant Church gathered in Paris and the French king saw this as an opportunity to attack them. Thousands were killed in what became known as the St Bartholomew's Day Massacre, which the pope chose to commemorate with a minted coin and a song of praise.

Gregory is primarily remembered for his revision of the calendar, named 'Gregorian' after him, which is still in use across the world.

Sixtus V (1585–1590)

Prophecy: Axis in medietate signi
Translation: Axle in the middle of a sign
Interpretation: His coat of arms has an axle passing through a lion.

Sixtus was a respected teacher and theologian from a humble farming background. As a pope he was anything but humble and at times could be severe and unforgiving. At one point during his reign he ordered the execution of hundreds of criminals in Rome.

His success was in putting the finances in order. His administrative skills were legendary and he set up a number of congregations of cardinals tasked with running specific parts of the Church. These would oversee the administration of the day-to-day running and appointing of offices and provide continuity as popes came and went. Previously the cardinals had individually attempted these roles but had lacked the power to curb the more outrageous actions of the popes.

By the end of his reign Sixtus was one of the wealthiest men in Europe, through implementing new taxes, which allowed him to spend money on completing the many projects taking place around Rome.

THE AGE OF REASON

Just as the political and territorial disputes began to subside, the teachings of the Church came under attack. With Copernicus and Galileo came the Age of Enlightenment and scientists began to use measurable results to refute the beliefs of the Church. In every area of science and philosophy advances would be made as critical thinking and scientific method became considered the only path to true knowledge.

Urban VII (1590)

Prophecy: De rore cæli
Translation: From the dew of the sky
Interpretation: He was Archbishop of Rossano in Calabria, where sap called the 'dew of heaven' was collected.

From a noble family, trained in law and capable of handling negotiation, Urban proved himself to be very capable in settling disputes prior to being made pope. He spent seven years in Spain as papal representative in the royal court of Philip II and was promoted to inquisitor-general of the Holy Office. A popular choice as pope, he also chose the name Urban as it means 'kind'. He was tragically short-lived as a pope but during his time he opposed nepotism and worked to feed the poor of Rome.

THE PUBLICATION OF THE PROPHECIES

We must pause here to consider that at this point in history the prophecies first came to light. They were said to be in circulation as early as 1590 within the Vatican and were printed and disseminated for public release in 1595.

Their limited release in 1590 would have coincided with the long drawn-out conclave that eventually elected Urban VII, but the actual printed publication did not find its way into the public domain until five years later. This raised many accusations of forgery and claims that the entire work was fabricated to support a papal candidate.

Before we return to the prophecies and their place in the history of the popes we must gather the evidence and consider the impact of the release and the accusations of forgery.

CHAPTER 7

RELEASE AND INTRIGUE

INTRODUCTION

R umoured to be in circulation within the Vatican in 1590, the *Prophecy of the Popes* was first made publicly available in 1595. Considering the authorship of Malachy was nearly 400 years before, it would seem they were languishing somewhere in the archives for all this time. This raises a number of questions, such as why did it take so long for the prophecies to appear, and what caused their eventual release? As they appear so many years later, and are noticeably absent from St Bernard's biography of Malachy, critics have also questioned whether Malachy actually wrote them himself – to which we must add the further question: if not Malachy, then who?

What we do know is that in the 16th century the prophecies found their way into the hands of a Benedictine monk, Arnold de Wyon of Flanders in Belgium (born in 1554, death unknown). De Wyon was a credible historian, and in 1595 he published a 900-page, two-volume book called *Lignum Vitae*, meaning 'tree of life'. The two volumes were bound into a single book and there exists a first edition of this in the British Library in London.

The first volume is a study of the family tree of St Benedict with attendant genealogies, and the second is a history of famous Benedictines in history. In the midst of these books is a short chapter recounting the prophecies attributed to St Malachy, the presence of which he explains as a response to there having been a great interest in them. It appears on page 307 in the second volume as a short essay under the heading 'Prophecies of St Malachy Archbishop, of the Popes'.

Although appearing for the first time in print in de Wyon's book, the author was not the source of the transcription or interpretations of the prophecies from the original. This he credits to a Father Alphonsus Chacón (Giacconus or Giaconis, born in 1540) of the Order of Preachers, whom de Wyon identifies as the 'interpreter' of the prophecies. It is likely that the term interpreter is used to mean translator and editor in this context. Author M J O'Brien claims that the original list would have been a list of obscure Latin phrases to which Giaconis added the popes' names up to the time of publication. The text in de Wyon's book is not a direct copy and had been reworked with the addition of interpretations for the popes up to the time of release in the 16th century.

There is no mention of the prophecies prior to their 1595 publication, but de Wyon introduces them as being famous and the source of much speculation. He states that the prophecies have never before been published, 'though many have been anxious to see it.' This claim might only refer to the rumoured circulation of the prophecies in the conclave of 1590, said to have been released by Alphonsus Chacón to support the cause of Cardinal Simoncelli. This was only five years before de Wyon went to print and there is no evidence that they were known about prior to this date.

I have discovered a single, uncredited reference claiming that the prophecies were one of the earliest documents printed on the Gutenberg press in 1455. If this were true then it would pre-date Chacón and de Wyon's publications by over 130 years. I have researched in the Vatican Secret Archives, the main Vatican Library and the British Library and have yet to track down a copy. In 1455 the Gutenberg press was certainly being used to produce copies of Catholic works, as this was the time that the first printed Bible was created, but the list of documents produced at this time are generally known and there is no mention of the prophecies among them.

We cannot be sure if the prophecies were always known about within the Vatican and only released when it was deemed useful to make them public. Or perhaps they were purposefully leaked for political ends at that time. It is not clear how they came to be released and if it was in any way sanctioned by the pope at that time. It might be that rumours were spread at the time of their existence by de Wyon as a means to promote his book or that a rediscovery of the prophecies within the Vatican archives had been leaked.

François Cucherat (1812–87) in his *La Prophétie De La Succession Des Papes*, published in 1873, quotes de Wyon's *Lignum Vitae* and claims that the prophecies had been hidden in the Vatican archives for 400 years. His detailed explanation – for which he gives no source – begins by explaining that, during a visit to Rome in 1139 or 1140 for the coronation of Innocent II, Malachy had a vision which he recorded of the succession of the popes. In this account Malachy presented the prophecies to Pope Innocent II for safekeeping in the Vatican archives and to console the pope that he might take comfort in the knowledge that the papacy would endure for centuries to come.

Cucherat gives no source for this account, but if we take it at face value there are a number of possible reasons why they were not advertised at the time.

It is difficult today to envisage how steeped in superstition the Middle Ages were for priests and lay people alike. Science had yet to shine a light into the darkest corners of existence and much of what we now learn as children about how the universe works was at the time consumed by the shadows of ignorance. At the time of St Malachy the prophecies would potentially have had immense influence as both an example of prophecy and as a political tool with which to control the future of Christendom. Just as Jesus rode an ass into Jerusalem, aligning himself with an earlier prophecy of the coming Messiah (Zechariah 9:9–10), so it would be possible for papal candidates to try to align with the prophetic words of Malachy.

At that time in history it was not inconceivable that a candidate who was certain to take the seat would be assassinated or kidnapped in favour of another. Knowing what we do of the politics and factions around the papacy it would be easy to imagine a pope being assassinated to hurry into power another candidate who might fit the next prophecy. Eventually each faction would have presented a candidate based on how well they could be seen to fulfil a prophecy and in many cases future popes would have been decided before the conclave had gathered. The conclusion would have been that this was a very dangerous document for its time. The potential damage the list could have done would have been reason enough to keep it out of the public domain at that point in history.

It is possible that Pope Innocent II swore Malachy to secrecy, realising that the prophecies would hold power over future elections of the popes. There are other accounts of happenings in Malachy's life where secrecy is sworn. An example is when he was praying in the company of a deacon and a dove entered through a window and the entire basilica filled with glowing light. After the event Malachy took the deacon to one side and warned him never to speak of this event if he valued his life and never to reveal the mystery for as long as he lived.

There is also evidence that St Malachy would bind people with oaths of secrecy concerning his spiritual experiences. If he had made an agreement to do so with Pope Innocent II over the prophecies this would account for their absence in St Bernard's biography and history in general. It is also possible that he was commanded by the pope to keep these prophecies secret, even from his good friend and trusted biographer. Perhaps it was another power play by Pope Innocent II to keep St Bernard in check, as whoever had possession of the prophecies would be able to wield power over the elections to the throne of St Peter.

THE HIDDEN

If the decision was made to keep Malachy's prophecies a secret it is possible that the popes passed them down privately or they were placed in some form of 'time capsule' to be opened after a number of years or following some specific event. It might even be the case that Pope Innocent II entrusted them to a noble family who were tasked with protecting the document until it could be released. Another possibility is that they were lodged in the archive in a manner that made them difficult to locate.

The idea that such an important document could go undiscovered or remain hidden for so long initially seems unlikely. However, this is not the first time documents under the control of the pope have either gone astray or been wilfully kept out of circulation. There is a more recent example of a specific prophecy being withheld – the third secret of Fátima. This was held within the Vatican for 60 years before a version of it was released in the year 2000, and even now there are questions over whether the version released is accurate or if the true prophecy continues to be suppressed.

An earlier example, closer to the time of Malachy concerns an important letter written by Clement V that remained hidden in the Vatican archives for centuries.

CHINON AND MISSING DOCUMENTS

In April 2004 Vatican archivist Barbara Frale published an article called *The Chinon Chart: Papal absolution to the last Templar Master, Jacques de Molay*, in the *Journal of Medieval History*. Her essay, and later her book, on this subject described the discovery of a document in the Vatican archives that had been lost for 700 years. The document was of immense importance to historians as it was a letter from Pope Clement V absolving the Knights Templar of all wrongdoing at the time of their persecution. The Templars were being targeted by King Philip IV of France, who had already persecuted the Jews in France in order to seize their wealth and land, and saw the Templars as his next source of income. As the pope was in Avignon and under the control of King Philip, he was unable to deliver the pardon to the Templars and it remained a 'dead letter', allowing the king to persecute the Templars. The letter was secreted in the Vatican archives, where it remained undiscovered for seven centuries.

The initial purpose of hiding the Chinon document would have been to keep it out of circulation long enough for King Philip to seize control of the Templars' wealth and lands, while later absolving the pope of any wrongdoings, but, like many items, it became lost in the mists of history. That such an important document could be forgotten for so long gives some credence to the idea that Malachy's prophecies were languishing for some four centuries before coming to light.

I contacted Barbara Frale, who discovered the Chinon document and continues to work in the Vatican archives, to enquire about Malachy's *Prophecy of the Popes*. I asked how likely it was that other documents could have gone unnoticed for so long. Her response was that there were many documents from the medieval period that were reprinted or released for the first time around the 16th century. The Chinon parchment had been missed because it was not clearly identified and catalogued. I also got the impression that there are many boxes of material in the Vatican archives that remain uncatalogued to this day, some of which may date from Malachy's time and before.

THE QUESTION OF FORGERY

The overall accuracy of the prophecies we will consider once we have completed our reading of the interpretations to the present day. Then we will know if the prophecies stand up to rigorous investigation as a whole.

Historically there are many within the Catholic Church who have undertaken to explore the prophecies of St Malachy and arrived at one of two conclusions. They are either convinced that the messages were from the Holy Spirit working through St Malachy, or that the prophecies are outright forgeries concocted in the 16th century. I doubt it is such a black and white situation and have no desire to force an absolute conclusion. Real or fake are too extreme as proclamations and there is evidence to support and contradict both points of view. The ambiguity of the past allows us to see both sides of the mystery contained within those prophetic pages.

To consider the 'who' and the 'why' of a forgery is not without some interest as it gives cause to test the prophecies rather than blindly accept them. It is for the individual to believe if the prophecies are real or not, but note that 'believe' is a very loaded word – sometimes used to protect what we perceive to be real, even though it remains unproven.

There are many fictional accounts of how Malachy was consumed by a feverish vision and related the stream of prophecies to a scribe in his party who recorded them, but there is no known evidence to support that this event ever took place. The details of how Malachy received the prophecies and gave them to Pope Innocent II come down to us from no earlier than Father Cucherat's account in the 19th century. Cucherat gives no source for this information and, as he was writing 800 years after the event, his account is not something we can entirely trust. With so little evidence for the prophecies existing prior to de Wyon's release many authors have reached the conclusion that they were a more modern creation, authored and released in 1690 to give credibility to a candidate during that conclave and therefore the author could not be Malachy.

Claude-François Ménestrier (1631–1705), a Jesuit priest, also argues that because St Bernard of Clairvaux omits to mention them from his biography of St Malachy they could not have been authored by the saint. The gap in St Bernard's account is in no way conclusive but it does add to the question of who actually authored the prophecies. St Bernard's biography of Malachy describes in broad strokes the actual events of Malachy's stay in Rome. At other times in the biography St Bernard describes Malachy performing many miracles and even claims that Malachy was a prophet. It seems extraordinary that St Bernard would not mention such a defining event in Malachy's life, or the existence of such a document so important to the papacy.

THE AUTHOR QUESTION

It is possible that they were an anonymous text and Malachy's name was associated with them to give them credibility, as he was known to have seen the future and also to have posted a document in the Vatican archives. There were certainly other prophets at the time of Malachy who would seem better suited to being credited as an author. St Hildegard von Bingen (1098–1179) was a good candidate as she had visions all her life but only began to disseminate them publicly from the age of 42. What happened to the visions she had prior to this is unknown and they may have been recorded and given to the pope to decide their fate. Hildegard's many visions identify events in the future of the Church, including great tribulations. That she was supported, like Malachy, by St Bernard of Clairvaux is an interesting coincidence.

LATE AUTHORSHIP

There is other evidence to suggest that the prophecies were fabricated in the 16th century. The presence of the antipopes has caused some to question the accuracy of the texts, as these are not considered true popes. The antipopes were created by the 'great schism' in Church history and lasted for nearly three centuries. Also, at least one antipope is missing from the text, possibly others, as this tradition has continued in secret, and certainly to this day there can be found claimants of the throne of St Peter beyond the walls of Vatican City.

If anything, the inclusion of the antipopes supports the credibility of the list – if the prophecies were contrived, any Catholic would omit the antipopes as they are not considered true popes. But the antipopes were pope to *someone*, and it is only after the event that subsequent popes have confirmed which of the rival popes from that era were to be accepted as legitimate. It would seem in hindsight that the prophecies erred on the side of caution by backing both claimants. For them to be included seems to indicate something that was not decided by a Catholic but given from another source.

THE SOURCE OF THE EARLY PROPHECIES

In 1557 Onuphrius Panvinius (b.1529, Verona) wrote a history of the popes called *Epitome Romanorium Pontificum usque ad Paulum IV*. In this work papal coats of arms were not always given, but when they were present they were used as clues in the prophecies. Panvinius' work also contained a number of inaccuracies, such as some of the coats of arms being assigned to the wrong pope. These errors are also present in the *Prophecy of the Popes*, proving that they were in part copied from this source. Even the antipopes are included, making this almost conclusive were it not for the fact that the prophecies continue on after the Panvinius book in the same coherent manner. As we will see from the next chapter the prophecies post-release are no less accurate than those that came before. This puts an interesting light on the idea that the prophecies were written in the 16th century. If they were forged, whoever wrote them was also a prophet who could go back and write the past but then continue on into the future.

Nostradamus (1503–66) must be considered at this point as he was alive in the early part of the century when the prophecies first appeared. As mentioned earlier, he was Catholic, and to make such prophecies would require a Catholic mind. He could have drawn on the past from the Panvinius book and added his own prophecies to complete the work, but it would require the ability to 'direct' the gift of prophecy to produce a specific result. This runs counter to what we understand of prophecy and how it takes form in a part of our consciousness that is beyond our control.

THE MOTIVE FOR FORGERY

Certainly there is motive for forgery and for the release of the prophecies. Their sudden appearance would have generated interest among the cardinals and other Church members as it coincided with a papal election in 1690. We can be suspicious of the timing of the release because if the incoming candidates for pope included someone who was aligned to the text it would have provided strong propaganda to support their cause.

Claude-François Ménestrier claimed in the 18th century that the prophecies were written by Cardinal Simoncelli in 1590. He believed Simoncelli's intention was to influence the papal election that took place that year and that later de Wyon was duped into including the prophecies into the *Lignum Vitae*. That they were thought to be able to influence the papal elections shows how seriously the prophecies were taken within the Catholic Church.

Simoncelli hailed from Orvieto, meaning 'old city' and the prophecy for this pope is '*Ex antiquitate Urbis*', which translates as 'of the city of antiquity'. Simoncelli failed to be elected and the papal tiara went to Gregory XIV. Gregory was from the ancient city of Milan so could also be considered as having fulfilled the prophecy at a stretch. Not all the prophecies are ambiguous enough to allow two popes to fit the criteria; the fact that they would have been capable of indicating either candidate is interesting in itself.

The promotion of Simoncelli answers the question of why they were released at this time, but this must not be confused with whether or not they were created at this time for this purpose.

The short-term purpose of a forgery would be immediately obvious as it attempted to promote Simoncelli as the next pope, but the long-term objective is much harder to understand. If the prophecies were a forgery, why include the fall of Rome, or, indeed, why include any of the future popes beyond that century? Why go to such effort to make them credible with information going so far into the future?

The prophecies conclude with a final passage that describes the fall of Rome and the last pope, Peter the Roman, which seems out of place. Its presence is unlikely to add to the credibility of the work, other than in keeping with the tradition of apocalyptic literature by lending it a certain gravitas. And if the document was entirely forged, why did the forger include so many future popes? It would have created an unnecessary burden of work to have invented so many predictions without any value, other than perhaps to try to give the document more credibility.

Since the time of publication debate has raged over whether the prophecies were a fabrication purely for political purposes, or if there is a genuine lineage that dates back to the time of Malachy.

The picture that is forming is one of the prophecies being compiled in the 16th century for the purpose of promoting a specific candidate rather than having been withheld until that time and then exploited for that purpose. But this only works if, following their release, the accuracy of the prophecies falls away or the text itself becomes entirely ambiguous. Ultimately, the prophecies are only valid if they prove accurate beyond the date that they were released.

POST RELEASE

The argument for forgery requires that after the date of publication in the 16th century there is a decline in the accuracy of the prophecies. The first observation to make is that there is no change in the style of writing and the prophecies continue as simple two- or three-word descriptions in the same manner as prior to publication. These descriptions are equally specific in many cases and continue to use very precise language. Admittedly some of the later descriptions do not score so highly in relevance and it is difficult to find a conclusive explanation for a few of them – though nothing like the number that pure guesswork would have introduced. There is, as will be seen in the following chapter, a very high level of accuracy for many of the prophecies, continuing up to present day.

We had previously explored the accuracy of the prophecy regarding Innocent XII (1691–1700) whose family name 'Rastrello', the Italian for 'rake', featured in the prophecy for his reign.

In another case of accuracy the pope who was in place in 1914 was described as 'religion depopulated'. That epithet perfectly describes Benedict XV's time, as Spanish flu, the rise of Communism and the First World War greatly contributed to the depopulation of Catholicism. The term 'religion depopulated' itself is not something a Catholic author would casually include in a forged prophecy – again, due to these worldwide events being outside the control of the Vatican there are no possible grounds for suspecting collusion.

There is a break in the text at the time of publication but once the writing settles back into a rhythm the descriptions are often too specific and accurate to be chance. We would expect a vastly different set of outcomes to follow publication if the entire work was fabricated, but this is not the case.

RESPONSE TO FORGERY

The accuracy of the later predictions proves that this cannot be a simple case of forgery for political ends. That would require our forger to have been a prophet or have one in their employ, but even this is unlikely in the extreme as seers are not known for being able to focus on anything so specific. The act of receiving visions is like opening to grace: it cannot be directed in such a controlled manner.

One option to consider is that the prophecies were not forged outright but were a reworking of an original document. If the prophecies in their original form could not always be explained in terms of the pope that they were meant to identify, it would pose a problem for anyone wishing to use them. If the list was specific and accurate in some cases, while being vague and seemingly off in others, they would risk being dismissed as intermittently accurate and not to be trusted. In order to manipulate these to promote a specific cardinal as pope, the prophecies would need to appear completely accurate up that point in time, and therefore the forger would need to correct all the errors and confusion of the earlier prophecies. To do this they used Panvinius' history of the popes, bringing with it all the inaccuracies that this book contained. After publication no such alterations could be made and this would explain why there is a lower rate of accuracy post-publication but many of the prophecies still ring true.

CONCLUSION

Even in the hands of a coercive force the prophecies are strangely robust. The promotion of Simoncelli from Orvieto or the 'old city' of the prophecy failed, and he lost out to Gregory XIV who had an equally archaic birthplace.

Beyond the claims and counter-claims of forgery there is another level of truth. The question is not just if they are real but if they are believed to be real. If they were entirely fabricated but had gained credibility within the Vatican, the fact that they are in the public domain from this point onwards means they could potentially influence the outcome of an election. From the politics and power struggles that had underscored the papal elections, and continued to do so after publication, it would be impossible for the prophecies to play a central role in promoting candidates to the Holy See of St Peter.

Even today the interest in the prophecies in the Vatican rises at time of a pope's death, although the cardinals maintain that they do not influence the election in any way. Among Italians 'Santa Malachia', as St Malachy is known, is revered and widely studied by Catholics and his prophecies are greatly sought after and discussed when a pope has passed on.

St Malachy might have been the true author and source of the prophecies, but without the originals we may never know for sure. We must accept that the prophecies continue to stand or fall by their accuracy and this overrules the importance of identifying the actual author.

In prophecy credibility is not something that comes with status but with the quality of the communication.

CHAPTER 8

THE PROPHECIES –
PART 2

INTRODUCTION

In 1590, prior to de Wyon's publication, a high demand for the rumoured prophecies gripped those within the Vatican. Copies would have been scarce but gossip about the content would have quickly circulated throughout Rome, even among senior members of the Catholic Church. Candidates for the next conclave would have been inexorably drawn to the information. Some would have spent hours poring over the text to try to determine if they might in some way be eligible to fulfil the next prophecy: 'Of the city of antiquity'. In private, discussion would have been rife as to who would be a good fit and whether or not the conclave should actively discriminate against the prophecy. The cardinals would have to decide if they were to set about proving it wrong rather than risk being at the mercy of the author's predictions for the next 68 popes.

Clearly a number of high-ranking Catholics took the prophecies to heart and decided they must at least have some credibility but had the sense to block their influence. From the point of release it would have been possible for every pope that followed to be contrived from the prophecies, but that does not appear to be what happened. While there was a great interest in the clues they presented there is no indication that they ever had a direct influence over who was elected.

We resume the list of prophecies, with attendant popes and interpretations following the circulation and publication of the list, aware that these statements were known from this point onwards within the Vatican.

Gregory XIV (1590–1591)

Prophecy: Ex antiquitate Urbis
Translation: Of the city of antiquity
Interpretation: He was born in the ancient city of Milan.

Gregory was a reluctant pope who was appointed after a three-month conclave. He opposed Henry of Navarre, a Protestant who was to become the next French king. After excommunicating Henry he moved to fund his political opponents but died after just ten months as pope.

In his brief reign Gregory also spoke out against slavery and ordered the freeing of the slaves of the Philippines.

Innocent IX (1591)

Prophecy: Pia civitas in bello
Translation: Pious city in war
Interpretation: He was Patriarch of Jerusalem and was also born in Bologna, which had suffered constant wars until put under the control of the popes in 15th century.

Innocent also opposed Henry of Navarre and planned to revise the papal finances as well as publishing his prolific writings. Sadly his intentions were never achieved as he died just three months after taking office.

Clement VIII (1592–1605)

Prophecy: Crux Romulea

Translation: Cross of Romulus

Interpretation: His title as a cardinal was 'St Pancratius', who was a Roman martyr. Romulus is credited as the traditional founder of Rome, after whom it was named. Clement was also from the house of Aldobrandini, famous for Beato Pietro Aldobrandini, who performed a miracle in 1063, walking through fire unharmed while carrying a cross.

Clement was welcomed as pope by the people of Rome and by the conclave to rid the papacy of the influence of Spain's King Philip II. Of high moral standing, he devoted much of his time to spiritual matters and funded the creation of educational establishments across Italy. He was also skilled in politics and successfully negotiated the release from prison of Archduke Maximilian in Poland. His astute nature helped influence the end of the Thirty Years' War in Europe and lend financial support to the war against the Turks in Hungary. Too much intellectualism took a toll on his compassion and Clement was vindictive towards those he perceived to be the enemies of the Church, such as the Dominican friar Giordano Bruno, who was burned at the stake in 1600 as a heretic.

He is the last pope named in de Wyon's *Lignum Vitae* prior to its publication in 1595. From this point onwards the prophecies were in the public domain for all to read, discuss and interpret.

Both Clement, above, and Leo XI, who followed in 1605, have only a vague resemblance to the prophecy corresponding to their tenures as pope. It remains to be seen if this was an early indication that the prophecies were becoming vague, and allowing for a wider range of interpretations.

Leo XI (1605)

Prophecy: Undosus Vir

Translation: Wave man

Interpretation: He was made Bishop of Palestrina in 1602, a city said to have been founded by the sailor Ulysses. Also elected during a full moon, known to control the tides, and survived as pope for only 29 days, which is one full cycle of the moon.

Leo was of the Medici family, who were said to have spent 300,000 ecus to promote him as a viable candidate for pope. The conclave appointed him against the wishes of the French and Spanish kings but he died of illness shortly after his coronation.

The prophecy for the following pope has a surprisingly negative description that must have raised a few eyebrows when the conclave began. It is difficult to imagine who would want to be pope in the light of a prediction that they would be remembered as 'nation perverted', however Paul V fitted the description.

Paul V (1605–1621)

Prophecy: Gens perversa

Translation: Nation perverted or race perverted

Interpretation: The family coat of arms displays a dragon and an eagle, signifying the marriage of two opposing households.

Paul V is chiefly remembered for promoting his nephew to the College of Cardinals to make him eligible to be elected as a future pope. This is thought to be the origin of the word 'nepotism' from 'nephew', although he was one of many popes at the time who favoured family members for positions within the Church.

Paul was born in Rome into the noble line of the Siena family and related to St Catherine. Studious and an expert in legal matters, he cut an uncompromising figure but held a holistic view of the Church and took interest in matters in all countries. He oversaw the completion of St Peter's, which had been 100 years in the making, and invested in the Vatican Library, the arts and education.

Gregory XV (1621–1623)

Prophecy: In tribulatione pacis
Translation: In tribulations of peace
Interpretation: The Thirty Years' War spread across Europe during his reign which he mediated against for peace.

A graduate of law, Gregory had been a leading judge of Rome. The experience would serve him well as pope as he was successful in politics across Europe and in the Near East.

Elected in bad health at 67 years of age, Gregory published clear instructions for electing popes, stipulating that all votes should be secret and outlawing self-promotion and other abuses in an attempt to prevent further political influence creeping into the conclave. However, the stemming of abuse did not go so far as nepotism, as he immediately promoted his nephew to cardinal, chiefly to act as a personal assistant. He also promoted his brother to an important role, though both figures proved themselves worthy of their positions.

Gregory supported the religious orders that were flourishing and went so far as to canonise Ignatius of Loyola, the founder of the Jesuits. He also organised and supported the missionary outposts across the world and took a more tolerant view of witchcraft, limiting the death penalty to only those who were proven to have been in league with the devil.

The year 1621 saw the start of the Thirty Years' War and carnage raged in Western Europe as the Catholic and Protestant states of Europe fought for control. The war concluded with the Treaty of Westphalia in 1648 and saw the protection of states from the influence of the Holy Roman Empire, but by this point much of Europe, especially Germany, had fragmented into smaller states.

Urban VIII (1623–1644)

Prophecy: Lilium & rosa
Translation: Lily and rose
Interpretation: He was born in Florence, which has a red lily on its coat of arms and three bees. Bees were thought at the time to prefer the lily or rose to all other flowers. Both the lily and the rose were used prior to publication to describe previous popes. This prophecy also continues the established tradition of describing coats of arms.

Urban was raised in Rome by his mother after his father's early death. Educated by the Jesuits, he became papal legate to France. As pope he was always loyal to the Church and continued funding the religious orders and their missions, especially in the Far East.

Like his predecessors he continued the tradition of nepotism by promoting his nephews and brother to positions which brought much wealth to their families. He also supported their petty political endeavours, while investing heavily in the defence of the Papal States.

At the time Urban was criticised for excessive military spending, forging arms and building fortifications and castles, but considering the spread of war this was not surprising.

While he had the good sense to prohibit slavery, he allowed the condemnation of Galileo by the inquisition and failed in his attempts to restore Catholicism in England. Galileo was forced to live out the end of his days under house arrest as part of the suppression of the idea that the solar system was heliocentric, which had been proposed by Copernicus in 1543.

Innocent X (1644–1655)

Prophecy: Jucunditas crucis
Translation: Delight of the cross

Interpretation: He was made pope on the Feast of the Exaltation of the Cross. (Note: this could have been any of the conclave members as whoever was chosen near this day would fulfil the prophecy.)

A bachelor of law, Innocent had been a member of the inquisition prior to becoming pope. A difficult conclave saw the French cardinals refuse to support any Spanish candidates, and the Spanish were equally intolerant of the French. Innocent X was a compromise. During his reign he was accused of having an inappropriate relationship with his brother's widow, Olimpia Maidalchini. While this may not have been a physical relationship, she is known to have exerted a strong influence over his papal decisions for a period of time.

Alexander VII (1655–1667)

Prophecy: Montium custos

Translation: Mountain custodian

Interpretation: Said to be responsible for setting up the 'Mounts of Piety' in Rome, a form of bank that had more in common with today's pawnbrokers, Alexander also hailed from the old and powerful Chigi family of Sienna, whose coat of arms was an image of six hills lit by a star.

Alexander had links to the papacy through his family: his father was the nephew of Paul V. Armed with doctorates of philosophy, law and theology, he rose to the role of Inquisitor of Malta and then was appointed by Innocent X as secretary of state.

The conclave lasted 80 days and eventually, to prevent international or factional influence, it was agreed to appoint Alexander because his wealth would allow him to remain above influence and bribery.

To guard against nepotism Alexander banned members of his family from coming to Rome seeking promotion. It made for a promising start, but after just a year in power he was swayed into giving control of the administrative office to his father and brother. While attempting to remain aloof by refusing to profit directly, he allowed his family to become obscenely wealthy by exploiting their positions.

His time in office was mixed, as the ongoing disagreement with Louis XIV of France led to the temporary loss of control of Avignon and was only resolved by conceding to the king's demands. In the pope's favour, in 1655 Queen Christina converted to Catholicism and abdicated from the throne of Sweden. She went into exile and came to Rome, where she became friends with Alexander. His legacy also includes creating a library for the University of Rome and the furnishing of many churches.

Clement IX (1667–1669)

Prophecy: Sydus Olorum

Translation: Swan constellation

Interpretation: The conclave was said to have taken place in the 'Chamber of Swans' within the Vatican. This identifies the location but does not identify the specific pope, so anyone elected from this conclave would have suited the prophecy.

A professor of philosophy and former secretary of state, Clement had a good reputation in Rome for his down-to-earth approach and charitable actions. A man of the people, he took confessions for common people that would visit him and visited the sick in hospitals.

Within Rome he shunned fame and avoided nepotism while balancing the books and putting the economy in order. On the world stage Clement reorganised the Church of the newly independent Portugal and took a firm stance against the warmongering Louis XIV. He also funded the defence of Crete, which was eventually lost to the Turks.

True to his life Clement chose a humble burial but his successor had a lavish monument erected in his memory. He is considered one of the greatest popes in history, a man who carried the burden of the Holy See in an exemplary manner.

Clement X (1670–1676)

Prophecy: De flumine magno
Translation: From a great river
Interpretation: He was born in Rome on the Tiber, which is known as the 'great river'. This is not the most specific of prophecies as many of the major rivers have been known by this title at some point. Almost any candidate who hailed from a major city would likely have resided near a 'great river'. A later account states that on the day of his birth the Tiber flooded and he had to be rescued from the great inundation by his nurse (Massey, 1718). His name, Altieri, can also mean 'deep'.

Another Roman, Clement was appointed after the conclave had gone on for four months, more because his advanced years would ensure a brief reign than for any merit of his own. Such mechanisms were used when an agreement could be found and what was required was a temporary pope to delay things until a time when the conclave could agree on a candidate.

As he was in his eighties Clement needed help from those he could trust, so he immediately promoted his two sons-in-law who over time took control of the Vatican.

He devoted his six-year tenure to keeping the Turks at bay on the European borders and at home he funded further works in Rome.

Innocent XI (1676–1689)

Prophecy: Bellua insatiabilis
Translation: Insatiable beast

Interpretation: Innocent had a lion and an eagle on his coat of arms, and was also said to be 'never without Cibo'. Cibo was the name of a cardinal who was a great influence on the pope. Cibo is Italian for 'food', so the prophecy is also a pun on this saying, describing the pope as 'never without food'.

Innocent was educated by Jesuits and is remembered for his charitable nature, especially towards the poor. As pope he lived a frugal life, setting an example to the cardinals by curbing their excesses and publishing edicts forbidding nepotism. He quickly restored the papal finances and used these to fund the war against the Turks.

Innocent also attempted to curb the excesses of King Louis XIV, who had taken it upon himself to persecute the Protestants. They fought a battle of wills until eventually the pope excommunicated the king.

In 1687 Isaac Newton published his *Mathematical Principles of Natural Philosophy* proposing that the universe was governed not by God but by scientific principles. This marked the beginning of the Age of Reason in Europe, when science and philosophy sought to view the world intellectually, free from faith and superstition.

Alexander VIII (1689–1691)

Prophecy: Pœnitentia gloriosa
Translation: Glorious penitence
Interpretation: Alexander's first name was Peter, named after St Peter, who repented having denied Christ.

Alexander was also elected as pope on 6 October 1689, which is the feast day of St Bruno, a celebrated penitent and founder of the Carthusian order.

As we have seen with previous popes, the day of election can sometimes seem more important than the identity of the pope. According to the commentaries by Cucherat he was also pope at the time that the French priests returned to the fold and these could also have been described as penitents.

Descended from the noble family of Ottoboni, Alexander's father was chancellor for Venice. Wealth afforded him the finest education and he graduated in law from the University of Padua, but his reign was short, lasting of only 16 months due to his advanced years when elected. In such a brief time little could be accomplished but he regained control of Avignon from Louis XIV of France, cut taxes to the poor, supported the war against the Turks and funded the Vatican Library. Encumbered by his traditionalist nature, he condemned the growing philosophical movement in Europe and regressed to appointing his relatives to positions of wealth and power within the Church.

Innocent XII (1691–1700)

Prophecy: Rastrum in porta

Translation: Rake in the door

Interpretation: His family name was Rastrello, Italian for 'rake', and originally there was a rake in the family coat of arms. It cannot be denied that 'rake' is a specific term and it perfectly matches the surname of Pope Innocent XII. This prophecy, and others like it, can be held up as evidence against the accusation that the prophecies are vague enough to be interpreted in a multitude of ways. 'Rake' is unquestionably a clear and direct reference to the surname and could not have been chance on the part of the author. A century after the publication of the prophecies and we have an exact match.

After a long and torturously hot conclave that lasted five months the Archbishop of Naples was elected and took the name Innocent XII. Strongly adverse to nepotism and the selling of offices, he issued a papal bull with strict guidelines preventing the promotion of family members on anything other than pure merit. It did not eradicate nepotism from the papacy but certainly enforced the stigma against it. Innocent XII also made peace with Louis XIV of France but failed to wrest control of the French Church from him.

Clement XI (1700–1721)

Prophecy: Flores circumdati
Translation: Surrounded by flowers
Interpretation: Of the Albani family, whose coat of arms is surrounded by flowers, Clement also strongly advocated the use of the rosary to honour Mary, the mother of Jesus. Regardless of these links, some of his supporters felt that it was important he conclusively fit the prophecy so they struck a medal in his name with the 'Flores circumdati' motto on it to validate the prediction.

At only 51 years old Clement was chosen more for his virtue than his experience when appointed pope. Widely considered to be an intellectual, he had been Senator of Rome, providing legal advice to Innocent XII and a keen follower of his stance against nepotism. Clement was devout and steeped in humility, choosing to forgo food while distributing wealth to the poor.

As his coronation took place Europe was on the brink of descending into turmoil following the death of the Hapsburg king, Charles II of Spain. The king had died without a natural heir and a bitter feud began as both Hapsburg houses of Austria and France made claims to the Spanish kingdom. As Austria and France went to war Clement mistakenly supported the French, who failed to take Vienna and were repelled. The Austrian armies retaliated against the pope by marching on northern Italy and eventually seizing the Papal States.

Innocent XIII (1721–1724)

Prophecy: De bona Religione
Translation: From good religion

Interpretation: Innocent was of the Conti family, which had produced a number of popes including Innocent III, after whom he took his name.

Innocent had attended the College of Rome and been appointed Archbishop of Tarsus prior to becoming pope. His election was the result of a difficult conclave but he proved a good choice as he worked to maintain the Church beyond Rome. He funded the Catholic James III's campaign to regain the throne of England and supported the Venetians as they fought the Turks for possession of Malta.

Innocent was coerced into making the singularly unsuitable French prime minister a cardinal. He also promoted his own brother to cardinal but limited his revenue to prevent any abuse of position.

Benedict XIII (1724–1730)
Prophecy: Miles in bello
Translation: Soldier in battle
Interpretation: A life of zeal and strict discipline was seen by some to be the battle he fought throughout his term as pope.

Benedict's early calling in life was to join the Dominican Order against the wishes of his family. He rose to become archbishop and retained the title Archbishop of Benevento while pope.

When elected, Benedict was initially very reluctant to accept but finally relented and took the title Benedict XIII to replace the antipope of the same name. His aim as pope was to return discipline to the Church by publishing decrees on strict dress code and the abolition of luxuries. He was zealous in his faith but also sought peaceful solutions to political issues.

Clement XII (1730–1740)
Prophecy: Columna excelsa
Translation: High column

Interpretation: He bought two Doric columns from the Parthenon for his family chapel at Mantua.

Hailing from the noble Corsini family, Clement was old and ill from the start but lasted ten years. In the second year of his pontificate he became totally blind, and in his later years he was compelled to keep to his bed.

Clement came to power with a good reputation, having held a number of offices in Rome. He had inherited bad finances but set out to balance the books. He brought to justice those within the Church who had abused their positions for financial gain and reinstated the public lottery to bring in revenues. This blatantly disregarded Benedict XIII's moral stance against gambling, which had seen it outlawed. The wealth Clement generated was spent on great building projects, including the restoration of St John Lateran and the Arch of Constantine. He also paved Rome and instigated the building of the Trevi Fountain.

Benedict XIV (1740–1758)

Prophecy: Animal rurale

Translation: Rural animal

Interpretation: He is remembered for the sheer number of papal 'bulls' he wrote, making the prophecy a pun on his profuse writings.

Benedict was scholarly, supporting art, science and medicine, but he was also traditional and conservative in matters of faith, so he stood against reform and change. He was at odds with society as it was the time of the direct criticisms of the Church by Rousseau and the indirect challenge of Diderot. Diderot had published the *Encyclopaedia*, a comprehensive overview of arts and sciences of the day.

Within the Church Benedict sought to limit the abuses of power, especially among the unruly cardinals, and to replenish the Vatican finances. Politically he was inspiring in his character but too quick to compromise with the European heads of state. Ultimately his legacy is one of bringing peace to the role of pontificate and finding a way to connect to the Eastern Churches of Greece, Israel and Egypt.

Clement XIII (1758–1769)

Prophecy: Rosa Umbriæ
Translation: Rose of Umbria
Interpretation: He was the former governor of Rieti, in Umbria; the state emblem of Umbria is a rose. Clement had also been a cardinal at the Santa Maria church in Aracoeli, famous for its blue rose window.

A Venetian of Jesuit education and graduate of law, Clement is recorded as being an exemplary individual who gave away his wealth to the poor and lived like a saint. His election marked the inauguration of another reluctant pope. The papacy was mired in politics and besieged by critics, with Voltaire heading the philosophical charge against the Church. The critics targeted the Jesuits, whose educational reforms and missionaries were a driving force in the dissemination of Catholic doctrine, both in Europe and abroad. These philosophers sought and found allies among the powerful of Europe and looked for ways to insidiously persecute the Jesuits.

The Jesuits were suppressed in Portugal, their wealth seized and they were deported to Italy. France and Spain followed suit and eventually demanded that the Jesuits were outlawed worldwide. Clement died within a month of receiving the demands, proving he was right to be a reluctant pope: the weight of the role had quickly proved too much for him.

Clement XIV (1769–1774)

Prophecy: Ursus velox

Translation: Swift bear
Interpretation: The family coat of arms has a running bear.

Bowing to political demand, Clement XIV issued a papal bull to disband the Jesuits. The overall effect was highly detrimental to Catholicism as it removed all the Church's centres of teaching from around the world. The Church would never regain such a capacity to educate. However, it also showed the in-fighting and politics that were poisoning the Church from within, and proved how little power the popes now had on the world stage.

Pius VI (1775–1799)

Prophecy: Peregrine Apostolic
Translation: Apostolic pilgrim
Interpretation: Exiled by the French Revolution, Pius was described by contemporary writers as the 'apostolic pilgrim on earth'.

When he visited Vienna he became the first pope to visit a foreign country for centuries. He also travelled again in his reign but was captured and imprisoned, dying in exile.

Pius VI was too blunt an instrument to handle the subtle politics that enmeshed the Vatican and its dealings with foreign powers. In his ignorance he published works condemning the ideas of the Enlightenment as the work of the devil. His vitriolic attack on scientists painted them as atheists when many were nothing of the sort. It was an attitude that alienated the Church and showed how out of step it had become with culture compared to its leading role in the Renaissance over a century before. Pius also managed to once again squander the Vatican finances and sink to nepotism by promoting his two nephews.

In 1789 the effects of the French Revolution reverberated throughout Europe. Not only was the French monarchy deposed, but all power structures, including the clergy, came under attack. Pius was powerless to object, other than to suspend members of the clergy who allied themselves with the new regime. This reactionary response was counter-productive, as failure to support the regime was seen as a treason that was punishable by death, giving the priests a choice of death or excommunication. As a result many thousands of priests were forced into exile. Equally destructive was the seizing and selling of Church possessions and property, ridding France of its long tradition of monasteries and attendant holy orders.

Fifteen years later stability returned to France as Napoleon seized control and proclaimed himself emperor, and in 1804 the subsequent pope was summoned to his coronation. It marked the turning of the tables after hundreds of years of the papacy holding sway over the French kings, with the new emperor demanding that all Christians within his domain be primarily answerable to him and him alone.

Meanwhile, Napoleon marched on Rome, forcing Pius to offer a treaty at great strategic, political and financial cost. He literally sold off the family silver to pay the debt and allowed Napoleon to choose from works of art and documents in the Vatican Library to buy his way to peace.

It was a short-term solution as the following year the French army invaded Rome, deposed Pius and exiled him to Florence, and then as a prisoner to France. It was a humiliating end to such bombastic beginnings as Pius would die powerless in exile.

Pius VII (1800–1823)

Prophecy: Aquila rapax

Translation: Rapacious eagle

Interpretation: This describes the relationship between the pope and Napoleon, whose banner was an eagle, and who pressured the pope to crown him emperor. Pius VII resisted, but the battle of wills defined his time as pontiff.

Following the death of Pius VI the conclave elected Pius VII with no other thought in mind than how to deal with Napoleon. Pius VII was learned and read widely beyond theology, but was also approachable and friendly. He was versed in new ideas and philosophies, so would have a seemed a capable choice to reinstate the Church. For the first half of his long 23-year reign, he was in the shadow of Napoleon, with whom he signed a concordat protecting French Catholics and clergy from further persecution. He managed to turn the French Church back to Rome again, filling the void for those whom revolution had left bereft of structure and order. Pius also blessed Napoleon at his coronation, his humble approach a stark contrast to the self-aggrandisement of the man who had proclaimed himself emperor.

Leo XII (1823–1829)

Prophecy: Canis & coluber
Translation: Dog and snake
Interpretation: His family name was Sermattei, an Italian variation on 'serpente'. Also in terms of slander, as he was widely disliked.

In contrast to Pius, Pope Leo XII's reign was both short-lived and short-sighted. He ghettoised the Jews of Rome and created nothing short of a police state to enforce his rule. He lasted only four years but managed to alienate the people of Rome from their pope.

Pius VIII (1829–1830)

Prophecy: Vir religiosus
Translation: Religious man
Interpretation: There is no clear link between this phrase and the pope other than that he chose Pius as his papal name.

Pius was elected at a conclave in Venice and was the last pope to be elected outside of the Vatican. As a successor to Leo XII he was also brief, lasting just one year. Pius VIII was too ephemeral to have any real impact on the papacy or quell the growing unrest caused by Leo.

Gregory XVI (1831–1846)

Prophecy: De balneis Ethruriæ
Translation: From the baths of Etruria
Interpretation: He was a member of the Camaldolese Order founded by St Romuald in Balnea, Etruria (now Tuscany).

Gregory XVI came to power at the behest of the more conservative members of the conclave. He was a throwback to pre-Enlightenment popes who struggled with modernity; as a result he chose to ban railroads from Rome. To his credit he spoke out against the trading of humans as slaves and also reinvigorated the missionary movement, but the unrest set in motion by Pope Leo XII had turned to uprising and the Papal States were besieged by civil unrest. Austria was called upon to send troops to reinstate order but civil unrest would continue to impose itself upon Gregory to the end of his life.

Pius IX (1846–1878)

Prophecy: Crux de cruce
Translation: Cross of the Cross
Interpretation: His family coat of arms was a white cross on a red background. The prophecy has also been interpreted as the burden Pius bore in relation to his time as pope.

Pius IX replaced Gregory as a more amenable pope. His reign started well as he immediately set about undoing some of the damage done by Gregory, diffusing some of the tensions that had arisen by pardoning a number of political prisoners and spending on civic improvements around the Papal States. The Austrian army were still at hand, having occupied the northern territories of Italy, and this probably brought Pius some comfort as they could ensure law and order could be quickly restored. His failure to expel the Austrian forces made him many political enemies in Rome, but his dependence on the support of Austria and France would keep him safe throughout his term.

Although widely read, he was also traditional and took up the battle against the Age of Reason. Pius published a critique of the various forms of government, institutions and philosophies that had found a footing in modern Europe. Among these he took issue · with communism, socialism and rationalism. The publication was widely condemned by governments and individuals, with some countries banning its publication. To support his ideals he convened the First Vatican Council in 1869, through which he restated the infallibility of the pope. Not surprisingly the claim made Pius many enemies among European leaders and even drew complaints from within the Church.

In 1870 the Papal States that surrounded the Vatican and covered up to a third of Italy fell to the Italian army when King Victor Emmanuel II declared Rome the new capital of Italy. Having retreated into the Vatican, Pius IX never left the city again and died there eight years later.

Leo XIII (1878–1903)

Prophecy: Lumen in cœlo
Translation: Light in the heavens
Interpretation: His coat of arms contains a shooting star, but he also wrote a series of exemplary encyclicals for which he is recognised to be a guiding light within the Church.

The next pope had another long reign: Pope Leo XIII lasted 25 years but he proved to be more diplomatic than his predecessor. Leo attempted to reclaim the Papal States but failed to generate support from other European powers. Further afield he was more successful, having expanded the Catholic Church in Africa, India and Asia. His outlook was more inclusive and he saw other forms of Christianity not as heresy but as an opportunity for re-integration. For the first time Christianity and democracy were seen as compatible by a pope. The open-minded rule of Leo continued with the opening of the archives and the Vatican Library to scholars of all religions. The one enduring point of contention for Leo was with Communism, which was continuing to gain support and threatening to bring atheism to the masses. In response he wrote of how the salvation and wellbeing of individuals could not be separated and that workers should unite to achieve a fairer wage. Education was also moving beyond the control of the Church and Leo expanded the list of banned books, though it lacked the influence of its first incarnation.

Pius X (1903–1914)

Prophecy: Ignis ardens

Translation: Burning fire

Interpretation: In one sense this can be seen as the fire of faith that burned within Pius. He was the first pope to be made a saint for over 400 years. More likely is that the end of his reign coincided with the beginning of the First World War.

Pius X was another contrast – a return to a simple man of God as leader of the Church. He was very traditionalist and fought against modernism, though he suited the needs of the Church at the time. Arguments over politics and modern philosophy were threatening to overshadow the purpose of the Church, so electing Pius would have appealed to those who wanted the Church to stand above such matters. Unfortunately political involvement was unavoidable and Pius was ill-equipped to deal with the complex machinations of the world leaders of the 20th century. His outlook was simple: the purpose of the pope was to direct others, who should listen and obey, but this had no influence on modern leaders.

Having come from a pastoral background, he understood how detached the parishioners had become from the process of mass. His remedy was to increase the amount of interaction they had by allowing the lay parishioners to take duties within the Church and increasing the regularity of communion.

The rise of methodical scholarship in line with philosophical and scientific advances was encroaching on theology, with a mechanistic outlook that lacked the mystical elements of religious studies. Pius countered this by supporting biblical scholars through building monasteries across Europe, but again his outlook was too simplistic and he attacked modernists for separating politics from religion. The result was a banning of more books and expulsion from Church education of anyone seen to be teaching ideas outside the accepted dogma.

Benedict XV (1914–1922)

Prophecy: Religio depopulata
Translation: Religion depopulated
Interpretation: The reign of Benedict encompassed the entire First World War, in which an estimated 20 million people died, the 1918 pandemic outbreak of Spanish flu that ravaged Europe and the Bolshevik Revolution which made Russia officially an athiest state. This has to be considered one of the most accurate of the post-publication prophecies, and one of the most accurate prophecies in history – if asked to sum up this period for the Catholic Church in two words, 'religion depopulated' would be a perfect description.

At the outbreak of the First World War a new pope was inaugurated. Benedict XV was an intelligent diplomat. He toned down the vitriol of his predecessor to be more inclusive of the different forms of Christianity, and as the war ravaged Europe he openly condemned those responsible while working to help reunite prisoners of war with their families. Benedict became an inspiration to the popes that followed, as at last the papacy had found its true calling: to act as an advocate for peace for all peoples of the world.

Benedict continued his relief efforts after the war, supporting the wounded and orphaned. At the time of his death he was one of the most respected men of his time.

Pius XI (1922–1939)

Prophecy: Fides intrepida
Translation: Intrepid faith (meaning faith without fear)
Interpretation: As Italy descended into Fascism and Mussolini supported the rise of Hitler, Pius spoke out against the Nazi regime and criticised anti-Semitism.

In 1922 the conclave elected Pius XI. His wealthy family had provided a good education for him and he had worked at the Vatican Library, which he continued to support throughout his time as pope. He also supported research into the science of archaeology. Although conservative and traditional in some respects, he understood the world stage and was the first pope to speak publicly via radio. He also went to great lengths to create Chinese and Japanese bishops and canonise many saints.

Under his rule the Vatican City gained full independence from Italy through an agreement signed with Mussolini. In 1922 Mussolini had risen to power on a wave of Fascist propaganda. He was no longer a Catholic but valued the support of the Vatican and gave the Vatican sovereignty, with the pope as head of state. He reinstated mandatory religious education in schools with Catholicism as the state religion and allowed for the Church to once again have a say in political matters.

That Mussolini was a Fascist was ignored by Pope Pius XI, who openly supported him. He could see in Mussolini an ally in the battle against Communism, but later, when Mussolini allied himself with Hitler's fascists, Pius' attitude towards him cooled and he publicly spoke out against anti-Semitism.

In 1933 Pius signed a concordat with Hitler, which has since been criticised as an act of showing support for Hitler when his intention should have been to protect the Catholic people in Germany. By 1937 Pius instructed every priest in Germany to devote a Sunday service to voicing his criticisms of the Nazi regime, including their obsession with racial purity.

Pius' support of Mussolini and Hitler may well have been in response to the growth of Communism in the East that was driving Catholicism underground in those countries. Having witnessed first-hand the Red Army attack on Warsaw during the First World War he became vehemently anti-Communist. It was almost a polar reaction that took place – avoiding one extreme by adopting the other – but the support deeply compromised the Vatican and the lack of a stand against Fascism would echo throughout Europe in the decades that followed the Second World War.

Pius XII (1939–1958)

Prophecy: Pastor angelicus

Translation: Angelic shepherd

Interpretation: This is an interesting point in history, where the public perception of the pope caught up with the prophecies. Initially there was no clear explanation for the prophecy relating to Pius so the public and press of the day conferred the title upon him. It was true that in his nature he was seen as 'angelic', but a better interpretation might be drawn from his passion for the writings of St Thomas Aquinas, known as the 'angelic doctor'. Aquinas was a great influence on the pope.

Pius XI had passed away in 1939 and was replaced by his own secretary of state, Pius XII, a gifted political diplomat who had spent ten years in Germany and so was an obvious candidate at such a turbulent time in history. The German occupation of Rome began in 1943, and although publicly the Vatican was declared neutral, the pope was secretly hiding refugees, which put the fragile relationship at risk. For many this was not enough and critics have long argued that the pope should have made a public stand against the atrocities that were unfolding.

His lack of action was in itself a failure to stand for what was so obviously right. That some 5,000 Jews were hidden in Vatican properties around Rome during the occupation shows that this man was no Nazi sympathiser. In his final radio address before the war ended he openly proposed democracy as the future of government. But in the year 2000 Pope John Paul II attempted to reconcile the public view of Pius when he apologised to the Jewish nations on a visit to Jerusalem for the inaction of the Vatican during the war. It was clear to many after 1945 that the pope was no longer infallible and John Paul II, while rightly attempting to make amends, had evidenced this through his apology. The death and destruction of two world wars in living memory challenged the faith of many Catholics and set in motion a decline in the European Church that continues today.

In 1950 Pius published an encyclical rant against new ideas in theology. It was a throwback to the inquisition and he chose to enforce it by ejecting those who held unorthodox views from office. In retrospect it seems like an extreme reaction for its time but faith had been badly shaken by the devastation caused by the Second World War. A number of new religions and ideologies were surfacing and the discovery of alternative scriptures such as the Dead Sea Scrolls and those at Nag Hammadi had raised interest in research into the origins of scripture. The Catholic Church kept a tight control over the Dead Sea Scrolls, preventing their publication until the 1970s. Communist political parties were also gaining ground in mainland Europe and Pius responded with the threat of excommunication for any Catholic who became a party member. The shadow that will always remain over Pius XII is the question of whether he could have done more to challenge the Nazis. In private he made it very clear that he found them objectionable, but in public he kept the peace for fear of reprisals.

In 1958, as Pius was gravely ill, he was exploited by his future embalmer who took photos of the dying pope and sold these to the press. Following his death, Pius XII suffered the final ignominy of his career as he was so poorly embalmed that his corpse began to rot while lying in state.

John XXIII (1958–1963)

Prophecy: Pastor & Nauta
Translation: Shepherd and mariner
Interpretation: He was patriarch of Venice.

John XXIII, a large and jovial man, came from an Italian farming family. He understood the struggle of the poor and working classes and yet was surprisingly scholarly. During his career in the Church he had spent a number of years in Istanbul, so was suited to international relations, and his war record was unambiguous in his attempts to save Jews and others from the Nazis. Of interest to researchers is that he kept a thorough account of his life in diary form, which has since been published in Italian.

John made a point of visiting local prisons and hospitals at Christmas each year and was informal and approachable to all. But while his appeal was apparent to the working class of society, he seemed reluctant to get involved in politics. With growing support in Italy for the Communist party, John was expected to take an active role in supporting the Christian Democrats. His silence on these matters initially brought criticism, probably exacerbated by the recent memory of the previous pope's failure to make a public stand against the Nazis. But John, like all good popes, chose reconciliation over rejection. He chose to be inclusive and communicate that inclusiveness to all, especially those who were deadlocked in the arms race of the Cold War.

He also aimed to reconcile the different Christian groups by welcoming all to his table in the spirit of acceptance. In 1962 he set in motion the Second Vatican Council, which, among other intentions, would be an opportunity to modernise the Church but he would only live to see a small part of what it achieved.

Among other achievements, the Second Vatican Council was a sign of openness and a radical response to changing attitudes within and without the Church. It saw the translation of mass into local languages, and priests coming down from the pulpit to address parishioners from the floor. The Church had been drifting further away from the congregation but now it threw open the doors and welcomed them in again.

Paul VI (1963–1978)

Prophecy: Flos florum
Translation: Flower of flowers
Interpretation: The family coat of arms has three lilies.

Paul VI had little in common with the humble beginnings of his predecessor, coming from a wealthy Italian family and working his way up through the ranks of the Church until he became Archbishop of Milan. He did share John's open-mindedness and inclusive nature and decided soon after being elected to undertake a pilgrimage to the Holy Land, defining his time as pope through travels around the world, which gained him great support within the Church.

His visits were televised and crowds welcomed him wherever he went, although the presence of extremists could not be avoided and he survived an assassination attempt while travelling to the Far East. He visited the United Nations in the USA, where he spoke out against war and on the importance of the family.

He sounded to all like a wise diplomat and gave hope to many Catholics whose faith had waned since the Second World War. At the Second Vatican Council he failed to clarify the Church's views on birth control, but ultimately prohibited it, which appeared out of touch with the cultural upheavals of the 1960s. He died of a heart attack in the summer of 1978.

John Paul I (1978)

Prophecy: De medietate Lunæ
Translation: From the half of the moon
Interpretation: Born in diocese of Belluno ('beautiful moon'), his brief reign lasted a single cycle of the moon, from one half-moon to the next.

Pope Paul VI was followed by the tragic Pope John Paul I. Humble in nature and origin, John Paul eschewed the pomp and trappings of his coronation and refused to wear the papal crown. He was a man of the people and would have made for an interesting pope, but after being in office for only a month he was found dead in his quarters from what was most likely a heart attack.

Conspiracy theories abounded concerning a scandal at the Vatican Bank that was about to unfold, but as the average age of popes is so advanced in years the likelihood of such a short reign occurring was inevitable.

St Hildegard had also predicted the assassination of a pope by a cardinal who would take over the role of antipope, but one could hardly imagine that hard-line conservatives had deposed him or that his replacement had had a hand in his demise, as he was succeeded by someone seemingly more progressive.

John Paul II (1978–2005)

Prophecy: De labore Solis
Translation: From the labour of the sun

Interpretation: John Paul's acceptance of the heliocentric view of the solar system meant that Catholics no longer had to maintain that the sun moved around the earth. This act of accepting such an obvious fact as the mechanics of the solar system would seem a good symbol of his work. While it is not the clearest of connections, in hindsight he might well be remembered by this epithet as a symbol of his modern approach. He marks a turning point where the Catholic Church could make amends with the past and begin to face the future.

Pope John Paul II understood the theatre of modern media and having studied drama in his native Poland he almost seemed to thrive on publicity as a means to get his message across. He was a man of incredible energy and charisma who travelled extensively across the world, using his trademark of kissing the tarmac wherever he landed. This simple gesture translated into every language as a symbol of blessing and humility. John Paul was a sprightly 58 year old when elected and during his time in office held hundreds of meetings with heads of state.

Along with millions of others who witnessed his travels, I saw him in Warsaw in 1991 as he toured in his open-top 'pope mobile'. John Paul visited Auschwitz and attempted to make amends for how the Vatican had behaved historically. His experience of living through the Warsaw uprising against the Nazis and during Communism that followed the war compelled him to seek peace, wanting the past to be healed and the present to be whole. He attacked the war on Iraq and the unfairness of capitalism, and stood against what he saw as the tyranny of consumer culture.

John Paul's career would seem without blemish but his popular image hides a rigid decision maker of traditionalist sensibilities who expected absolute loyalty from his subjects. That he took a stand against contraception at a time when AIDS was emerging, and condemned homosexuality as well as refusing women a role in the Church showed an ultra-conservative side to him. It is likely that these views will see historians balance their appraisal of him over time.

An assassination attempt in 1981 was almost successful and John Paul attributed his survival to the Virgin Mary apparition at Fátima on the same day in 1917, restating the importance of visions and prophecy to the Church.

As brightly as he shone in life, his decline was slow and arduous, reducing him to a shell of his former self. He died in April 2005 and over four million people visited his body as it lay in state in St Peter's Basilica. John Paul canonised more saints than all his predecessors put together, and in time it is likely that he too will join their ranks.

Benedict XVI (2005–2013)

Prophecy: Gloria olivæ

Translation: Glory of the olive

Interpretation: Prior to Benedict XVI being appointed, many pundits commented on how the prophecy might relate to a future pope. The most obvious being that he would be a Benedictine, as the olive branch is their symbol. Instead the prophecy was potentially fulfilled when Joseph Ratzinger adopted the papal name Benedict. He could not have done this unknowingly. Another interpretation is that Benedict was previously the cardinal bishop of Velletri and the Velletri coat of arms has three olive trees. The olive branch is also a symbol of peace – some consider that during his reign there will be peace in the Middle East. Certainly the 'Arab spring' is working towards such ends, but Benedict can claim no part in this process of change. As there is no clear interpretation we might have to wait until hindsight of Benedict's reign gives us some perspective to fully understand the correlation.

After John Paul II power shifted again towards the conservative as the cardinals appointed Joseph Ratzinger, former head of the Congregation for the Doctrine for the Faith. He took the name Pope Benedict XVI.

Benedict had proven to be as traditional as expected. Hope for positive reform or modernisation faded and his stance on matters such as the ordaining of female priests was a clear signal that he was unwilling to change his views. Although Benedict had met with other religious leaders and shown respect for their beliefs it is clear that he did not see them as being equal to Catholicism. The more progressive members of the Church and the outsiders who looked on, bemused by such a hard-line traditionalist, have had to wait for the election of Pope Francis in the hope that he will bring the Church into the 21st century.

Peter the Roman

Prophecy: In psecutione, extrema S.R.E. sedebit Petrus Romanus, qui pascet oves in multis tribulationibus: quibus transactis civitas septicollis diruetur, & Judex tremêdus judicabit populum suum. Finis.

Translation: In the final persecution, the seat of the Holy Roman Church will be occupied by Peter the Roman, who will feed the sheep through many tribulations, and when these things are finished, the city of seven hills will be destroyed, and the formidable Judge will judge His people. The end.

Interpretation: For the full interpretation of this prophecy see chapter 12.

On receiving the final prophecy the prophet would have been shocked by the vision of a distant future where a blackened sky over Rome is stirred by the billows of smoke and ashes floating on a cold wind. Imagine as he watched the man in the white robe rise from the throne of St Peter for the last time. The frescos are crumbling from the walls, reduced to dust and rubble, and somewhere someone is shouting, 'La cupola è in calo, la cupola sta scendendo!' The voice is choked and dies away. The final pope is leaving the ruins of the Vatican, to where his judgement awaits.

Should the end of the papacy be approaching, we, like the 'formidable judge' of the final prophecy, can look back to the time of St Peter and to the present 'Peter the Roman', seeing the context of the popes who expressed all aspects of humanity in their time. Those that were elevated above the masses were prone to the same desires and distractions that we all face, but with the added pressure of power. They would be judged on how they rose to the challenges of heresy, Communism, Fascism, Protestantism, exile and the antipopes of the Great Western Schism.

As some popes fell into darkness, tainted by crimes, indiscretions, nepotism, political intrigue, wars and persecutions, these are weighed against the work of the popes who sought peace, helped the poor and brought light to the world. Through the turbulent history some popes remained faithful, beacons to those who sought guidance on the spiritual path.

The popes will be remembered also for the monuments and art that they lavished upon Rome, along with the funding of the Renaissance artists with their passionate celebration of faith at the forefront of that cultural revolution. They left a legacy of fine art and sculpted figures that spill out from the canvasses and podiums of churches across Rome. But these were grand statements often paid for by selling offices and favours.

Finally they attempted to fix the errors of the past and to survive into the 21st century. Perhaps the fate of the popes rests on the smallest of actions – like the gesture of humility acknowledged during the Second Vatican Council, that priests should cease to speak from the podium but stand on an equal footing with their subjects.

CONCLUSION

At this point in time we have reached what the prophecies claim will be the final pontiff. It remains to be seen if this final revelation is accurate but we can now see how little the prophecies change in tone, style and content before and after they were published. Once revealed, the expectation of a sudden drop in clarity did not come, and those who judge them to be forgeries can only do so by ignoring a number of accurate predictions. In the next few chapters we will reflect on the prophecies and examine what the final prophecy of Peter the Roman might mean and, more importantly, in which way it might describe the current pope.

CHAPTER 9

REFLECTIONS ON THE PROPHECIES

INTRODUCTION

If everything were perfectly obscure, we would have no idea of divine truth. If everything were perfectly clear, we would have no merit in deciphering it.

Pascal

Since the publication of the prophecies, for every papal election people have tried to interpret the clues associated with the final pope. Many had predicted the conclave of 2005 would result in a Benedictine pope because the prophecy included the term 'olive', and the olive branch is the symbol of the Benedictine order. Those who believed the prophecy were at a loss when a non-Benedictine was appointed the role. Then, to everyone's surprise, Cardinal Ratzinger adopted the papal name Benedict. He did this in honour of a former pope and not the founder of the Benedictines, but it is difficult not to see this as evidence in support of the prophecies. Ratzinger was certainly known to give credence to prophecies as he has commented at length on the secret of Fátima. He has held mass at the site of the visions and has even endorsed a book on this subject called *The Last Secret of Fatima* by the Vatican secretary of state.

With a keen interest in prophecy Cardinal Ratzinger would have been well aware of the *Prophecy of the Popes*, so we must wonder if it was a conscious decision on his part to effectively enact the prophecies. He certainly gave weight to the idea that they are still relevant after all this time. If Ratzinger did contrive a link to the prophecies it threatens to invalidate those that followed de Wyon's publication, as it could signal that there could be some internal decree within the Vatican to honour the prophecies and attempt to fulfil them at that point in time. As the Church would have us believe the choice is divinely inspired by the Holy Spirit working through the members of conclave, there should be no possibility of Malachy having a mundane influence on those involved. However, as the members rarely decide on a pope at the first vote, it would appear other factors come into play. Those who are less inclined to believe that the Holy Spirit puts in an appearance might argue that the prophecies were sometimes fulfilled by design. This scenario is highly unlikely but a compromise could exist where members of the conclave are influenced by their knowledge of the prophecies and choose accordingly.

This raises a wider consideration. As the prophecies conclude with the fall of the Vatican and the destruction of Rome there would need to be a strong apocalyptic affinity among those involved. If the intention is to live out the prophecies then there needs to be an acceptance within the Catholic Church that they are colluding with the End Times. The immediate lack of an obvious link between Pope Francis and the description 'Peter the Roman' would seem to indicate a conscious decision was made to try to avert the prophecy or it had no influence on the conclave of 2013.

I doubt it could be so clean cut – in the conclaves over the last 400 years some cardinals might have voted for a candidate that upheld the prophecies while others would have voted without any mundane influence. Certainly the predictions involving the rise of Napoleon and the First World War could not have been contrived as they were beyond the control of the cardinals. Either way, the prophecies can be interpreted in hindsight and we can establish if they are accurate post-publication, be they contrived or divinely inspired.

THE LANGUAGE OF THE PROPHECIES

At first glance it would seem that Cucherat's story of Malachy having received the information as a vision is apocryphal. If the information was communicated via a vision then the clues should be visual unless the prophet also heard voices or saw a written description. The language used in the descriptions contains too many specific terms that are abstract and could not be communicated visually – qualities such as 'good', which appears a number of times, or place names, of which there are many. We might conclude that the visual aspect of these insights would have needed to be accompanied by a voice: a description of some kind that gave the additional level of information to describe what was being seen.

It is possible for visual prophecies to include words. There is no biblical precedent for this but in the centuries that followed, words have sometimes formed a part of a vision. An example mentioned earlier was the prophetic dream of Emperor Constantine, in which he witnessed the legend 'By this sign you will conquer' written in the sky. There are also visual entities that speak, such as the Virgin Mary apparitions or the appearance of some other divine messenger. However, this does not seem to be what the prophet experienced.

Cucherat, who provided the earliest description of Malachy receiving the vision, fails to describe any such communication. He simply recounts how Malachy had the visions and described them to a monk who acted as scribe. If we begin with Cucherat's (albeit untrustworthy) account that the prophecies were received as purely visual we can test this hypothesis to see if it stands up to further investigation.

A clue to supporting this theory can be found by examining the language used. With visions, as with dreams, there is often a residual memory that holds a reasonably clear image and then it is up to the viewer to convert this into language. Why the prophet chose to reduce each pope to two- or three-word descriptors was never explained but there is a link between the brevity of the text and the state of consciousness accessed to achieve visions. Like we read in poetry, the language of higher states of consciousness becomes very economical, eventually reducing complex ideas down to simple symbolism. Religious symbols, for example, hold a wealth of information that can be accessed through contemplation. The language of the prophecies is an example of maintaining meaning while simplifying the message. As the prophet rises through the levels of consciousness to witness visual images they remain on the cusp of language and symbolism. It is a place where images can inspire a few specific words in the mind of the author, in the same way that Jacob saw the ladder with angels ascending and descending and knew to interpret it as the gateway to heaven (Genesis 28:17).

METHODS FOR INTERPRETING THE PROPHECIES

Having travelled the length of the prophecies and nearly 800 years of the papacy we can get a sense of how many of the prophecies are accurate and to what extent. We can also recognise a pattern of points of reference.

The methods of decoding the prophecies do not change much over time as the prophecies are simple enough in nature and consistent both before and after publication. They also benefit from being written in such a direct manner as to protect them from vague psychological projection or leaps of imagination. We are not looking for patterns, like hearing a voice on the wind or seeing a face in the folds of a crumpled cloth. On the contrary, many of the phrases in the prophecies reference something absolutely specific and immediately identifiable about the elected pope. Where the correlation is entirely clear, after the event we look back and wonder how the candidate avoided being identified prior to entering the conclave.

Prior to publication the popes could mainly be identified by the family name, coat of arms or their place of birth. Post publication the prophecies continue to use these clues but also broaden to include a wider variety of factors. There are wider signals in birth, death and life events. Some seem entirely abstracted from the actual pope, such as the prediction identifying Napoleon, who at the time was far greater in fame and power than the corresponding pontiff. Then there are world events, such as 'religion depopulated' describing the events around the First World War, which are not linked to a specific individual becoming pope but to factors surrounding the papacy. Some of the descriptions cover the location of the conclave, or the feast day that coincides with the election. These are less about the individual and more focused on events surrounding the papacy as any pope would have fulfilled the brief.

The use of coats of arms recurs throughout the prophecies as an identifier. Popes who were not of noble origin were appointed a coat of arms when they took office, otherwise they used their family coat of arms. Papal armorial bearings were first introduced for the popes in the 13th century with Innocent III (1198–1216). The issue with the papal coats of arms is that they have less credibility as they are easier to contrive after the fact, though in many examples there are also other supporting details. For example, the prophecy for Clement V (1305–14) was 'Ribbon of Aquitaine' and the papal crest he adopted has three 'fesses', or ribbons, but he was also the archbishop of Bordeaux in Aquitaine.

In a number of cases there is more than one possible interpretation. For Innocent XI (1676–89), whose unfortunate description was 'Insatiable beast', the prophecy could either be referring to the lion on his coat of arms or be a pun about his adviser Cibo, a word also meaning 'food', whom he was never to be seen without. This ambiguity is held by some to be evidence against the accuracy of the prophecies, but it can also be seen to further validate the prophecy as the short phrase can be applied in more than one way to a single pope.

ACCURACY

From the initial visions as a point of origin through to the conversion of these images into words to be relayed to a scribe, the potential for inaccuracies increases. The margin for error increases with each subsequent communication. The first scribe to record the prophecies should have produced an accurate account with little room for error. Later copyists – such as Alphonsus Chacón, to whom was attributed the 1590 release that found its way into de Wyon's publication – might have introduced inaccuracies of their own. Added to this the Latin that appears in de Wyon's publication is not perfect, which brings an additional risk of error, though for the most part the terms used are specific and unambiguous.

Taking into account minor errors in transcription and translation, we should now view the entire set of prophecies as a whole. Previously we saw how the earlier prophecies were likely to have been subjected to changes to make them look more credible and accurate. To this end, they were correct until the 16th century, whereas the later, post-publication entries had no such 'interference' and should be less accurate or less specific. In truth, it is difficult to find explanations for some of the later prophecies but many are still surprisingly accurate.

As a comparison we can briefly look at a few examples of pre-publication accuracy. The first pope in the list, Celestine II, reigned during the 12th century and was predicted to be 'Ex castro Tiberis': from the castle on the Tiber. Celestine was born in a castle on the Tiber so the prophecy is confirmed. Urban III, whose wonderful description translates as 'pig in a sieve', had the surname 'Crivelli' meaning 'sieve', and a pig adorned his coat of arms, which is equally specific and accurate.

The prophecies continue in much the same way, although some of the interpretations are not immediately obvious, even though prior to publication. For example, the prophecy for Julius II (1503–13) is unnecessarily convoluted to decipher. The description of 'Fructus jovis Juvabit' translates as 'Fruit helped by Jupiter'. The explanation for this is that the pope's family name was Rovere, meaning 'oak tree' and that the oak tree and its fruit were consecrated to Jupiter in pagan times. It is difficult to reconcile this pagan description with Catholic authorship when it would have been far simpler to have 'oak tree' as the prophecy.

Following the publication of the prophecies in 1595 they continue to reference the name, birthplace or coat of arms of the corresponding pope. The few that seem without explanation are so small in number that it could well be that either history has failed to record their link to the prophecy or that something was lost in the transcribing, from either the words of the prophet directly or by subsequent authors. For some prophecies it would have been possible to fit the pope to the prophecy after the event of his coronation by collusion – examples of this are those that describe the papal coat of arms, which was adopted after the pope had been elected.

The important prophecies are those that came true without any possibility of intervention from within the Vatican. The prophecy for Pope Pius VII could not have been contrived. His reign coincided with the rise of Napoleon, whose fame and power overshadowed the pope considerably. The prophecy for the time of Pius was 'rapacious eagle', and the eagle was the symbol by which Napoleon was identified. There are other prophecies that were also based upon external factors, such as the location of the conclave, historic events or feast days that coincide with the election. Clement IX (1667–9) was prophesised as the 'Swan constellation'. He was elected in the 'Chamber of Swans' within the Vatican, although any cardinal could have been elected in that place and would therefore have fitted the prophecy. This does not invalidate the prediction but it changes the focus from the identity of the individual to the environment.

Further evidence for the sustained accuracy of the prophecies can be seen in Pope Clement XIII (1758–69), whose prophecy was 'Rose of Umbria'. Clement was a former governor in Umbria, which has a rose for its state emblem. Pope John XXIII (1958–63), whose prophecy described him as 'shepherd and mariner', was previously the Cardinal of Venice, and Pope Leo

XIII (1878–1903) is described in the prophecies as 'Light in the heavens': his coat of arms shows a shooting star. These examples and numerous others are accurate 700 years after being written and 400 years following publication.

Innocent XII (1691–1700), whose prophecy translates as 'Rake in the door', had the surname Rastrello, Italian for 'rake', and originally had a rake on his family coat of arms. This has to be the most accurate and one of the hardest to contrive. Innocent's election came at the end of a very difficult five-month-long conclave, so it is unlikely that his selection was a simple attempt to fulfil a prophecy.

Another important example of the accuracy of the prophecies is the reign of Pope Benedict XV (1914–22), in which he witnessed the Bolshevik Revolution outlaw Catholicism in Russia, the 1918 Spanish flu pandemic that ravaged Europe and the outbreak of the First World War, which killed a further 20 million people. His correlating prophecy was 'religion depopulated'. It must be noted that these world events could not have been averted so it would not have mattered which pope reigned during this time. The prophecy is linked to the timing of historic events and not to the man, but it is clear that the link to the pope could not have been contrived in any way.

CREDIBILITY

The main threat to the accuracy of the later prophecies comes not from interpreting them but their credibility due to the various ways in which a potential pope might try to align himself with the prediction. The existence of such descriptions is a risk if they are thought to influence the selection of the popes. Any link between a candidate and the phrase for that pope could be used as propaganda to support their election campaign and it is likely that the prophecies were originally released with that intention.

Even after becoming pope it was still possible to try to fulfil the prediction. Pope Clement XI (1700–21) was elected under the prophecy 'surrounded with flowers' but his followers could find no such link, so they struck a medal in his name with this motto on it to validate the prediction. Pope Pius VI (1775–99) was described by contemporary writers as the 'apostolic pilgrim on earth'. Malachy accurately described him as the 'apostolic pope', but he was only named so after his death, so it is difficult to conclude whether he fitted the prophecy or not. There exists a short black-and-white film of the life of this pope, with the title *The Pilgrim Pope*, which is both accurate but potentially contrived. There were other possible interpretations but the above illustrates that the prophecies were considered important enough to justify concocting links between a pope and their corresponding description.

It becomes a self-fulfilling action, where the prophecy is read and used to forge a link to an individual. The same might be said of those who became pope and chose papal coats of arms that are later seen to be described by the prophecy. We cannot know for sure if they selected the design to suit the prophecy or if they genuinely arrived at a heraldic device free from the influence of the text. It is a very real possibility that the prophecies might influence both the actions of the cardinals who wished to be elected and the minds of the cardinals who vote to elect.

FINAL THOUGHTS ON THE ACCUSATIONS OF FORGERY

If the prophecies were a 16th-century fabrication we would have expected the accuracy of them to fall away after the time of their publication. They should have become vague and easily applied to a number of candidates. This is not the case. The prophecies remain pointedly accurate and written in the same clear manner as those that precede publication. Some are exact fits to the pope they predict.

The above examples that are proven accurate, especially those of world events beyond the control of the pope, could not have been the lucky guess of the forger. Likewise if we take the idea that the earlier prophecies were amended to appear perfectly accurate, it would stand to reason at least some of the latter ones would remain obscure. The accusation stands that they were published for political ends during a particularly long and difficult conclave, but it is clear from the text that they were accurate before and after that point. To me it is clear that whoever transcribed them from the original may have made some changes to make the previous ones more accurate and then tweaked the current one to suit their own political ends.

In some ways it is entirely acceptable that whoever copied the original chose to iron out some mistakes, in the same way an editor will polish the work of an author before sending it for publication. If we are to accept the hypothesis that whoever transcribed the prophecies sought to 'polish' the earlier prophecies by revising any obscure parts of the text then they acted not as a scribe but as an editor. This distinction means that we can attribute the fabricated parts to the editor and the original text to the author, be it Malachy or persons unknown. The inaccuracies and mistakes in the alterations prove that the editor and the author are two different people as the prophecies are visionary in nature whereas the act of editing is not. The scribe would have used a current version of papal history, such as *Epitome Romanorium Pontificum usque ad Paulum IV* published in 1557 by Onuphrius Panvinius, to compare and rewrite any prophecies that were obscure in meaning.

This does not detract from the original text, which must have been produced by a gifted prophet. My conclusion on the question of forgery is that the prophecies are, for the most part, a true record of a genuine act of prophecy.

If we look beyond this there is also something new here, something challenging to be considered. When the prophecies were released they take on a different tone in that after the release the correlation between the pope and the identifying description often only becomes apparent after the pope has been elected. There are more examples where some act or event in their life post-coronation equates them perfectly with the prophecy or the connection is simply not identified until after they take office. This means the candidates could not have attempted to fulfil the role by aligning themselves with the clues and that the vision was self-protecting – as if, when it was initially revealed, it took into account that it would be circulated during the 16th century. From this perspective it could be said that the prophecies were both an act of transcending time and worded in a manner that pivots around the exact time of release. The difference is subtle and hard to prove but the concept is an interesting one.

THE FINAL PROPHECY

The final prophecy concerning Peter the Roman and the End Times is unlike any of those that precede it as it has a full paragraph of descriptive text. The short epithet to give a clue to the identity of the pope is in the same format but the surrounding text gives context to the events that this pope is predicted to witness.

Detractors have taken their cue from the position of this text to question whether it was a part of the original prophecy, or if the change in style indicates a break in the text where other popes may intervene that are not described. The opinion that the final prophecy in de Wyon's *Lignum Vitae* is a standalone paragraph that follows the prophecy the 'glory of the olive' suggests that because the last two popes are not adjacent they may not be consecutive.

There are two counter-arguments to this. The first is that it is highly unlikely to think the prophet would have received an incomplete vision. Having gone to the trouble of prophesising for 111 popes over 700 years and then to suddenly skip to the end is not credible. The second reason is that no indication is given in the text that we should expect a break in the narrative at this juncture. As the prophecies were originally said to be dictated as an unstructured stream of Latin sayings, it is possible that the original text was devoid of any line breaks.

Another accusation raised against this text was that it was a later addition to the text authored by someone else. The symbol of the Benedictines is the olive branch, so with the penultimate pope described as 'glory of the olive' it was assumed this pope would be Benedictine. According to some sources, including an entry in the 1913 *Catholic Encyclopaedia*, Peter the Roman was added by Benedictine monks to avoid the description of the final persecution of Rome being linked to the Benedictines. The motive being that this may have caused persecution from within the Church if their order were seen to be harbingers of the End Times. De Wyon, who published the text, was himself a Benedictine historian.

If the Benedictines chose to amend the text they could have done so by adding 'Peter the Roman' to the list of popes following 'glory of the olive' and dispensed with the description of the End Times. It would be less credible to insert this extra text into the final paragraph as we have seen the context of the final pope questioned for being a change of style. Added to this, the amount of revision required is not practical. If the final paragraph had no name prior to de Wyon, it would have needed the entire paragraph to be rewritten to accommodate it.

The question of authorship is also raised again, specifically citing the final paragraph as a separate entity in relation to the rest of the prophecies. The claim that the original list of names does not contain a reference to 'Petrus Romanus' and that the last lines were added to the printed text in de Wyon's *Lignum Vitae* cannot be proved without the original manuscript being released. From the content of the final paragraph it is clear that it is describing an event that coincides with the final pope and 'Peter the Roman' is mentioned within this paragraph. The special circumstances of this final prophecy warrant the inclusion of additional text, whereas the actual description of the pope as 'Peter the Roman' is entirely in keeping with the other prophecies.

If the original prophet witnessed this event he would be compelled to add it to his description of the popes. But if it was forged it would seem unlikely to serve any purpose other than to be very unsettling for those who read it. Its only purpose would have been to continue the tradition of apocalyptic literature in Christianity.

A PLACE IN THE CANON OF ESCHATOLOGY

Eschatology is the Greek word meaning 'last discourse'. It is used in Christianity to describe the four final events that mark the end of the world. These are the Second Coming of Christ, the resurrection of the dead, the Last Judgement of the living and the dead, and the separation of the saved and the damned.

Many of these prophecies are linked to St John's Apocalypse as well as the gospel of Matthew (24:5–30), which describe the upheavals that will accompany the End Times. In recent years many Christians who subscribe to eschatology focused on the millennium as a likely time for these events to unfold. This failed to materialise but it has not diminished the belief in predictions of the End Times.

The *Prophecy of the Popes* is not alone in making predictions specific to popes and the End Times. A group of prophecies published under the title *Genus Nequam* came into circulation in the late 13th century. The original publication in 1292 was linked to the cardinals of that time but later editions were expanded to include popes, starting with Nicholas III (1277–80). These prophecies are visual in that they contain images of the popes accompanied by short descriptions. The symbolism of the images has many heraldic animal elements accompanying the figures, such as lions, bears, unicorns and crows, as well as the fleur-de-lis symbol. There are currently 30 known prophecies in this group. The authorship and purpose of these texts is unknown but might have been as propaganda to influence a papal election of 1304, echoing the use of the prophecies released in 1595.

Around 1328 a second set of images for the *Genus Nequam* appeared, including the *Ascende Calve*, a continuation of popes that were influenced by the politics of the day. These also begin with Nicholas III but end with an apocalypse and the final pope is associated with the image of the great dragon from the biblical Revelation. More than one set end with the final pope depicted as the Antichrist. The text, when present, for the final prophecy is usually drawn from the destruction of Ninevah in the Gospel of Nahum, or the recognition of the sovereignty of God from Daniel.

The first edition of the *Genus Naquam* had twelve plates with images and descriptions, predicting an 'angelic pope'. The phrase 'angelic pastor' appears in a number of prophecies relating to the End Times, as one of the events that prefix or coincide with the coming of the Antichrist. In the *Prophecy of the Popes*, Pius XII (1939–58) is described as 'pastor angelicus'. The reign of this pope coincided with the Second World War and the peak of

Hitler's power. When the Nazis' crimes against the Jewish people and others are considered it is not a great leap to see Hitler as a figure who fulfils the criteria of being the Antichrist: a creature of hate and intolerance who failed in his plans to rid the world of race that Jesus was born into.

There are many other examples of the apocalyptic tradition of eschatology and some are specific to the fall of Rome.

COMING CHASTISEMENT

There are some key themes that repeat in Catholic prophecy for what is termed the 'coming chastisement'. The underlying points that many prophets agree on are that will be a worldwide war, natural disasters and an act of God. There are also similarities in the descriptions of members of the Church suffering many persecutions, resulting in the pope being deposed from Rome. The consensus concludes that eventually a figure of good will rally an army and drive the enemies of the Church from Europe. Then there will be peace until the time of the Antichrist.

The elements of this story are repeated by prophets and seers throughout history. Such ideas can be found in the writings of St Cataldus (5th century), who states that the 'Great King' will wage war; St Columba (6th century) wrote of great wars and the sacking of the Church; Monk Adso (10th century) wrote that a king of the Franks will go to Jerusalem to lay his sword at the Mount of Olives and immediately after, the Antichrist will come. St Thomas a' Becket (12th century) spoke of 'wars and wonders shall befall toward the end of the world'; St John of the Cleft Rock (14th century) wrote that the Antichrist would reveal himself in the year 2000 and that the pope would have to flee Rome; and Father Balthassar Mas (17th century) saw the land swallowed up by the sea.

St Hildegard von Bingen (12th century) predicted a comet causing the inundation of many countries, followed by storms, earthquakes and tidal waves. She singles out a 'great nation in the ocean that is inhabited by people of different tribes' to be devastated by earthquakes and partly submerged. Many have interpreted this to be Great Britain but Britain is not located on any major fault lines. It is more likely to be a description of America, where the west coast is already threatening to collapse into the sea. She also writes of how the sea will inundate the land and coastal towns.

Other prophets who are not recognised by the Catholic Church, such as Nostradamus, also made predictions regarding the popes and the End Times. The English prophet Old Mother Shipton was accurate in many aspects of her prophecies and published the following in the 16th century: 'Carriages without horses shall go, and accidents fill the world with woe. Around the world thoughts shall fly in the twinkling of an eye. Through hills man shall ride, and no horse be at his side. Iron in the water shall float, as easily as a wooden boat.' However, her prediction for the end of the world was a little premature, as she wrote that: 'The world to an end shall come, in eighteen hundred and eighty one.'

Malachy's Ireland was already steeped in such prophecy long before he was born. Part of St Malachy's appeal as the author of the papal prophecies would be the long tradition of apocalyptic prophecy in Ireland, dating back to St Patrick. St Patrick, the patron saint of Ireland, described how the sea would submerge Ireland a full seven years before the final judgement, so that the Antichrist would not be able take control of the people. This, according to the author Bander, is considered a 'blessing'. It is a story that is repeated in many histories of the Irish people from that time, although it seems odd that God would have to kill the people to save them, but this is often the way of apocalyptic thinking. The world will be destroyed but the people saved.

The final prophecy of the popes is rooted in this tradition of eschatology but also gives specific information with regards to the final pope. By examining the text we can get an understanding of what fate awaits the Church according to the prophet and the last papa: Peter the Roman.

CHAPTER 10

THE FINAL PROPHECY

INTRODUCTION

We have reached a point in the history of the Catholic Church where we can look back at the trials and turbulence of its history and consider this a time of relative peace. The final prophecy, which speaks of the destruction of Rome and the last pope, would seem a long way from the traditional and stable organisation that currently occupies the Vatican. However, the deeper we look into the current sheen of respectability, the more cracks appear and the entire edifice is still under pressure from its detractors both inside and outside the Church. Beneath the serene appearance there are many challenges facing the Catholic Church and the new pope Francis I.

At the conclusion of the *Prophecy of the Popes* there is a short paragraph predicting what will occur during and after the reign of the final pope. The original statement, rendered in Latin, is as follows:

In psecutione, extrema S.R.E. sedebit. Petrus Romanus, qui pascet oves in multis tribulationibus: quibus transactis civitas septicollis diruetur,& Judex tremêdus judicabit populum suum. Finis.

This translates as:

In the final persecution, the seat of the Holy Roman Church will be occupied by Peter the Roman, who will feed the sheep through many tribulations, and when these things are finished, the city of seven hills will be destroyed, and the formidable Judge will judge His people. The end.

With an initial analysis of the text it is apparent that it follows the tradition of apocalyptic prophecy and includes many key elements from eschatology such as the final judgement. The vision described appears to be the end of the Catholic Church, brought about by both external forces and persecutions that are followed by the Last Judgement. It has been stated by other prophets that cataclysmic events will occur prior to the End Times but many will fail to see these as divine in origin. For the event to be apocalyptic it would need to include both the physical and spiritual collapse of the Church.

With the time of the final pope at hand it should be possible to identify the forces driving these issues today as they build towards the last days. We must dissect the prophecy line by line to understand what might be the cause of these events.

THE PERSECUTIONS AND TRIBULATIONS

In the final persecution . . .

The opening line refers to the 'final persecution . . . of the Church' and a further reference to 'many tribulations' gives a brief idea of what is expected to befall the last pope. The use of the word 'final' implies that there have been, or will be, a number of persecutions preceding it. Certainly the history of the Church is rife with various persecutions, criticisms and attacks of all kinds, but if we take this to mean the final culmination of a spate of persecutions we can look for some explanation as to what these might be.

An act of persecution is directed: it is not some random cataclysm or accident but the actions of those who level accusations at the pope and the Catholic Church. In contrast, 'tribulations' can be a broader set of events that impact upon the Church.

The history of the Catholic Church appears to be one long battle against one enemy or another, but since the Reformation the very character of Catholic Church has increasingly come under scrutiny and found to be wanting. By the end of the 20th century many scandals had come to the surface to undermine the fabric of the Church and cast doubts on those who were once held in high esteem. The Catholic Church is currently besieged on all sides by critics.

These accusations could be seen as evidence that some of the persecutions are already happening and we shall look at some of these in detail. An example in recent years has focused upon leaked information from within the Vatican that all is not well with the finances. Where previous popes had spent with impunity we now live in a world of banking regulation and accountability, so the financial mismanagement of the past is no longer acceptable.

THE VATICAN BANK

The Church has suffered a long history of failing to 'balance the books' as various popes emptied the coffers to sponsor acts of extravagance or fund others to do their bidding. The challenge faced by the administration of the Catholic Church is that the cost of running such a vast organisation is dependent on ever-decreasing donations and the support of other banks. In recent times a solution was sought to address this issue and protect the Vatican from the financial duress of being dependent on the banks of Italy.

In 1942 the Vatican Bank was established by Pius XII and has remained one the most clandestine financial operations in the world. As the Vatican is its own state the accounting of the bank is closely guarded and is not independently audited. This has led to speculation over the years that there is the potential for financial malpractice and corrupt activities.

For many the worst fears were confirmed in the early 1980s when the Vatican Bank was implicated in the collapse of the Banco Ambrosiano, in which it was the major shareholder. Officials at the Ambrosiano were linked to money laundering, clearing funds for illegal arms deals and several murders, including that of Roberto Calvi, found hanged under Blackfriars Bridge in London in 1982. Calvi was the head of Banco Ambrosiano, had mediated with the Vatican Bank and was also listed as a member of P2. P2 became a huge political scandal in Italy as a quasi-Masonic lodge that was a front for recruiting politicians, military officials and civil servants with a view to overthrowing the Italian government and installing a fascist dictatorship.

Following the collapse of Banco Ambrosiano the Vatican Bank closed its doors again to inspection, but a number of scandals have leaked out in recent years hinting strongly that all is not well with the finances of the institution. Recently the bank has had to weather further accusations of financial wrongdoing from insiders. Staff within the current administration have taken it upon themselves to leak information about the financial situation and in 2011 Italian newspaper *Il Fatto Quotidiano* raised questions concerning possible illegal practices of the Vatican Bank. A leaked letter discussed how the bank could be used for money laundering and tax evasion. As usual, when such accusations arose the Church went after the person that leaked the letters but did not publicly address the issues raised by them.

There are wider implications to this story and it continues to make the news. A letter leaked to the press from March 2010 from Archbishop Carlo Maria Vigano, and addressed to Pope Benedict XVI, made allegations of nepotism and corruption within the office where he worked. There is no financial regulation from outside and if corruption is rife within then it is only a matter of time before the financial system of the Vatican State goes into meltdown.

As an unregulated entity the Vatican Bank is also in the perilous position of being capable of far over-reaching its true value in terms of borrowing and lending, putting it at risk of falling into catastrophic financial collapse similar to the disaster that befell the banks of Iceland in 2008. In that instance, following deregulation the three major banks in Iceland were able to accrue debts of €50 billion against the country's gross domestic product of just €8.5 billion. When the financial crises began and the debts were called in but could not be repaid, the Icelandic banking system collapsed. Similar financial malpractice could expose the Vatican Bank to the risk of collapse and trigger a shift in opinion against the Church.

The effect on public opinion of such scandals emerging calls into question the ethics of the Church. It is already possible to view the bank as an anachronism, seemingly ignorant of the irony of its position in relation to Jesus expelling the money-lenders from the temple.

Another questionable area of the Vatican's finances is its use of the stock market. Many are unaware that the Catholic Church is collecting donations from the congregation and investing these on the stock market. The nature of playing the stock market is to bet on the value of shares rising and in its simplest form is pure gambling. Gambling was outlawed in the Catholic Church by Benedict XIII in the 18th century and to my knowledge has never been reprieved.

Adding to the financial situation is the question regarding the wealth surrounding the Vatican. The *Compendium of Social Doctrine of the Church* was published by the Catholic Church in 2005. It includes the basis for the seven 'social sins' that include birth control, stem cell research, polluting the environment and, surprisingly, 'excessive wealth', which is does not seem to recognise as a failing of its own. The embarrassment of riches on display in Vatican City have not gone unnoticed by critics. Many outside the Church already see Catholicism as a control mechanism for the masses, and a taxation of the poor to preserve the power and wealth of Rome.

In embracing South America and Africa the Church also found itself facing the issues of poverty and famine. As the Vatican remained aloof from these issues the priests who lived in some of the poorest neighbourhoods in the world were less sanguine about the state of affairs. Since the 1950s challenges have arisen in South America, calling on the Vatican to alleviate the poverty of its people. The lack of a response to this situation from the Vatican is rousing a revolution against poverty, using the idea of Marxism as a stealthly way of moving the Church towards addressing these issues.

These issues are adding to a growing discontent in attitudes towards the Church in both its ethical stance and how it responds to scandals. They add to a public opinion of the Catholic Church that is already tarnished by the scandal that has shocked followers of the Church in recent years – that of child abuse.

CHILD ABUSE AND THE CATHOLIC CHURCH

During the 1980s a number of stories made the press worldwide regarding sexual and physical abuse suffered by children in the care of the Church. A spate of accusations were made in many countries across the world, and in the US alone over $60 billion has been paid out in compensation by the Church to victims. In the largest case to date, over 500 reported cases of sexual abuse were settled. This might not be a new phenomenon, as the scale of sexual abuse would not have been realised or reported so widely in previous times. The issue of abuse in the Church has rightly cast a long shadow over a Church that, until recently, was held in high esteem among a large percentage of the population.

Investigations uncovered systematic failings throughout the hierarchy of the Church in acknowledging and addressing the issues that were being reported. Individual cases received little or no response when brought to the attention of bishops, and in some cases the individual accused of abuse was merely moved to a different area without any involvement of the police.

Even at the level of pope it seems that the Church was unable to act on the matter in a responsible manner. Pope John Paul II was not without his critics, and while the Church paints a saintly picture of him, he failed (or chose not) to address the volume of serious accusations of child abuse that occupied the world's media on a weekly basis. This has continued to this day, with the Church appearing to protect those amongst its ranks who have abused the innocent.

In recent years there were child abuse cases in Ireland that were covered up by Cardinal Brady, which again greatly undermined the public's trust in the Church. Brady had neglected to pass on allegations of abuse to the police on a number of occasions (reported by BBC News, 8 May 2012).

Child abuse is the last taboo in any civilisation in the world. It is one of the actions that could be described as truly evil and yet the 'holy' fathers of the Church seem the most susceptible to such crimes. As those in such positions of power are seen to exploit those in their care they lose all respect that would normally be associated with their position and rank. Such a vast loss of trust could eventually bring down the Church as the public fears that the Church is rife with paedophiles. The conclusion many draw from these scandals of abuse is that the Catholic Church somehow creates perversion. The reality, equally disturbing, is that the Catholic Church is being exploited by paedophiles.

It is understandable that the conscious mind would realise that inappropriate feelings towards children must be stymied, and logically a vocation such as that of a celibate priest would look attractive. But perversion directs not from the conscious mind but from the unconscious part of the psyche. It puts the individual into the environment of the very children they had sought to avoid. So consciously the paedophile chooses to repress their sexuality by joining the priesthood, while unconsciously they are putting themselves in a position of power over others and gaining access to children.

As the public's opinion of the Catholic Church has fallen so far, only by directly addressing these issues will it continue to survive. As an organisation, in response to the scandal the Church must report any suspicion of abuse to the police immediately. Past crimes should be admitted to and atonement should only come through sentencing, not be avoided through bribery. Unfortunately prison does not help paedophiles address their condition: it just removes them from society for a while.

In the immediate term, if children cannot be protected they should never be alone in the company of priests. In any other profession no adult would be allowed access to children unless they have been properly vetted and subject to police checks – and only then with supervision or in the company of a parent or guardian. Finally, the pope should decree paedophilia a 'blasphemy against God', as blasphemy is the only 'unforgivable sin' according to the Bible (Luke 12:10, Mark 3:29, Matthew 12: 31–32).

While there are physical boundaries to be put in place, the issue of child abuse comes down to both the failing of the disturbed individual in facing up to their need for help, coupled with the failing of the Church to recognise that the repression of sexuality attracts perversion.

The Catholic Church attracts those who are shamed about their sexuality and are joining to be 'celibate', while their affliction subconsciously steers them towards a position of power. This issue would be alleviated if the celibacy rule was revoked to allow priests to marry. The Church would become a less attractive proposition for those who should be seeking help instead of a place to hide. The practice of celibacy in the Church comes from Matthew 19:12, where Jesus is quoted as saying that there are those 'who have made themselves eunuchs for the sake of the kingdom of heaven'. The term 'eunuchs' is known to mean having been castrated but is being misinterpreted as 'celibacy', which is wrong. And celibacy was never that big an issue for the many popes who had wives and concubines, sometimes even when they were pope.

The issue of celibacy is part of a wider issue of the Church not facing up to sexuality. As late as the 16th century, with Paul III, popes were still siring children, sometimes out of wedlock. Since that time the Catholic Church has continually failed to address issues of sexuality. Aside from the impact of celibacy noted above, the Church has remained stuck on issues such as divorce, abortion, contraception, gay marriage, the marriage of priests and the appointing of female priests. None of this dogma can be found in the Bible. Contraception is a modern invention needed at a time when the population of the world far outstrips its resources. To object to its use among millions of Catholics displays a shocking ignorance of the world situation. These include some of the poorest people of earth and yet the Catholic Church will allow them to have children they cannot afford and then fail to help financially support them. To refuse contraception for people in abject poverty is to condemn their children to death by starvation or disease.

On 14 November 2012 a young woman in the Republic of Ireland died during childbirth from a complication that was identified with her unborn baby. She could have been saved by an abortion but this was refused on religious grounds because Catholicism is the state religion. She was not a Catholic but the law was imposed upon her. As a man I do not feel that I should have any say over the matter of abortion – at most I would say it should be for the individual to decide and they should subsequently be supported in their decision. The issue here is not one of whether or not abortion is right or wrong, but that there are circumstances when it should be allowed as a medical emergency.

The Church has also struggled with issues such as homo-sexuality, due to a simple failing to see it as natural. People do not learn to be gay or choose to be gay – they are born gay – and to deny them this is to deny them life, which is the opposite of what Jesus taught. A former Catholic priest who studied at the Vatican once told me that an apocryphal scripture existed within the Vatican stating that the apostle Paul was 'capable of physical love with another man'. This should come as no surprise considering the entirely male-dominated New Testament, but the Catholic Church refuses to accept the existence of same-sex relationships as anything other than immoral.

The hypocritical attitude towards homosexuality is starkly illustrated by the resignation of the United Kingdom's only papal candidate on 24 February 2013. Cardinal Keith O'Brien was due to travel to the conclave following Pope Benedict XVI's resignation but resigned his position following a number of allegations that claimed he had made improper advances towards young men in the priesthood. This was compounded by his incongruous public stance against homosexuality. So often it is the case that those who try to repress their own sexuality become the most judgemental towards it.

The damage these outdated views are doing to the Church is immeasurable. Great swathes of the population are excluded or denigrated by the Church. Women in particular go unrecognised by the Church and remain sidelined in all but the most basic of Church activities.

These issues are becoming fatal to the Catholic Church as public understanding and opinion has moved on and what was once a place of guidance and wisdom is becoming a new inquisition against modern society. This new inquisition fails to understand the needs of the congregation and those outside the Church see it as ignorance and indoctrination.

The call to change is not a purely external pressure. Even among the most devout communities there are critics speaking out from within the Church. Ireland has long had a reputation for being a bastion of Catholic faith but even here there is a sense of uprising among the priests. A group of Irish priests have spoken out about the need for reforms within the Church that must be led by the pope but so far have only managed to invoke the censorship and ire of the current incarnation of the office of the Inquisition: the Congregation for the Doctrine of the Faith (CDF). The issues they raise are the need for the ordination of women as priests and objecting to the stance that gay and lesbian relationships are immoral. These radical modernising ideas are likely to be the last chance to retain the dwindling congregation and attract younger people to the Church.

THE DECLINE IN PRIESTS

The corrupt image and outdated attitude of the Catholic Church has resulted in a fall in the number of applicants who wish to become priests and the closure of many churches that cannot be maintained. The vow of celibacy has also deterred young men from entering the priesthood. To take a vow so early in life to the exclusion of having a family is too great an expectation to place on any individual – rather than submit to this there are plenty of alternative Christian groups that are not so strict in their approach. As a result of this the average age of priests is now thought to be over 50, which is almost 20 years older than Jesus was when he began his ministry. The lifeblood is draining from the Church.

Aside from the decline in the number of those joining the priesthood, thousands are asking to leave. By the 1980s in the Republic of Ireland 1,000 of the 7,000 priests alive at that time had resigned and it is estimated that in the US alone there are 17,000 ex-priests (*Vicars of Christ*, Peter de Rosa). Once, priests were trusted and respected spiritual guides, who supported their communities, but increasingly they are viewed with distrust as some have exploited their positions to harm others, and even more disturbing, those above them have sought to cover this up. The bad press and continuing scandals that have plagued the Church have irrevocably damaged the public perception of the Catholic Church's hierarchy.

THE DECLINE IN CONGREGATION

A few years ago I attended the christening of a friend's young child at a local Catholic Church. During the service the priest chose to use to use the quote 'And the sins of the father will be visited upon the son', which is not actually present in the Bible. At the time it seemed entirely inappropriate for the occasion of celebrating the welcoming of a child into the Church. For the other non-Catholics in the audience it was not an attractive spectacle and they must have wondered why anyone would want to subject their child to such a curse. For many the experience of going to Church is remembered as something that heaped guilt upon them, blaming and shaming them for human nature.

Congregations have declined dramatically over the last 50 years as Sunday has succumbed to commercial pressure for shops to open and other activities have been available. This has allowed apologists to cite consumerism as a distraction from faith – which has some merit, but at a spiritual level there is a growing disconnection between the Church and the congregation. Spirituality is experiential and progressive and this is making the Catholic Church seem outdated. To the outsider it looks antiquated and anachronistic with modern values. In such a climate members of the Church are driven away and others seek to explore their faith elsewhere.

To stem the loss within the Church there are some who would seek to help it evolve towards meeting the needs of the modern congregation, but these individuals often go unrecognised. There is a growing schism between those who wish to do good works and support their communities and the actions of the Church as a whole, which are producing a loss of faith among Catholics and excluding non-Catholics from the Church.

ALTERNATIVE RELIGION

Prior to the 10th century the Catholic Church was capable of sharing with other religions and in some cases allowing them to influence the Church as it sought to absorb comparative faiths into Christianity. As it grew in power its tolerance for other religions dwindled: it chose to persecute those that refused to yield to the new Catholic religion. The pagans were mostly absorbed into the Church but the Jews had a stronger faith and posed a bigger threat in terms of doctrine and ownership of Jesus.

In the centuries since the Middle Ages the Vatican has published thousands of documents condemning the Jews and blaming them for the suffering and demise of Jesus. Various popes throughout history have taken it upon themselves to persecute the Jews directly. Considering Jesus and all the disciples – including St Peter, the founder of the Catholic Church – were Jews, it is astounding that so many of these learned, seemingly intelligent people were anti-Semitic. The blaming of Jews is something that has been propagated for nearly 2,000 years and yet it ignores the fact that Jesus was Jewish.

Contrary to his depictions in Western art, Jesus would have looked like any other Middle Eastern Jew living today. The loincloth draped around the waist of Jesus in those countless renderings of the Crucifixion also hides a circumcision. So many Christians throughout history, Hitler included, have been content to place the source of the world's ills at the feet of the Jews, but few would acknowledge that their idea of salvation is also in the hands of a Jew. It is obvious really – but still difficult for many to grasp – that Jesus was not a Christian; he was a Rabbi, even a reformer, but still a Jewish teacher. Jesus taught tolerance and forgiveness, which is something people on all sides of this ongoing tragedy seem to have forgotten.

The older religions did not entirely die away and Christianity itself has splintered into many factions, some of which are growing in number, filling the void left by the decline in Catholic congregations. Spirituality has always been present: it naturally appears in every culture and at every point in history. It is inherent in humans and people have always looked to understand it and find an outlet for their spiritual needs. The decline in church attendance does not mean they have abandoned spirituality but that they have either chosen to hold it personally or have discovered another outlet for their faith.

For those who wish to investigate alternatives to Catholicism the last century has seen an explosion in the sharing of faiths and ideas. Publishing and translation has made available every religion, philosophy and heresy for all to read and decide upon; affordable travel has allowed us to visit cultures that only the rich could have considered investigating in past times. Added to this is the wide dissemination of faiths, the mixing of cultures from across the world as people become economic, political or environmental migrants and others choose to live where they wish. The mixing of cultures has greatly expanded our understanding of the mysteries of Eastern religions and through this exposure we learn of the sense of community among Sikhs or the meditative practices of Buddhists. Even in the last few decades the rise in New Age views and philosophies about spirituality has become widespread. The control of faith is passing from the Church to the individual as many choose to follow their own path.

Even among Christians there is now an array of different groups providing alternative paths to celebrating Christ. Groups such as the Quakers promote a very different experience of Christianity. Members of a Quaker group sit in a circle and share their experiences of what they find spiritual in their everyday lives.

There are some teachings on spiritual matters, such as tolerance or charity, but being among these groups feels like being part of an extended family of people who are genuinely seeking to live Christian lives. At the other end of the Christian spectrum members of the Pentecostal Church sing out from the pews to celebrate their Christianity and love of God. Followers could join the humble groups of the contemplative Quakers or the raucous carnival of a gospel choir, both of which offer a living experience of Christianity.

Other religions, such as Buddhism, also offer tools, such as mediation, to help individuals. They focus on personal spiritual evolution in contrast to the disconnected experience that often happens in church. As the spirit moves people to discover their own faith, some are finding new forms of Christianity while others turn away from the teachings of the Bible completely, which poses a vast challenge for the Church. Added to this we now have access to a wider canon of biblical texts and apocryphal writings. The Word of God is being explored in ways unthinkable a hundred years ago.

THE NEW HERETICS

Since the Bible was first printed in the vernacular the Church has steadily lost control of the Word. Lay persons have been able to make their own interpretation of scripture and researchers have pored over the various translations, biblical archaeology and alternative scriptures to widen our knowledge of biblical times.

In addition to this, apocryphal gospels have been discovered, providing insights into the time of Jesus. From the Nag Hammadi Library and the Dead Sea Scrolls come a new release of writings directly linked to the time of Jesus. They paint a broader picture of personal gnosis, a direct connection between the individual and God that eschews the need for a hierarchical Church. An example of this can be found in the Gospel of Thomas, presented as a collection of the sayings of Jesus that contains the following:

> Those who lead you say to you 'See, the Kingdom is in the sky'
> . . . it is within you.
>
> The Gospel of Thomas, 3

This gospel is potentially the most important of the apocryphal works as many academics agree that the four canonical gospels were probably drawn from an earlier single source, referred to by researchers as the 'Q source' or 'Book Q'. As it takes the form of a collection of sayings attributed to Jesus, the Gospel of Thomas is a good fit for a single resource of that nature.

As we can see from the above quote, it is not surprising that this gospel has never been accepted by the Vatican. It takes power from the Church and hands it over to the individual, which radically undermines the Church. That's not to say organised religions have no purpose, as there will always be those who need a simplified deity they can relate *to*, rather than an abstract, experiential phenomena they can relate *with*.

These apocryphal texts are not unknown to the Vatican and it is possible that there are secret enclaves where they are studied and respected. A former Catholic priest once confided in me that it is rumoured that those within the inner circle of the Vatican have a very different set of beliefs than what is taught to the general public.

The need for this subjugating of the mystical side of Christianity may have its roots in the problem of teaching mystical concepts to lay people at a time when formal education did not exist for the masses. At that time the teachings would tend to be pragmatic guidance on how to live a moral life based upon literal interpretations of the Bible. But now we live in an age of education, where all ideas and beliefs can be exchanged and contemplated by anyone with a rudimentary understanding of reading. The time has passed when the Catholic Church could control its followers by giving them simple rules on how to live, like using the Ten Commandments as the basis of all laws. Society has moved on and Church and state have separated, at least in the minds of the masses. Christianity gets lip service from the Western world leaders and they are happy to be photographed attending church, but their actions are driven by politics and commerce, not religion.

The influence that popes once commanded is dwindling, lost among the myriad signals that bombard us every day. In Malachy's time the church would be the tallest building in the village, often placed upon a hill – it would be a landmark, visible from miles around. Now, churches are lost among the skyscrapers and steel department stores, in every sense. At some point the Catholic Church will need to publicly reconcile what is truth and what is dogma or they will fail to remain relevant to a people who are now easily equipped to find a more spiritual belief system, or abandon religion altogether.

As the gulf between the individual and the Church widens it leaves a vast unfulfilled psychological need that will cause people to seek meaning for their lives in other places. Since the mass deaths of the Second World War many new religions and alternative faiths have gained traction with those who turned their backs on traditional forms of Christianity. Atheism has also increased dramatically as faith becomes too fragile to withstand the onslaught of rationalism and science.

SCIENCE

Aside from being sidelined in politics and issues of morality, the Church finds itself under direct attack from science and philosophy. The philosophers of the last few centuries raised many arguments against faith but only science has brought evidence to the table to directly undermine the Catholic view of the universe. Aside from explaining the mechanical underpinning of the universe, science has now become more abstract and delved into areas that were formerly considered to be the realm of mysticism. The march of science is threatening to shine a light of reason into the darkest corners of belief and prove that the shadows of the unknown have only given rise to superstition. Unfortunately scientists have often railed against religions to the extent that they have lost sight of the true nature of faith. The likes of Richard Dawkins, a one-man crusade to instil atheism in the masses, are attempting to reclaim the cosmos from religious dogma by applying what appears to be common sense. Dawkins' work is interesting but often feels like he is railing against a figure of God that is more like Santa Claus than any authentic religious experience. This is part of the current rift between the communities of science and faith, but over time I think we will come full circle as both science and psychology are beginning to see the nature of reality as a construct which we can influence directly. This returns us to a world of mysticism that allows for the divine to work through the individual and be present in the world.

PERSECUTIONS END

In conclusion to our examination of the 'persecutions' of the Church, we have seen that they are many and varied. It is possible that a schism will eventually develop within the Catholic Church over one of the many contentious issues in circulation. Returning to prophecy, we find that both St Hildegard and Nostradamus identified the end of the Church with a great schism and the presence of an antipope who will split the Church. In the worst case the prophecy of La Salatte will be realised and 'Rome will lose faith and become the seat for the antipope.'

PETER THE ROMAN

. . . the seat of the Holy Roman Church will be occupied by Peter the Roman, who will feed the sheep through many tribulations . . .

The next line of the prophecy names Peter the Roman as the pope who will preside over the Church at the end. Contrary to the prophecies that state the final pope will be the Antichrist, he is described as continuing to attend to the spiritual needs of his congregation until the fall of Rome. Identifying this Peter the Roman is important, as it may have some bearing on the tribulations that are to overtake the Vatican. In the next chapter we consider the current pope and how he might fit the prophecy.

As the prophecies consist of a long list of popes and Peter the Roman is the last, it is seems logical that no more popes will follow. There are a number of possible reasons why no further popes will be created. In spiritual terms the remainder of the prophecy speaks of the Last Judgement, which would account for the end of the Catholic Church, as all are judged. Also described in the prophecies is the destruction of Rome, which could indicate a cataclysm on a global scale, and the nature of this event is what we must look at next.

THE DESTRUCTION OF ROME

. . . the city of seven hills will be destroyed . . .

Rome has always been identified as the city of seven hills and the destruction of Rome may have been predicted in the Book of Revelation. The number seven repeatedly appears in the Book of Revelation, referring to numbers of churches, spirits, letters, stars, seals, angels, crowns and hills. Revelation 17:9 describes the woman who rides the beast as sitting upon the seven hills. Later, in Revelation 17:18, it is stated: 'And the woman which thou sawest is that great city, which reigneth over the kings of the earth.' This is a fair description of Rome but aligns it with a harlot who rides the great beast that the angels must destroy. This is not a new idea: the Cathar heretics of the Middle Ages believed the Vatican was the 'harlot' of the Apocalypse (see *Heresy and Authority in Medieval Europe*).

As previously mentioned, the destruction of Rome forms part of the body of prophecies in eschatology. But these are the events that describe the time of the final pope and for the line of popes to come to an end the destruction of Rome must be more than just physical. The entire Catholic religion would need to be concluded in some apocalyptic form. There are many descriptions of how this might happen, from predictions of the saints, scripture, even popes. It is worth noting at this point that in 1514 Pope Leo X recounted a vision in which he learned that the end of the world would happen '500 years hence', in 2014.

PHYSICAL DESTRUCTION

In the 12th century St Hildegard von Bingen predicted the arrival of a comet that drives out the sea to inundate the land:

The Comet by its tremendous pressure, will force much out of the ocean and flood many countries, causing much want and many plagues . . . The ocean will also flood many other countries, so that all coastal cities will live in fear, with many destroyed. All sea coast cities will be fearful and many of them will be destroyed by tidal waves.

But even a flood, while devastating, will eventually recede. Should the cataclysm be more long term it could change the geography of the land mass across the world. The spectre of climate change also threatens to inundate the lowlands worldwide, but on a permanent basis. Evidence for the deluge we recognise from the Old Testament can be found on all continents; like ice ages, this is a cyclic occurrence, though mankind's progress into industrialisation has hastened the next partial extinction of humanity.

For the destruction of Rome to occur the actual bricks and mortar of the Vatican would need to be rent apart by some destructive force. On a global scale the geological record tells that there have been many major geological, environmental and astronomical events – such as the meteor that created the Yucatan peninsula, ice ages and the mass extinctions of pre-history. Active volcanoes, such as the giant caldera that spans Yellowstone Park in America, ring the earth. Should that erupt, the resulting dust cloud would plunge the western hemisphere into year-long winters and widespread crop failure. Earthquakes are not uncommon in northern Italy as the country is criss-crossed with minor fault lines; the country experienced at least ten earthquakes of magnitude 4.0 or more in 2012. In Isaiah 24:19–20 we read of a global cataclysm where the earth is shifted from its orbit. This would result in worldwide earthquakes and tsunamis.

The assumption among Christians is that such events are part of God's plan and set the stage for the End Times. Regardless of one's belief that God's wrath instigates such events and that the chosen will be saved from such cataclysms, once in motion nature does not discriminate. We know from recent history that natural disasters like earthquakes and tsunamis will destroy church, mosque and synagogue alike.

It is possible for a completely new threat to emerge and suddenly bring about the downfall of the Vatican as a physical entity. In the last century politics and war have been the driving forces behind the greatest loss of human life and physical property. Historically this was a constant threat from the kings of Europe, the Islamic empire and eventually both the Axis and Allies of the Second World War. Many opportunities to storm the gates of the Vatican have come and gone but in the current age it seems unlikely that a war would encroach that far into Europe. It is possible that an act of terrorism or an escalating conflict with the Middle East could target Rome, but this is not such a threat nowadays as the Vatican has been careful not to be too vocal about its enemies of old.

If Rome and the Vatican are destroyed by anything other than the rapture, over one billion Catholics worldwide will be dispossessed of leadership. As 'pope' means 'father' of the Church and some popes spent their time exiled from Rome, it does not seem likely that the prophecy is tied to the physical location of the city. If it were a natural upheaval such as an earthquake or any other localised event then I imagine the Catholic Church would revert to its primitive structure and become decentralised for a time. The control of the Church would pass into the hands of the surviving cardinals and bishops and then later they would try to recreate the papacy. There are plenty of Vatican-owned properties that would suffice as a new Holy See, and over time we would expect it to reform and appoint a new pope to continue the line.

History warns us that such a void could lead to schisms and rivalries where each diocese would compete to house the next Vatican headquarters, but the main challenge to this happening is that, according to the prophecies, there can be no more popes. They signal not just the fall of the Vatican in Rome but the end of the papal succession. For this to be the case the destruction must be wider than just the physical Vatican State, as 'Peter the Roman' will be the final pope and then the papacy must come to an end. Should the Vatican be destroyed and the line of popes come to an end without some recognisable divine intervention there would be a great crisis of faith among Catholics. Destruction on a worldwide scale would test the faith of Catholics to such an extreme that many would abandon their belief in God, creating a spiritual vacuum. If, however, the event is accompanied by any kind phenomenon that could be interpreted as divine intervention, many would welcome the end with open arms.

THE FORMIDABLE JUDGE

. . . and the formidable Judge will judge His people.

There are two types of judgement in Christianity. The first takes the form of 'personal judgement', which occurs when an individual dies, and the second is the 'general judgement' which occurs on Judgement Day. There has always been a confusion of the two, as it would appear that after death we are judged and sent to our final place, be it heaven or hell. Then at the point of the Last Judgement we are resurrected and judged again and likely sent back to heaven or hell. This issue of contention was decided in a papal bull issued by Pope Benedict XII in 1336, which stated that we are to be judged upon death but failed to clarify how this would differ from the Last Judgement.

The identity of the 'formidable judge' is not given in the prophecy but can easily be identified from scripture. According to the Book of Revelation, the 'Great Judge will return to Judge his people' (Revelation 5:28). Revelation goes on to identify the Great Judge as Jesus, who returns during the End Times, and whose voice can be heard but only by the saints. Christ returns to judge the living and the dead and a number of these are saved. This is considered by the Catholic Church to be the Second Coming of Jesus, and differs from other Christian groups that believe Jesus will reign for 1,000 years either before or after an apocalyptic event.

It is difficult to find a rational way to discuss the Last Judgement according to the Book of Revelation as the language veers from factual events to seemingly symbolic reverie. For example, during the opening of the fifth seal the dead are described as being 'given robes to wear and told to wait', which, as even theologians concede, is not possible without a body. The use of the term 'dead' here might be symbolic for atheists and other non-believers, but like much of Revelation the passage remains open to interpretation.

Revelation is supported in its reference to a Second Coming by many other prophecies that describe the return of Jesus to pass judgement, including the gospel of Matthew. Matthew 24:31–33 describes a Second Coming and Last Judgement as:

When the Son of man shall come in his glory, and all the holy angels with him, then shall he sit upon the throne of his glory: And before him shall be gathered all nations: and he shall separate them one from another, as a shepherd divideth his sheep from the goats: And he shall set the sheep on his right hand, but the goats on the left.

The appearance of Jesus in the world as a divine intervention, or Second Coming, would also unseat the pope, which could explain why the line of popes would cease to exist at this point. Too often in history popes failed to hold both the spiritual and material aspects of the role without falling into corruption and this has undermined any claims to infallibility. In the conclusion of the *Prophecy of the Popes* the sins of the popes are visited upon their successors.

CONCLUSION

The end.

The idea of the final pope and Last Judgement must be both feared and welcomed within the Vatican and there are some who think this might be the only way forward. For them the Catholic Church has become a barrier to spirituality, an obstacle of its own creation. In the wake of an apocalyptic event perhaps a new structure would be agreed: a devolved leadership where the apostolic line is deferred to archbishops who take the role of local heads of the Church. This outcome might be a better political and cultural fit for ministering to such a diverse and geographically dispersed flock than the current structure.

The immediate challenge for the Church is to stem the loss of both members of the congregation and the priests that serve them, who are abandoning the old structure. This is due to the persecutions and issues that have befallen the Church but when such times of difficulty are experienced by an entire group this can call for an archetype to actualise, that is to attract someone who exhibits the qualities needed to fill the psychological void in the group. The needs of the Church as a whole can be met by a leader such as those who rose up in the Old Testament, or the heroic figures of mythology. We have seen from the issues facing the Church in the last century that there is already a need for such a figure, and the next pope will be required to fill the current spiritual vacuum and reignite the passion of the faith among the followers. In the final prophecy this is Peter the Roman and the conclave of 2013 had the power to elect this pope to be both a self-fulfilling prophecy and the path to self-destruction.

And so we come to the question of whether Pope Francis is the last pope. The list of favourites for the role had been circulated in 2012 and the criteria for selecting a pope are well known. The reign of 'Peter the Roman' has arrived and with some detective work we can identify if the conclave chose to uphold the prophecy or to try to stave off the time of the final pope and deny the prophecy its conclusion.

CHAPTER 11

CANDIDATES AND CARDINALS

INTRODUCTION

Since the publication of the prophecies they have been scrutinised prior to every papal election to fathom who might be appointed pope. As one pope dies or retires the candidates for the conclave are examined and rumours circulate regarding who might be elected.

Prior to the conclave of 2005 speculation was rife that the candidate would hail from the Benedictine Order. The prophecy described the coming pope as 'glory of the olive' and the olive branch is a symbol of the Benedictines. Cardinal Ratzinger was not from the Benedictine Order but surprised everyone when he adopted the papal name of their founder, St Benedict. The statement 'glory of the olive' is also ambiguous and is thought by some to mean peace will come to the Middle East. Certainly during Benedict's time the Middle East was in upheaval and in recent years we have seen uprisings all across the Arab world as citizens have demanded a more moderate rule in what is being termed the 'Arab spring'. Perhaps this will be how future generations will view this period of history, as a time when the Middle East sought to establish a democratic peace.

As the prophecies have often accurately identified the incoming popes it would be naïve to think that they are not without some influence over the elections. In some cases cardinals have taken the prophecies seriously enough to try to align themselves to the predicted outcome. *The Prophecies of St. Malachy* (Bander, 1969) includes an anecdote of the 1958 papal election regarding the prophecy 'shepherd and mariner'. A candidate for the election, Cardinal Spellman, took the prophecy to heart and hired a boat on which he transported sheep up and down the Tiber to try to influence the election in his favour. His ruse proved unsuccessful and the less-contrived patriarch of Venice was appointed as Pope John XXIII. This is probably not the first time something like this has happened and it shows how much credibility the prophecies have among the cardinals. The election for the current pope saw a surprising number of leading candidates that could be linked to the name 'Peter'. Both Cardinal Peter Turkson of Ghana and Cardinal Odillo Pedro Scherer of Brazil were strong candidates that had 'Peter' as a part of their name. Papal commentators had already singled Scherer out as the leading candidate to succeed Benedict (see Gurugé) and he also had the benefit of not having lost out to Cardinal Ratzinger in the 2005 conclave.

Cardinal Bergoglio attended the 2005 conclave and was seen by many as front-runner in the election; he was supported by the more moderate factions of Church, but he lost to the conservative Cardinal Ratzinger, who became Pope Benedict XVI.

CARDINALS

For the first thousand years of the Catholic Church the election of the pope was subject to external influence from the ruling bodies of Italy, such as the emperor or the senate. Politicians who sought the power and support of the pope soon learned that it was in their interest to have a say in who occupied the seat of Rome or they risked being sidelined. This led to the schisms of the High Middle Ages and since that time the papal electors have struggled to rid themselves of such influence. As early as 1179 attempts were made to ensure that only cardinals could choose a pope but for centuries to follow nepotism and the promoting of cardinals could not be so well policed. Only in the last few centuries have they managed to close their doors to the politically motivated. Now popes are selected in the gathering of cardinals called the conclave and these cardinals can only rise through the correct channels to hold such prestigious positions.

Technically anyone can be made pope, but the position has, for hundreds of years, been conferred to one of those who cast the votes. To be pope it is now expected that the individual will be drawn from the College of Cardinals. The role of cardinal is the most senior position in the Church and can only be appointed by the pope. There are currently over 200 cardinals alive today and the number is steadily increasing. In November 2010 Pope Benedict XVI held a consistory to create 24 new cardinals and in February 2012 he appointed a further 22 cardinals, reaching the upper limit of the College of Cardinals who are eligible to become pope. The average age of those in the college at the time was 78, almost three times that of Jesus when he started his ministry.

For the purpose of papal elections the number of cardinals allowed to take part is limited to 120, though in the conclave of 2013 only 115 were present. Cardinals are traditionally identifiable by their red biretta hats and for the purpose of papal elections they wear the hats adorned with tassels. The cardinals converge on Rome in the days that follow the death of a pope.

THE VACANT SEAT

Sede vacante is the term given to the vacant seat of the Cathedral of St John Lateran following the death or abdication of a pope. An abdication has not taken place since Pope Gregory XII in 1415 so it was a major shock to catholics worldwide when Pope Benedict XVI announced his resignation in February 2013. It was expected that he would remain in power until he drew his last breath.

The resignation received some criticism from within the Church, as some thought the act risked setting a precedent whereby unpopular popes could be urged to resign. The opposite is true, as it would, in the case of the very old and infirm, allow a pope to resign gracefully without waiting for his health to decline to a terminal state.

Others have raised the possibility that conflict within the Church moved Benedict to resign, but it is reasonable to assume that it was Benedict's own decision to relinquish the role due to illness – at such an advanced age illness is often accompanied by a loss of faculties. In living memory there was the sad decline of John Paul II, who was reduced to an incoherent, almost vegetative state that seemed to slowly strip the Church of leadership.

Pope Benedict was able to announce his own departure, whereas usually the death of the pope is confirmed and announced by the Cardinal Camerlengo, a senior cardinal responsible for death duties. Prior to the 20th century the death was verified by the Camerlengo striking the pope's corpse on the forehead with a small silver hammer and saying his name three times. Now he need only announce the death. The dead pope's ring and seal are taken to be destroyed, symbolising the end of the pope's reign. This act has its origins in necessity more than tradition as the ring would contain the papal seal and its destruction prevented it being misused after the pope's death.

The General Congregation of Cardinals then maintain the running of the pope's affairs and instigate the plans for his funeral and the appointing of a new pope. With Pope Benedict's planned departure it was possible to ensure a smooth handover and for the cardinals to gather prior to the event. We think of the pope primarily as a religious leader but the role carries a further eight titles aside from Bishop of Rome. These have varied through history but the pope is not just a spiritual leader but also a political ruler and the sovereign of the Vatican City State. As such he has the power to issue currency and raise an army should he so wish.

Following the death or departure of a pope there are nine days of mourning during which the cardinals travel from around the world to Rome to attend the pope's funeral in St Peter's Basilica, or in the case of the recent election the time was spent by cardinals discussing the issues facing the Church, which would help identify the type of qualities expected of the next pope. In the days that follow the funeral the cardinals who are eligible to vote for the next pope meet in the conclave of the Sistine Chapel and the election of a new pope begins. Contenders for an incoming pope are unofficially called *papabili* (singular *papabile*).

THE VATICAN CONCLAVE

The gathering of cardinals to decide the next pope is called the conclave and was first convened in its current form in the 13th century. The conclave has been responsible for choosing every pope for nearly 700 years. The word 'conclave' comes from the Latin words meaning 'with a key' and hails from the time the cardinals were first locked into the room to make a decision. They were held in a sealed building, in part to assist a quick decision as it can become an uncomfortably hot environment, but mostly to prevent outside influence. The closed nature of the conclave dates back to the election following the death of Clement IV in 1268, when it took three years to elect a new pope. They eventually settled on Gregory X and, having been subjected to this prolonged ordeal, Gregory made a rule that in future the cardinals would be locked up together until they came to a decision. Food would be rationed and conditions within the conclave would deteriorate, forcing the cardinals to make a decision.

Pope Gregory XV published the papal bull *Aeterni Patris* in 1621 outlining the rules for all future papal elections. He decreed there would be one vote per cardinal to be made in secret, and no candidate could vote for himself. Gregory's intention was to remove political influence from the elections but it also implies that there were common abuses of the voting process – which may call into question a number of the previous outcomes of the conclave. It is still seen as inappropriate for cardinals to promote themselves during the elections, so it is likely that they debate on each others' behalf and the future of the Church.

The conclave is a closed session and the election is private but democratic. The cardinals vote four times per day until a two-thirds majority for one candidate is reached and the new pope is elected. Until the election is completed the cardinals are forbidden to leave the conclave. If the voting continues for more than ten days a final vote is taken with any majority counting as a decision. Not since 1831 has any conclave exceeded five days days and with time to meet and prepare beforehand it was no surprise when the 2013 conclave reached a decision within 24 hours.

Anyone is eligible to be pope as long as they are male, unmarried and under 80 years of age. There are no further criteria beyond this, but tradition has it that a pope is always elected from among the cardinals. As mentioned above, the cardinals are collectively referred to as the College of Cardinals and they are called together to advise the pope and to provide temporary leadership in the event of the pope's demise or abdication. Cardinals were said to be eligible to become pope from AD 769.

Within conclave ballot papers are distributed containing the words 'I Elect _____ as Supreme Pontiff'. Each cardinal adds a name of their choosing, and deposits the paper into a metal dish that serves as a ballot box. The ballot papers are then collected and counted.

After every vote the collected papers are burned in a small stove to indicate to the waiting crowds in St Peter's Square if a decision has been reached. For the duration of the conclave a chimney connected to a stove is installed in the Sistine Chapel for this purpose. Smoke is released from the chimney: black to signify no decision has made and the Holy See remains empty, or white to announce that a new pope has been elected. The smoke is caused by the burning of the ballot papers, as both a signal and to destroy the evidence of the voting. To ensure there is no confusion for the waiting crowds and TV viewers around the world, the precise colour of smoke is achieved by adding chemicals. If it is white 'We have a new pope!' is announced from the balcony on St Peter's Square to the masses that await their new spiritual leader and this message is echoed worldwide.

If the conclave were to exceed the ten-day limit and no compromise had been found the cardinals would move to a final vote. At the conclusion of a successful majority vote the elected cardinal is asked if he accepts the role. If he does, and as far as we know none have declined, though some have tried, he then gives the papal name by which he wishes to be known. Popes can choose any papal name they wish. With the conclave at an end all that remains is for the new pope to make himself known to the flock by appearing on the balcony overlooking St Peter's Square.

In recent elections a media frenzy has taken place in St Peter's Square as one billion Catholics worldwide await the announcement. The papal elections are one of the most influential events in world history and even countries that have a low Catholic population widely report the election. With developments in television and the internet providing 24-hour coverage the result of the last conclave was known almost instantly worldwide.

CONCLUSION

There is a double-edged sword at play in the election of Pope Francis. In previous elections the choice of pope could potentially be swayed, albeit privately, by the prophecies. This could cause some candidates to try to appear to fit the prophecy in the hope that others would see how well predisposed they were to the role. The problem with the conclave that determined the current pope is that, according to the prophecy, he will be the last. Pope Francis has inherited the role of 'Peter the Roman' and if he fits the prediction, he has the burden of knowing he is said to be the final pope who oversees the fall of Rome and the Vatican.

The election of the popes is said to be inspired by the Holy Ghost so it should be that no man will have a say in these matters. If a match for Peter the Roman was chosen and the prophecy believed to be fulfilled would the cardinals have invoked an apocalyptic event? It is an expectation of the Catholic masses and as such is welcomed by many Catholics across the world, but it theoretically comes at a price of great death and destruction. It is difficult to reconcile the coming of heaven on earth with the natural disasters portrayed in the Book of Revelation. So into this conundrum came the final conclave as the cardinals elected the next pope. It may well be that they decided to try to postpone the apocalypse by specifically choosing a candidate that in no way can be compared to 'Peter the Roman'. Although, like Cardinal Ratzinger who chose the papal name 'Benedict' which fitted his Benedictine prophecy, the incoming pope, Francis, might well have chosen a name that fits the prophecy or we may find that over the course of his reign events unfold that will identify him with Peter the Roman. It is possible that the pretence that the prophecies had no influence will be maintained, but in secret the cardinals may well have voting for, or against, a coming rapture. More likely is that so many of the leading candidates were in some way linked to St Peter; just by becoming pope they are all following in the footsteps of saint, that it would have been almost impossible to avoid some kind of link.

CHAPTER 12

THE FINAL POPE

INTRODUCTION

For much of the Middle Ages the papacy was in turmoil. Papal elections were often contested and various schisms and political wrangling challenged the primacy of the Catholic Church. It was a time of antipopes, with rival factions appointing their own pope to challenge the Holy See. Tradition has it that Malachy presented the list of 112 future popes as a gift to Pope Innocent II to bring some comfort to his troubled reign. Innocent, who had returned to Rome from exile in France, may have delighted in knowing that papacy would last another 700 years. But now that 700 years is drawing to a close, and with it the succession of popes is coming to an end. Pope Francis must take little comfort from the prophecies today as they reckon him to be the final pope.

To identify the last pope according to the predictions of Malachy is akin to unravelling a detective story. The choice of Francis from the candidates that were summoned to the Vatican conclave after Pope Benedict XVI resigned had to fulfil a more pressing set of criteria than simply fulfilling the prophecy. After examining Malachy's enigmatic description of the final pope to establish what this means and how it might apply to Pope Francis, we must bring the strands together and attempt to identify if he is the last pope – the pope who will witness the fall of Rome.

CHOOSING THE LAST POPE

On 12 March 2013 the conclave was ceremoniously opened and 115 cardinal *papabili* filed into the Sistine Chapel. The door was locked behind them and they would not be allowed out again until a successor to Pope Benedict XVI had been appointed.

While the actual voting is secret, there are a number of criteria by which the pope is chosen, and a greater number of unofficial factors that will also influence the vote. By considering these factors we can build a case for why Francis was elected as the current pope.

As mentioned previously, the only fixed rules for who can be pope are that he must be male, unmarried and younger than 80 years of age (the imposed age limit was implemented by Pope Paul VI in 1970). As yet there is no retirement age for popes, regardless of the risk of senility, degenerative diseases and diminishing faculties. Within the 80-year limit the choice will also be influenced by the 'young' or 'old' debate. If the candidate is nearing 80 and in poor health, the risk is that he will spend much of his time as pope incapacitated and have a potentially short tenure. However, if the candidate is young or particularly healthy there is the risk that he lasts far longer than had been expected and, if he is discovered to be unsuitable for the role, he will have more time to cause harm as he cannot easily be deposed. The obvious route to take would be that if the candidate was controversial, he might only be considered if he elderly, but a younger man would be welcome if he was considered a 'safe' choice.

On 13 March 2013 Jorge Mario Bergoglio became the first non-European pope for 1,300 years, which surprised many of the pundits, who seemed to have forgotten that St Peter was a 'non-European'. He is also the first Jesuit pope, finally drawing a line under the persecutions the Society of Jesus had suffered under previous administrations. It was announced shortly afterwards that he would take the name Pope Francis, which he chose in honour of St Francis of Assisi. Soon after that, he emerged on the balcony of St Peter's to address the awaiting crowds who had braved the rain to hear the first address by the 266th pope.

Born Jorge Mario Bergoglio on 17 December 1936 in Buenos Aires, Pope Francis was ordained as a Jesuit in 1969. He was made Bishop of Auca in 1992 and then Bishop of Buenos Aires in 1998. He became a cardinal in February 2001 at the behest of Pope John Paul II and, prior to becoming pope, he was Archbishop of Buenos Aires.

At 74 years of age he appeared in good health and good spirits as he spent his first days welcoming the crowds who came to see him. Although 74 years of age may appear elderly, the fact that the rules have changed to limit the age to 80 would seem to indicate there is now a trend in the Vatican towards electing a younger pope who will be more active and likely to live and reign longer.

This factor may have narrowed the number of eligible cardinals a little but other factors also influenced the voting. A key factor in choosing the pope involves the issues faced by the Catholic Church at this time in history, and the qualities needed in a pope to address them. While the armies of Europe may have receded – the emperors and warlords having been replaced by public opinion, politicians and bankers – the threats to the Church are just as challenging, if not more so, than in the past.

As the cardinals made their decision, some of these issues would have been considered critical in order to sustain the Catholic

Church. So at the back of their minds, the cardinals would have been considering the following criteria:

1. The pope would have to be capable of connecting with the Catholic communities beyond Europe. These congregations have more potential for growth than their Western counterparts but are also facing very different challenges. The needs of the congregations would be greatly helped if the pope was one of their own and capable of speaking to them in their own language. Seemingly counter to this, there would be a strong desire by the Italian cardinals to appoint an Italian pope, as the previous two had been German and Polish. This role is, after all, also the Bishop of Rome and, prior to Pope John Paul II, all the popes had been Italian since 1523.

Pope Francis is half Italian, so he bridges the gap between Europe and South America without being too extreme a step from the safe European leadership the Vatican State had become accustomed to. He is fluent in Italian and can manage the role of Bishop of Rome without the need for an interpreter. The compromise is palpable as Pope Francis can both placate the Italian Catholics and engage the vast South American congregation who feel dispossessed by European indifference to their needs.

Pope Francis is devoted to alleviating the suffering caused by poverty and this will likely remain his focus and mission as he attempts to re-engage those who feel the Church no longer speaks to them. His Jesuit background is also well suited to stemming the Pentecostal tide sweeping through South America.

2. A non-European pope would also prove that the Catholic Church is moving towards addressing the issues facing these countries. It will also be important to reach out to

other faiths and try to build bridges to the various factions of Christianity that exist today.

Pope Francis is also committed to social justice: his mission is clear in the name he has adopted as pope. That Bergoglio chose the name Francis is likely to have been based upon his natural affinity with St Francis of Assisi. St Francis was the son of a rich merchant and was raised in finery and feasting, but he abandoned his life of luxury and followed a spiritual path that led him to Rome, where he witnessed poverty. So moved was St Francis by the plight of the poor that he renounced his wealth and chose to lead a life of poverty and humility.

As Cardinal Bergoglio, Pope Francis shunned the palatial dwellings and chauffeurs afforded his position and chose instead to live in a modest apartment and travel on public transport. He spent much of his time among the poverty-stricken population of Buenos Aires and was a leading voice on their behalf.

3. The new pope will need to put the Vatican finances in order in the wake of the banking scandals that dogged Pope Benedict XVI in his latter years.

St Francis was also subjected to visions and mystical experiences and had been commanded by God to 'Go, Francis, and repair my house.' Such a mission must weigh heavily on the mind of Bergoglio. But before he can make gestures of financial support to the poor he must balance the books and ensure that the Vatican is free from banking scandals. Should he radically divert the wealth of the Church he risks leaving the coffers empty, like so many of his predecessors. Not afraid to speak out against injustice and corruption and having been a major critic of corruption in the Argentine government, Pope Francis must now get his own house in order.

4. Pope Benedict XVI was a strong advocate of the strict adherence to doctrines and was considered a very conservative choice of pope. A more moderate pope might be more attractive to the wider congregation, many of whom are currently leaving the Church for religions with less prescriptive expressions of faith. Benedict's views did not help to quell public concern that the Church is outdated. To look at the history of the popes as a whole there would seem to be a pattern of alternately appointing a hard conservative and then a moderate. This has played back and forth over the centuries like a system of checks and balances to curb the failings of each pope. As Benedict was so conservative it was highly likely the following pope would be a moderate.

True to the historical pattern the papacy has swung back towards a moderate in the appointment of Pope Francis, who was considered in opposition to Benedict's traditionalist outlook in the previous conclave. He speaks against discrimination of all kinds, could reach out to Africa through poverty and appears to be possessed of the humility required to meet with other faiths on an even footing. His opinions on tolerance for same-sex couples is a welcome development for the Church, although he strongly objects to same-sex couples adopting children, which indicates a somewhat-outdated view of the family unit.

5. It is important for the new pope to be free from scandal and be politically aware. Bad publicity or failure to be firm and decisive around issues such as child abuse, or to have shown intolerance of any kind as a cardinal, might prove embarrassing 'baggage' for a pope in the eyes of the media. The next pope must have a transparent attitude to ridding

the Church of abuse and corruption and be capable of understanding and acting against both decisively.

In the days that followed the election the more cynical aspects of the press scrutinised the pope's public and private history in search of scandals they could link him to. A story circulated about his possible collusion in human rights abuses of the Argentine government in the mid-1970s. The Vatican immediately issued a statement refuting the accusation. Considering the number and scale of scandals that have been levelled against the Church in recent years, any inaction on Bergoglio's part at that time seems trivial by comparison. The real challenge will come when scandals arise through other members of his Church and he will be assessed on how he responds to these. He has previously spoken out against child abuse in his native country but it remains to be seen if he is willing to take decisive action against abuses by members of the Church. Only by expelling transgressors will he alleviate the public view that the Church cannot be trusted to address the perversion in its ranks.

6. It was thought likely that a candidate would be chosen who had not been present in the 2005 conclave. Anyone who was eligible to be pope and attended the previous conclave will have lost the vote to Cardinal Ratzinger, and this might be seen to reflect badly on them. Having previously failed to be elected might imply they are inferior to Ratzinger or that the wrong choice was made in 2005.

The maturity and experience Bergoglio has achieved since that time might counter this, but at such an advanced age one would think that the additional years would make little difference. It was for this reason many considered that Cardinal Scherer would be a more likely candidate, as he had not previously attended the conclave and yet shares many of Bergoglio's positive strengths.

7. Finally, and it is certainly not an explicit requirement, after the success of Pope John Paul II – who was universally popular and did much to attract the disinterested back to the Catholic Church – the role would benefit greatly from someone charismatic and capable of reaching out via modern media. We live in an environment of mass communication that could be used to the advantage of the Church instead of being avoided or ignored.

Even Pope Benedict XVI was encouraged to connect with his audience via Twitter in the last few months of his reign. Pope Francis is widely educated, having studied theology at San Miguel and earned his doctorate in Germany; he is fluent in Spanish, German, Italian and, of course, Latin. His humble but approachable manner and speech will serve him well as pope, though he is considered a quiet man. He is known as someone who only speaks when there is something important to be said, and this might actually work in his favour in a world where we are constantly bombarded by the inane witterings of modern mass communication.

CARDINAL BERGOGLIO

In the light of the above issues I think the factor that most influenced the papal election was the pope's country of origin. Popes have traditionally been Italian or at least European, but the percentage of Catholics in Italy compared to the total number of Catholics worldwide is significantly lower, and the main areas of conversion for the Church are now beyond the borders of Europe.

If Rome had appointed another Italian, this would have alienated Catholics worldwide, who already feel disenfranchised by the continued European focus of those in the Vatican. To choose an Italian could have been seen as a snub, and caused a schism in the Church, like the creation of the 'antipopes' of the Great Western Schism in the Middle Ages.

In contrast to this, a non-European pope has so rarely been elected that it would have been seen as too big a step to be choosing a purely African or South American pope. There have been Italian, Greek, Syrian, African, Spanish, French, German, Dutch, Polish and English popes, but never one from the Americas. In recent decades North America has been rife with sex abuse scandals and cover-ups among the Church leaders, which has tainted public opinion of the Church. This would have cast a long shadow over any American cardinal and therefore been unpalatable to members of the conclave. For South America, one of the main challenges comes from competing faiths and a perceived lack of local support for the poor. Therefore the current pope needed to be multilingual and at least part non-European, or have strong links with non-European countries. A less conservative pope than Benedict XVI was also welcome.

As the conclave began, of all the potential candidates, Argentine Cardinal Jorge Mario Bergoglio in particular fulfilled these criteria.

Poverty is a huge issue between the clergy of South America and the Vatican, as there is so much wealth in Rome and yet so many Catholics in Brazil are mired in destitution. Bergoglio is a devout Catholic but has criticised the Catholic Church for not doing enough to fight poverty or recognise the needs of common people, far from Italy. To this end he is aligned with some aspects of 'liberation theology', a movement dedicated to demanding relief from poverty for the millions of Catholics in South America. If, as pope, he fails to represent these local congregations, millions of people could collectively turn their backs on Rome. This shift may continue anyway, as it is possible that, with so many branches of Catholicism across the world, local representation is demanded at some point in the future. There may come a time when there is the 'equivalent' of a pope in each country, speaking the local language and able to address local cultural needs and issues – a situation that would end the rule of Rome.

Politically it is as much a matter of representation as taxation: a sizeable amount of wealth leaves Latin American states to fill Rome's coffers – funds that could perhaps be put to better use closer to home.

By failing to address the poverty issue and meet the needs of the people the Church is in decline in some areas. Its followers are not abandoning their faith but turning to other religions to find an outlet for their spirituality. While the Catholic Church has seen numbers fall in many areas of South America, over 75 million Christians have converted to Pentecostalism. The Pentecostal Church promotes an emotionally charged and sometimes ecstatic experience of faith. It employs singing and dancing, and a passion entirely absent in the dry monotone of a Catholic sermon. The people of South America identify with it readily because it mirrors their own vibrant nature and speaks directly to their Latin American spirit. Gospel choirs sing out the anthems of people celebrating their faith and life. Against such an attractive experience it will take someone as engaging as Bergoglio to win back the opinion and the faith of the masses.

Having deduced that Cardinal Bergoglio was the most appropriate candidate for the current pope we can compare what we know of his life to the final prophecy made by St Malachy.

'PETER THE ROMAN'

With Cardinal Bergoglio the successor to Pope Benedict XVI, we must establish if he can be readily identified by the prophecy. In terms of the prediction the single clue we have to identify the next pope is the brief epithet 'Peter the Roman'. It is this Peter the Roman who will 'feed his flock among the many tribulations' until the Last Judgement takes place.

Throughout the prophecies the clues provided by Malachy consist of a single short description. In most cases this can be linked directly to some aspect of the corresponding pope. As the description of each pope often refers to their country of origin, their name, their coat of arms or insignia and their title or position they held prior to becoming pope we can consider these identifying traits for Bergoglio to see if he can conclusively be linked to the prophecy. Like Pope Benedict, the link can now be made after the election. For example, for Pope John Paul II (1978–2005) St Malachy described the pope as 'shining star'. The papal coat of arms adopted by Pope John Paul II was the image of a shooting star. This belated assignation fulfilled the centuries-old prophecy but could not have been used to predict his election. The papal coat of arms has very little historical merit and many were pure invention but the prophecies refer to these devices on a number of occasions. In the case of Peter the Roman neither part of the prophecy lends itself to heraldic symbolism so we can perhaps exclude that from the interpretation.

As Bergoglio is half Italian he could not truly be said to hail from Rome in terms of his family. His father hailed from Bricco Marmorito near the Alps in northern Italy so this cannot be construed to indicate Pope Francis is a 'Roman' but the Italian cardinals would certainly have seen him as being one of their own and the people of Rome are more likely to accept him as their bishop. There is also, it seems, more than one way to be a 'Roman'. On the BBC news website an article dated 19 November 2010, entitled: 'Pope to shape College of Cardinals at consistory' contained the following:

> However, 13 of the new cardinal-electors currently work or have worked in the Roman Curia – the Vatican's bureaucracy – and Curial officials now make up nearly a third of all cardinal-electors, prompting speculation the next Pope is likely to be a 'Roman', if not an Italian.

This is a clear example of how members of the Curia are automatically referred to as 'Roman', having held a position in the Vatican administration. Bergoglio held five such positions in the Roman Curia, although he has publically spoken out against the political factions that are present and how it is open to exploitation by careerist cardinals. So while it could be said that he is a 'Roman', it very likely that as pope he will also be known for radically reorganising and taking control of it.

All that remains is to connect him to the name 'Peter'. Incoming popes choose their own papal name and some of the previous prophecies have used this to establish a link to a pope, but in the case of 'Peter' this is very unlikely. Although a Pope Peter did exist, it is generally frowned upon to appropriate the name of the saint in whose footsteps all subsequent popes follow. It is now generally accepted that no pope would choose or include Peter in their papal name.

The links to the 'Peter' aspect of the prophecy were not clear until Bergoglio chose the title Pope Francis. He took this name from St Francis of Assisi, whose full name was Francesco di Pietro di Bernardone – Pietro being a variant of 'Peter'. This is not the first time the middle name of a pope has been used in the prophecy. It is not even the first time the middle name in question was specifically 'Peter'. In 1555 Pope Paul IV was elected with the prophecy describing him as 'from the faith of Peter'. Paul's middle name was 'Peter', creating a precedent for this in the prophecies. It also mirrors how Pope Francis' predecessor had come to be identified by the papal name Benedict with its link to the olive branch mentioned in the prophecies.

CONCLUSION

After hundreds of years of speculation we have discovered Cardinal Bergoglio to be Peter the Roman: the final pope according to the *Prophecy of the Popes*, as attributed to St Malachy of Armagh.

Not only have we reached the final pope but we are aware of the connections between Pope Francis and the prophecy. Should the link have been made prior to the election there is a possibility that this might have influenced the decision. The notion of a cardinal fitting the prophecy once learned cannot be unlearned. The cardinals who came to know of this cannot easily purge the thought from their minds and will go to the conclave knowing that there is an option to support or reject the prophecies. It would have been difficult to limit their choice to meeting the needs of the congregation – they were also in a position to try to delay the Last Judgement or embrace the final prophecy and lay the foundation for what could be the End Times. All Christians hope for the return of Jesus, but at what price?

As it stands, following the abdication of Pope Benedict it fell to the College of Cardinals, the Holy Spirit that inspires them, and to fate that Bergoglio took on the role.

The fate of the Catholic Church now hangs in the balance.

CHAPTER 13

CONCLUSIONS

INTRODUCTION

For too long science and religion have railed against each other, yet in prophecy they might find some common ground. The Church should not fear scientific progress as, when everything known by science has been measured, categorised and considered, what remains is the divine. The *Prophecy of the Popes* transcends the science of time and space and is also divinely inspired.

For me, the real revelation is not that the prophecies foretell the fall of Rome and the popes that precede it, but that prophecy itself appears to be possible.

Prophecy stands or falls by its outcome. We can be wise after the event like the interpreters of Nostradamus, or see meaning in vague predictions like the tabloid astrologers, but what elevates the *Prophecy of the Popes* above this is that it is not vague. It has continued to be relevant hundreds of years after it was discovered and possibly 800 years after it was written.

The descriptions it contains are often so direct, and so accurate in their summation of the popes, that they uphold the idea that humans can witness other points in time. The method for achieving this dislocation is likely to be triggered by a change in the states of consciousness in the individual, but whoever received such a clear view of the papacy unfolding over hundreds of years had a religious fervour that invoked this state of being.

RELEASE

As our earliest copy of the prophecies dates from 400 years after they were supposedly written, we cannot conclude that they exist in an original form. Even the author of the 1595 release, de Wyon, quite likely never saw the original document. The final whereabouts of the original *Prophecy of the Popes*, potentially the most important document about the Catholic Church today, remains a secret, and without access to the Vatican we cannot examine the original text or follow the clues to where it might currently be hidden.

The original text, should it exist, has never been made public, shown to exist or even mentioned as existing prior to de Wyon's publication. It is recorded in the Vatican that Malachy deposited a document in the archives on his final visit to Rome in 1139 but no details are given about the nature or content of the item.

It is also written that the prophecies were in circulation within the Vatican in 1590 and there is mention of them existing in the 1450s, although no evidence has been provided to support either claim. If the prophecies existed for de Wyon to copy and distribute, then why has it not been possible since that time for any scholar or researcher from within the Vatican to produce the original document? This would seem to hint that not all is what it seems with de Wyon's find, but perhaps the prophecies came not from the Vatican but from a private collection.

It is possible that, having caused so much controversy at the time of their release in 1595, they were removed from any catalogue listing and allowed to sink back into the unmarked boxes of documents within the archive. Perhaps the pope himself had them removed and lodged in a private safe to prevent the threat of endless speculation consuming the cardinals every time a new pope was to be elected. We can imagine a safe somewhere in the pope's private apartment that contains this dusty text, and who knows what other wonders.

Will the original document ever be released? Like the final secret of Fátima that has remained hidden from view for nearly 90 years, is it considered too controversial to be revealed? The Vatican claims that no prophecy given after the Bible can be pronounced upon as catechism, and yet it remains withheld. Now that the final pope, as identified in the prophecy, has been elected, now would seem to be the right time to release the original or earliest-known form of the prophecy.

I have requested from the Vatican – both directly and via an Italian intermediary – a copy of the earliest version of the prophecies, but nothing has arrived to date. Now I call upon the Vatican for the release of the original text of the prophecy and to put all questions of age, authenticity and authorship to rest before it is too late.

ACCURACY

Without an original in circulation why should we even consider the prophecies as having merit? Of all the predictions directed at the Catholic Church over the past two millennia, the *Prophecy of the Popes* has proven the most reliable. The accuracy of many of the descriptions of popes before and after publication cannot be denied. Going forwards, with Pope Francis in place, according to the prophecy the pieces are set for the destruction of Rome and the end of the Catholic Church. There are those who can deny this and claim that Francis does not fulfil the prophecy or that the final stanza was added to avoid the connotation that a Benedictine would be the last pope but there was a certain inevitability in this election. So many of the leading candidates had 'Peter' as part of their name or embedded in their life in other ways that it was almost impossible to choose from the top five candidates and not get a 'Peter the Roman'. This can be seen as demonstrating that either the final prophecy is too vague to be considered a true prophecy or that it was always broad enough to seal its own fate regardless of how the cardinals voted. That the Catholic Church has survived this long through so many precarious points in its history also testifies to the robustness of the prophecies.

EMBRACING THE PROPHECY

The urge within the Vatican has always been to protect the status quo but, as so much of Christianity stems from prophecy, to ignore it at this late stage would be to undermine the foundation of the Catholic religion. If they had tried to avoid the prophecy, would a cataclysm have been averted or would it have come anyway and by its very appearance confirmed the new pope as Peter the Roman?

There is also the possibility that the senior members of the Catholic Church want to embrace the Last Judgement. Perhaps they actively seek to bring about their own destruction as an opportunity to surrender all power, wealth and possibly life, in what might be their only chance to earn a place among the saints.

It may seem a strange notion that the Vatican would want a final pope to occur in accordance with the prophecy, but for some the apocalypse is a necessary step towards establishing the kingdom of heaven on earth. Members of the conclave may have seen their role as instigating all that is prophesised in the Book of Revelation.

STAGNATION

For many, the image of the papacy is as an unchanging institution that has been stuck in its ways for nearly 20 centuries, but, as we have seen, the history of the papacy is one of upheaval and turmoil. There has always been change. The history of the popes, as summarised in the previous chapters, has often seen Rome besieged by uprisings, with the pope forced to flee for his life and live in exile. The schisms have been so radical in the past that we have seen a slew of antipopes challenge the supremacy of the incumbent pope. Where once the Papal States included much of northern Italy, the Vatican is now a single city state within Rome. At just over 100 acres, it is one of the smallest independent states in the world. And yet the pope commands control over the lives of more than 1.3 billion people, just over 17 per cent of the world's population.

CHALLENGES

We have reached a point in history where the Church seems so out of touch with the lives and cultures of its congregation that attendance is in steep decline. There is dissent within the ranks as priests call for changes on matters of marriage and homosexuality, highlighting the outdated Catholic worldview. It is no surprise that there is a vacuum in the recruitment of new priests. The young men of today have more to sacrifice if they take up positions in the Church. Opportunities to experience life, relationships, travel and learning have all evolved. Even spirituality can now be found in a myriad of places. There are choices far beyond what even our parents could have accessed.

As we have seen, the collapse of the Church as an organisation could come from many quarters. The Church that Pope Francis rules is unrecognisable from the loose coalition of Christian groups that came together almost 20 centuries ago, yet so much has become rigid and cast in stone. Where once Christian belief was growing and evolving, now fixed and immutable dogmas pervade. So much has been decreed that it is almost impossible for a pope to be progressive without contradicting the rules laid down by his predecessors. Pope Francis is a strong pope but may find his hands are tied when it comes to making the radical changes needed to bring the Church into the 21st century. He is held in place by traditions and in many cases he stands to enforce them. The traditions that held the Catholic Church in place for so long are now its biggest enemy. It has become a stumbling block of its own creation.

REFORMATION

The Church has undergone many reforms in its history but in recent years it seemed to be stagnating and entering a decline. The Second Vatican Council attempted to update the Church but further wide-ranging reforms are needed to be driven by a more tolerant, progressive pope. Such a pope could find a place in the 21st century if they upheld the morals that the Church preaches, otherwise even without an apocalypse the Church will continue to decline. As the beginnings of reformation, the Second Vatican Council was an inspired and brave step in the right direction but it did not go far enough. A Catholic Church that reformed to feed the poor and allow its hierarchy to live and act as Jesus did would be an inspiration. In short, a Church that people would want to be part of.

For the Catholic Church to be reformed and revitalised it would need to openly embrace the diversity of the modern age. It needs to be seen as charitable and the wealth of the pope and the Vatican must be replaced with something that has the humility of the saints. Just as Hildegard von Bingen predicted many persecutions for the Church, she followed this by stating that when the priests accepted a path of poverty, things would become easier. Pope Francis might well be the antidote to this stagnation.

Aside from the external threats, the internal politics of the Church are just as potentially disruptive. Bergoglio's criticisms of the Curia might go against him now that he is in office, and his intention to align the Church with the poor will no doubt create further enemies but if a religion does not reflect the life of its members it inevitably risks being usurped by other religions. He must also be seen to take a hard line on the immediate expulsion and transparent reporting of transgressions, be it the abuse of people or finances. If he were to realise the shackles of celibacy both deter new priests from joining and are an attractive factor for paedophiles entering the Church, he might give blessings to marriage for all members of the Church and also open the doors to female priests. Not all mistakes will be forgiven but it would help if they were learned from and some form of balance was restored in way of response.

EVOLVE

The Church needs to evolve faster to mirror a society that is making leaps in all areas of development. While the regimented nature of the Church hierarchy and strict routes of progression are clear and unambiguous, the spiritual side of the Church seems at odds with this. For the Church to evolve would also require that the religion on which it is based also evolves. Once a Bible is cast in print the growth of religion stops at that point in time and everything that follows is just an attempt to interpret or support what was written at that time. And yet the Catholic Church, as we have seen from its history, has developed constantly over the last two millennia.

It should not deny this, but should embrace the ability to keep up with societies' needs. The spiritual development of individuals, wherever they find a connection to the divine, has an important place in faith and modern society and should be supported. Only then, by reaching beyond the stone walls of Vatican City, can there be a central role for the Church to support the diverse communities encountered across the world. From this an opportunity will arise for the unification of all forms of Christianity and a respect for all religions and faiths.

This approach mirrors the range of beliefs based upon the Bible, which is as vast as the text is complex, and works on many levels. There are symbolic sections and parables, mystical events and miracles – and, certainly in the Old Testament, many, many prophecies. Jesus acts in support of these prophecies when he fulfils the role of the prophesised messiah, thus bringing the Old Testament tradition of seers and sages into the New Testament along with his own progressive teachings. The Bible is overflowing with prophecy: there are literally hundreds of prophecies, from minor events to major cataclysms, in the Old and New Testaments. It is an integral part of the Christian tradition. What the *Prophecy of the Popes* also indicates is that prophecy is not only possible but integral to spiritual development. The final challenge for the Church would be to reinstate prophecy as an experience of divine union and to recognise its status as an important tool. It is a means to revealing the present and future will of God.

If the methods of prophecy were disseminated to a wider audience the experience of the individual would be more important than the words they hear from the pulpit. It would also negate the need for priests and popes, as individuals would have their own direct relationship with the divine. In this way the Church would be challenged not only by the prophecies but by the methods through which they were received.

St John's Book of Revelation concludes the Bible, his words passionately recounting the events of the future on a worldwide scale, but this is where the Church would have us believe prophecy ends. It is doubtful that the Holy Spirit would be silenced simply because man gathered a selection of scriptures and bound them together in a book. And the silence has been deafening as we have witnessed popes, saints and laymen prophesising through the ages. The voice of the Holy Spirit continues to make known the unknowable to those who reach out with an open heart. We are not abandoned, but the popes may wish to keep this method of divine discourse a secret from the masses. Perhaps this is why, ultimately, the prophecies had to end with the destruction of the Church. The pope and all his cardinals and clergy may finally step aside to allow the power of knowing the will of God to come down to the people. In Catholicism without a pope, prophecy would find its place again.

At the core of Catholicism is something very spiritual and precious but over the centuries this has become obscured by dogma and scandal. The opportunity is to strip away the outer construct and return the Church to an experience of the divine through simple faith and a spiritual life. Imagine then the experience of the prophet who wrote of the time of the Last Judgement. To see the destruction of Rome would have been a terrifying experience, and unsettling for a long time after. To have one's faith challenged so deeply, to have an insight into the demise of something at the core of your existence would gnaw into the spirit.

Yet between the long shadow of its past and the potential for a cataclysmic event in the future there is still hope. If a cataclysm engulfs the Church and the organisation becomes decentralised or is forced to recreate itself from the ashes of Rome it could engender both a physical and spiritual renewal. The challenge would be to rebuild the religion in the image of Jesus, to let go of the past and reform to meet the needs of humanity as it now stands. Belief cannot be switched on and off. It will always endure in some form – even in the wake of a major upheaval within the Catholic Church something of the religion will remain. Even if the spiritual centre, Vatican City, was destroyed, the millions of Catholics across the world would continue to practise their faith.

And so in the conclusion of the prophecies there is a challenge to all who have faith in Catholicism. If God will allow the Catholic Church to fall into ruin both physically and spiritually, what does this mean to the faithful? The challenge facing the final pope is that, in spite of the destruction, we must reach beyond the veil, the physical manifestation of the Church, and look to its spiritual counterpart, not in the books and words of popes but in our own souls. If God removes our relationship with the Vatican, in the space remaining we are called to find other paths to the divine. If that be His will then let Rome fall, let Catholicism evolve and become something else: perhaps a way for individuals to seek an experience of God for themselves.

Robert Howells
March 2013

SELECTED BIBLIOGRAPHY

Anon, *Compendium of the Social Doctrine of the Church*, Libreria Editrice Vaticana, 2005

Anon, *Complete Illustrated History of Catholicism and the Catholic Saints*, Hermes House, 2011

Anon, *Prophecy of the Popes Attributed to Joachim of Fiore*, British Library, 1340

Anon, *Prophecies. Prophetic Visions about Popes and the Oracles of Leo the Wise.* Oxford Bodleian Library, 16th century

Anon, *The Eclipse of the Church*, Magnificat Editions, 1971

Attwater, D, *The Penguin Dictionary of Saints*, Penguin, 1983

Bander, P, *The Prophecies of St. Malachy*, TAN Books and Publishers, Inc., 1969

Bertone, T and De Carli, G, *The Last Secret of Fatima*, Doubleday Books, 2008

von Bingen, Hildegard, *Mystical Visions*, Bear & Co, 1986

Catholic Encyclopaedia, online at www.newadvent.org/cathen, 1913

Cooke, G, *Developing Your Prophetic Gifting*, Sovereign World, 2003

Coxhead, D and Hiller S, *Dreams, Visions of the Night*, Avon, 1976

Cucherat, M F, *La Prophétie De La Succession Des Papes*, British Library, 1873

Duffy, E, *Saints and Sinners: A History of the Popes*, Yale University Press, 1997

Dunn-Mascetti, M, *Saints: The Chosen Few*, Boxtree, 1994

Dunne, J W, *An Experiment with Time*, Hampton Roads Publishing Co, 2001

Dupont, Y, *Catholic Prophecy*, TAN Books, 1970

Fleming, M H, *The Late Medieval Pope Prophecies: The Genus Nequam Group*, University of Arizona, 1999

von Franz, M L, *On Divination and Synchronicity*, Inner City Books, 1982

Ghilardi, A, *Life and Times of St Francis*, Paul Hamlyn, 1967

Gurugé, Anura, *The Next Pope*, CreateSpace Independent Publishing Platform, 2011

Hall, M P, *Sages and Seers*, Philosophical Research Society, 1981

Hall, M P, *The Secret Teachings of All Ages*, Philosophical Research Society, 1928

Herolt, J, *Miracles of the Blessed Virgin Mary*, Routledge, 1928

Hogue, J, *The Last Pope*, Element, 2000

James, W, *Varieties of Religious Experience*, Dover Publications Inc, 2003

Kramer, H, *The Malleus Maleficarum*, Speyer, 1486

Lawlor, H J, *St Bernard of Clairvaux's Life of St Malachy of Armagh*, SPCK, 1920

Lewis, B R, *Dark History of the Popes*, Park Lane Books, 2009

Levillain, P, *The Papacy: An Encyclopaedia*, Routledge, 2002

Maitre, J, *The Prophecy of the Popes attributed to St Malachi*, Librairie G. Loireau, 1901

Massey, E, *The Destiny of Rome or, The Probability of the Speedy and Final Destruction of the Pope*. Roberts and Dodd, 1718

McClure, K, *The Evidence for the Visions of the Virgin Mary*, Aquarian Press, 1983

Norwich, J J, *The Popes*, Chatto and Windus, 2011

O'Brien, M J, *An Historical and Critical Account of the So-Called Prophecy of St. Malachy Regarding the Succession of Popes*, MH Gill and Son, 1880

O'Malley J W, *A History of the Popes*, Sheed and Ward, 2010

Palmer, E, *History of Prophecy*, self published, 1862

Panvinius, O, *Epitome Romanorium Pontificum usque ad Paulum IV*, 1557

de Rosa, P, *Vicars of Christ: The Dark Side of the Papacy*, Poolbeg Press Ltd, 1998

Rucker, R, *The Fourth Dimension*, Penguin Books, 1985

Swift, E L, *The Life and Acts of St. Patrick, translated from the original Latin of Jocelin, Cistercian monk of Furnes of the 12th century*, Hibernia Press Company, 1809

Wakefield, W L. Evans, A, *Heresies of the high Middle Ages*, Columbia University Press, 1991

Wales, F H, *Prophecy in the Catholic Church*, A R Mowbray & Co, 1898

Walsh, M (ed.), *Butler's Lives of the Saints*, Burns and Oates, 1995

Walvoord, J F, *Prophecy Knowledge Handbook*, Victor Books, 1990

de Wyon, Arnold, *Lignum Vitae, Liber Secundas*, Angelerius, 1595

INDEX